Winning by Design

Winning by Design

Technology, Product Design and International Competitiveness

VIVIEN WALSH, ROBIN ROY, MARGARET BRUCE AND
STEPHEN POTTER
*of the Design Innovation Group, The Open University and
The University of Manchester Institute of Science and Technology*

First published 1992

Blackwell Publishers
108 Cowley Road
Oxford OX4 1JF
UK

238 Main Street, Suite 501
Cambridge, Massachusetts 02142
USA

British Library Cataloguing in Publication Data

A CIP catalogue record for this book is available from the British Library.

Library of Congress Cataloging-in-Publication Data

Winning by design: technology, product design, and international
    competitiveness/Vivien Walsh . . . [et al.].
        p.   cm.
    Includes bibliographical references.
    ISBN 0-631-16437-5   0-631-18511-9 (pbk)
    1. Design, Industrial – Management.   2. Technological innovations –
Management.   3. New Products – Management.   I. Walsh, Vivien.
TS171.4.W56   1992
658.5'752 – dc20   91-43640
                                                                CIP

Typeset in 11 on 13 pt Garamond
by Graphicraft Typesetters Ltd., Hong Kong
Printed in Great Britain by TJ Press
This book is printed on acid-free paper

Contents

List of Plates

List of Figures

List of Tables

Acknowledgements

Many individuals and organizations have contributed in a variety of ways to the work that led to this book. First of all we would like to thank all the firms, named and anonymous, both in the UK and abroad, that participated in our various studies and surveys. Without their cooperation we would not have had the empirical evidence on which much of this book depends.

We also wish to thank all the other organizations that at various times provided information and facilities. The Design Council provided vital access to the records of the Design Index/Design Centre Selection (now unfortunately discontinued) and Design Award schemes for Studies A and B. Special thanks are due to Anthony Key and Rachel Moon for their help at that time. The Rubber and Plastics Processing Industry Training Board, the Danish Design Council and several trade associations provided useful advice and information for both Studies A and B. Study C, although not the main concern of this book, would not have been possible without the enormous help given by John Benson and the staff of the Design Initiative Unit of the Design Council.

We are grateful to many individuals for their contributions to various aspects of the work involved in this book. In particular we wish to acknowledge David Walker for his contribution in helping to start the Design Innovation Group and for his work on the motor industry for Study A, and John Towriss for his work on Study B and especially for developing the special computer software which enabled us to analyse the business and design performance indicators. Jenny Lewis, Georgy Leslie and Veronica Mole provided invaluable help with the collection of information and analysis of data. Bill Evans and Paul Gardiner, as well as conducting some of the interviews in foreign firms for Study B, have on many occasions provided extremely useful comment and advice.

As well as to those who have helped directly with specific research projects, we owe a great deal to members and associates of the Design Innovation Group and many others who have provided us with ideas and insight. They include Jan Annerstedt, Colin Clipson, Mike Cooley, Barry Dagger, Christopher Freeman, John Langrish, Christopher Lorenz, Stan Moody, Mark Oakley, James Pilditch, Roy Rothwell, Alan Topalian and James Woudhysen.

We owe the idea for the main title of this book to a report, also entitled 'Winning by Design', published by the Warren Centre for Advanced Engineering at the University of Sydney, Australia. The project report (Lawrence, 1987) and its accompanying technical papers (Warren Centre, 1987), which were the result of a major study of how design could improve the competitiveness of Australian industry, cover similar topics to those in this book. We recommend these publications highly.

We would like to acknowledge the financial support of the Technology Faculty and the Research Committee of The Open University and of the Joint ESRC/SERC Committee which enabled us to carry out the research that forms the basis of this book.

Finally we wish to thank Sally Boyle and Gordon Lengden for providing graphic design support and Carole Marshall, Beryl Boswell and Mary O'Mahony who helped word-process and circulate the chapters of this book as they went through many drafts.

Vivien Walsh, Robin Roy, Margaret Bruce and Stephen Potter
Manchester and Milton Keynes

Introduction and Summary

The Background to *Winning by Design*

The starting-point for this book was the appearance in Britain in the late 1970s and early 1980s of several official and semi-official reports – notably the Corfield Report on *Product Design* (NEDO, 1979) and the Finniston Report, *Engineering our Future* (Committee of Inquiry into the Engineering Profession, 1980) – which stressed the role of product design and technological innovation in company success, international competitiveness and economic performance. Although by then the importance of R&D (research and development) and industrial innovation to company performance and national economic revival was acknowledged by government and parts of British industry, the same was not yet true of design.

The Design Innovation Group

It was this context which led to the formation of the Design Innovation Group (DIG), at the beginning of the 1980s' upsurge of interest in design. The DIG was established in 1979 in the Design Discipline at the Open University, but subsequently expanded to become a two-centre organization with members from Manchester School of Management at the University of Manchester Institute of Science and Technology (UMIST). In addition to the academics and researchers who form the members of the DIG, it has a number of associates from industry, the design professions and other academic institutions in the UK and abroad.

The aim of the DIG is to investigate the role of design and innovation in international competitiveness and to identify management strategies and product development practices associated with successful businesses producing well-designed products. Because there was already a substantial body of knowledge concerning technological and industrial innovation, especially from work done at the Science Policy Research Unit at Sussex University, upon which we draw in this book, the emphasis in the DIG's work has been on the commercial and economic role of design. This work includes studies of the design of products ranging from furniture to computers, but (until recently) excluded research into other areas of design such as graphics, textiles and interiors, except where they impinged on the design of products. The focus on products was not because the other design areas are not economically and commercially important – indeed, they are fields in which British designers excel – but because product design was the field in which British industry was facing the strongest international competition and in which there was the greatest need for improvement in both practice and management.

Research for this book

The book is based on the research into this area by the DIG and many others over the past decade, but in particular on a series of empirical studies of the management and practice of product design, development and innovation in a number of contrasting industries conducted by the DIG during the 1980s. These industries range from very mature sectors such as bicycles to new technology sectors such as office electronics. More details of these industry studies are given in chapter 1, but broadly they fall into two phases. Study A investigated the relationships between good design, the management of product development and business performance in (mainly British) firms from the plastics products, bicycle and motor industries. Study B was a major international comparative survey of design and business performance and the management of product development in British and world-leading Danish, Swedish, Dutch, Japanese and Canadian firms from the furniture, heating and office electronics industries. In parallel with these two studies, members of the DIG have undertaken other research into product design and technological innovation, their effective management and their role in international competition in a variety of specific cases and industries, including railways, aircraft, chemicals, videotex, lighting and consumer electronics, some of the results of which are referred to in this book. In 1990 the DIG completed a third major empirical survey (Study C) which investigated the commercial risks and returns on investments in design and product development projects, involving inputs of professional product, engineering and graphic design expertise, in a large sample of small and medium-sized British manufacturers. The results of Study C are only briefly reviewed in this book, as they are being published in detail elsewhere (Potter et al., 1991).

As a result of these various studies we have come to the conclusion that product design is a crucial, but often neglected and misunderstood, activity in the performance of firms and economies. Design is the vital link between a market need, an invention or innovative idea and its translation into a product suitable for manufacture and use. But we have found that being good at design is not enough. Putting effort and resources into design and product development is a necessary, but not a sufficient, condition for competitiveness and good business performance at the company level as well as for an improved trade balance and growth at the level of the national economy.

Using this Book

For the benefit of the busy reader, in the following sections the main arguments and findings of *Winning by Design* are summarized in more detail and the book's structure and content are outlined. As should become clear from the summary, the book tends to be analytical in tone and content, building on other research in the field of design and innovation studies, rather than being in the prescriptive 'how to do it' style of some management texts. Nevertheless, the book is intended to be of interest to practitioners in industry as well as to students and teachers of design management and innovation studies. There is much included about what successful (and less successful) firms actually do, and chapters 3–7 all finish with a set of 'Lessons and Conclusions' which are intended to provide some general guidelines to good practice for those who have to develop product strategies, devise organizational structures for product development and manage design and innovation projects.

In addition, much of the work of the DIG is aimed at providing material for educational courses on the effective management of product design and innovation, both of the conventional face-to-face type at Manchester School of Management, and those offered through the distance-learning systems of the Open University and other organizations. For readers who may be interested in these courses, published materials from them are included in the list of references, and details may be obtained from the institutions concerned.

Summary of the Main Arguments and Findings

Why design and innovation are important

Since the Second World War, and particularly since the late 1950s, the creation and manufacture of well-designed products, across the whole spectrum of technical innovation, have become essential to the success both of individual companies and national economies. In this period industrialized economies moved from a situation in which markets were often protected and there was relatively little choice of products, to one in which international competition has steadily grown and customers have a growing choice of products and suppliers. At the same time, rapid technical and market change has stimulated the flow of new and improved products, while greater affluence has increased the demand for well-designed goods of high quality and technical sophistication.

In this context far too few firms, in Britain especially, but also in other countries including the United States, have devoted sufficient resources and expertise to the research, design and development of new and improved products and to competing on design, innovation and quality as well as on price. As a consequence British and American firms lost markets to competitors from countries – notably West Germany and Japan – that recognized the need for advanced industries capable of supplying products of excellent design and high quality, often incorporating the latest technology and materials.

Investment in R&D and innovation is important to competition not just in new technology industries such as electronics, but also in established industries such as motor vehicles and traditional sectors such as textiles. The amounts required for R&D and innovation to compete in world markets may differ between sectors but, as Cox and Kriegbaum (1989) warn, 'Any industry that falls behind the going rate for its particular technology is courting trouble.'

Not all new or improved products, however, involve R&D or technical innovation. As is shown in chapter 1, only some of the investment that firms make in product design and development will be included in R&D statistics, and the vast majority of new products involve variations on existing technology, or incremental improvements on existing designs, rather than major innovation. Thus throughout this book we provide evidence from our own case studies and other recent research which shows that successful firms and industries place their emphasis not just on creating innovations, but on improving the design of their own or competitors' products, creating 'design families' and ranges of related products for different markets, and on designing and redesigning those products for reliability, quality and economic manufacture.

Our research has also shown that those firms that invest resources and professional expertise in product and industrial design in both traditional and new industries have been commercially more successful than firms that pay less attention to these aspects of design. It is significant that several of the world-leading firms noted for both good design and business performance in our studies are Scandinavian. Denmark, Sweden and Norway are countries noted for the use their industry makes of product and industrial designers. We might equally have chosen Italy in the field of fashion and furniture or West Germany for engineering design. The irony is that Britain was the first country to establish a national body to promote design, is recognized for producing some of the best designers in the world and has the world's strongest design consultancy industry; yet, while British industry appears to be reluctant to exploit this national resource, British designers are increasingly being employed by foreign manufacturers.

The roots of this problem lie deep in the history and culture of British manufacturing, but there are some hopeful signs. Our own surveys (see chapter 4) and various other studies (e.g. Ughanwa and Baker, 1989) show that the majority of British firms across all sectors now employ at least some full-time in-house design staff, and most also use design consultants at least occasionally. During the 1980s there has been a shift from traditional craft-trained to graduate-level staff in design. In the engineering industry especially, the proportion of graduate-level engineers and technologists has increased substantially, while that of non-graduate technicians and draughtspeople has fallen (Francis and Winstanley, 1988).

However, the issue is not just whether manufacturing industry is aware of design and has begun to employ suitably qualified designers and engineers. It is whether the scale of the resources and effort devoted to design is capable of matching those of competitors – the 'going rate for the technology' mentioned above in respect of innovation. Often British firms with one or two research, design and

development staff find themselves competing against foreign manufacturers with substantial R&D departments and large teams of specialist designers and engineers. Whereas the two major Japanese
corporations we visited in Study B employ many thousands of scientists and engineers and between fifty and 250 industrial designers,
our studies show that about a quarter of British manufacturers fail to
use industrial design at all, and only about a fifth employ in-house
industrial design staff. As is described in chapter 4, in some sectors
about a third of British firms do not employ any specialist design
staff and rely on individuals with other jobs (so-called 'silent designers'), suppliers and customers to do design. But the fact that British
firms of all sizes do manage to compete in world markets shows that
developing successful products is not just a matter of the resources
going into research, design and development, but of how well they
are managed and how well design and innovation are integrated
with other functions in the firm.

Why design and innovation are not enough

The second message of this book, therefore, is that product design
and technological innovation, however well-resourced, are not enough
on their own to ensure the success of a product, firm or economy,
at least in the longer term.

Apart from the examples from our studies given in the book, there
are many well-known cases of firms, noted for the design of their
products or for their ability to produce technical innovations, getting
into financial difficulties. Sinclair Research, first in the world to
popularize home computers, was forced to sell its computer business
to Amstrad in 1986. Jaguar, famous for the design of its luxury cars,
and soon after completing a £55-million investment programme in
new research, design and development facilities, was sold to Ford in
1989. The late 1980s saw several famous British retailers, including
Habitat, Next, Laura Ashley and Coloroll, which had grown rapidly
on the basis of their reputation for making and/or selling well-designed
furniture, clothes and household goods, losing sales and profits. In
1990 Coloroll went into receivership and Laura Ashley announced
that it was closing much of its UK manufacturing operation and
sourcing more garments from lower-cost suppliers in other countries.
There is a complex story behind each of these examples and it would
be a mistake to attribute what happened to any one factor. But clearly,
being good at design or innovation was not enough to insulate these

firms from growing competition at home or abroad, from the uncertainties of market and technical change, or from the high interest rates and the downturn in UK consumer spending of the late 1980s and early 1990s.

As is shown in chapter 2, competition in any market sector depends on a particular mix of 'price' and 'non-price' factors which together determine the 'value' of a product to a consumer. Our own and many other studies (e.g. Hooley et al., 1988) have demonstrated the importance to competitiveness not just of how well a firm's products are designed or how novel they are, but also of the firm's capabilities in other areas such as marketing, quality control, delivery, and after-sales service. In this book we show that, while design and innovation have a major influence on both price and non-price factors (by providing products that perform well, are attractive and easy to use, economical to operate, and that can be made at an affordable price), the success of a firm in international competition depends on all-round competence. We argue further that to get a 'competitive edge', excellence in at least one area is required: this could be good design, but might be excellent quality, low-cost manufacturing, or some other strength. The highly successful British retailer Marks and Spencer, for instance, is renowned for the excellent quality and value of the clothing that it sells, without attempting to be in the vanguard of design.

Although design and innovation on their own are insufficient to make a company's products successful, they are certainly areas in which companies can aspire to excel, as long as they do not lose sight of all the other factors. As is noted in chapter 3, only a few firms have the resources and technological strength to pursue an 'offensive' or 'defensive' innovation strategy successfully. However, paying special attention to design offers firms of all sizes across many sectors the opportunity to differentiate what they offer from their competitors' products, to tailor products to particular customers' needs and market niches and, for relatively small investments in professional design expertise, to achieve a competitive edge. But in order to achieve this competitive edge it is necessary for design to be properly managed and integrated with other key business activities.

Design management guidelines

The third message of this book, then, is that the process of design has to be properly managed. Our own surveys and several other studies (e.g. Oakley, 1984; NEDC, 1987; Service, Hart and Baker, 1989) have provided guidelines to help firms across a variety of industries manage design and innovation more effectively. And during the 1980s several organizations, including the British Standards Institution, the Engineering Council, the Design Council and the Department of Trade and Industry, began to provide courses, booklets and advice to increase industry's awareness of the importance of design management and to improve design management practice.

Although the guidelines in the various studies, courses and publications differ in emphasis, there is agreement that design management should be tackled at three levels: strategic, organizational and project. There follows a summary of some key design management guidelines from our own and other studies, focusing on those that are relatively independent of the industry concerned.

At the *strategic* level, considered in chapter 3, we argue that there is, of course, no foolproof recipe that will guarantee the success of a firm or project, given the risks and uncertainties of design and innovation. Nevertheless, it is essential for the firm to attempt as best it can to understand the likely longer-term changes in the market and the technology in which it is operating, and, together with a view of its own desired direction, to build a strategy for design and product development based on that understanding. For example, such a strategy might consider how the company might be affected by or exploit the emerging demand for 'environmentally friendly' products (see chapter 8).

Although in this book we tend to emphasize the merits of strategies based on market-led design improvement and incremental innovation, this is not to suggest that more radical change in the design and technology of products is not also important. Indeed, we show that the most successful firms usually have a strategy for product development that combines several approaches: for example, market-led continuous evolution of existing products combined with a longer-term programme of innovation in product design or technology to create or exploit new market demands. In other words, these firms are not afraid to run the higher risks of producing products that may be ahead of market demand or that make use of innovative design ideas or new technologies.

At the *organizational* level, we show in chapter 5 that some studies of design management tend to be rather simplistic, advocating multi-disciplinary project teams for most situations. In practice there is no ideal organization for managing product development, as the most appropriate form depends on the size of the firm and the maturity of the industry. The essential factor seems to be that there are organizational structures that somehow enable all relevant individuals and departments to participate in product development and ensure that their contributions are properly coordinated. In small firms good communications between designers, managers, marketing and production staff during the design/development process may be achieved informally. In larger organizations discussion and contact between the various departments and individuals will usually have to be formalized. The most appropriate means to achieve this may vary at different stages of a project; for example, starting with a development committee for planning, then using a project team for design and development, and finally moving into a conventional functional department for manufacture.

Another organizational issue, considered in chapter 4, is whether individuals qualified in design or technology should be on the board of a company and whether there should be a board-level director whose main responsibility is design. Although designers, technologists and design directors on the board have been widely advocated, the evidence that this will produce improved commercial performance is mixed. What seems much more important is that the senior management of the company should fully understand the role of design and product development in their business and hence make sure that there is clear responsibility for these activities. It is also vital that a company employ the best designers and engineers it can afford, and in sufficient numbers to provide the necessary spread of expertise. The main benefit of having a separate design director is that such an individual can ensure that the need for good design is taken into account across all the firm's activities – packaging, publicity, buildings, corporate identity – and not just in its products.

At the *project* level, considered in chapters 6 and 7, the most significant factors that distinguished the well-managed, commercially successful firms from the rest concerned the thoroughness with which product development was carried out from planning and briefing to design, development and manufacture.

At the planning and briefing stages we found that successful firms based product development projects on a full understanding of the market and user requirements, and achieved this understanding by using a variety of sources of marketing intelligence. In these firms management provided designers (whether in-house or consultants) with a comprehensive marketing brief at the start of the product development process, which formed the basis of a detailed product design specification. Customers and end-users, as well as marketing, design and production staff, often provided valuable input to the development of the brief and specification.

At the conceptual stage such firms allowed their designers to explore a range of options and typically provided facilities to enable models and mock-ups to be rapidly made for initial evaluation within the firm before proceeding to prototype development. At the stage of development and manufacture the successful firms subjected prototypes and pre-production versions of a new product to systematic customer evaluation and user trials (as well as to the usual technical testing and designing for ease of manufacture) in order to improve the design and reduce the risk of producing a market failure.

Finally, as noted in chapter 7, reducing the lead time from concept to market, or from order to delivery, is an increasingly important determinant of competitiveness. A variety of measures, in the organization of product development teams along the lines discussed in chapter 5 and in the use of computer aids to design and manufacture, is allowing firms to move from traditional 'linear' approaches to product development to faster 'concurrent engineering' methods.

Design, innovation and the quality of life

In the 1990s, therefore, the rules of successful competition are changing. Companies not only have to develop and manufacture well-designed, high-quality products at a price that offers the customer value for money, but this has to be done at least as fast as, or preferably faster than, the competition.

But although such measures may result in improved performance for individual firms, we argue in chapter 8 that they will not necessarily lead to long-term improvements in the economy as a whole. We further argue in chapter 8 that economic growth does not necessarily result in a better quality of life and is associated with a variety of major environmental problems. We conclude the book by giving examples of how design and innovation might be used in the 1990s not just to improve business performance and stimulate growth, but to enhance the quality of life and preserve the environment.

The Structure of *Winning by Design*

The book broadly covers the main areas involved in the successful product development process outlined in chapters 1 and 2.

Chapter 1 defines product design and explains how it relates to research and development, new product development, and innovation. This chapter shows that design is more pervasive than innovation, analyses the skills of the designer, and discusses the different perspectives from which design may be viewed.

Chapter 2 discusses the role of design in Britain's declining competitiveness. Design is usually treated as a factor contributing to 'non-price' competitiveness. This chapter shows that this is too simple a view because design also influences 'price' factors, for example, in reducing the cost of materials or the time required for manufacture. It shows that perceived 'value for money' is the basis on which purchasing decisions are made in many markets and that purchasers consider product features and price together when deciding what to buy. However, on the basis of our studies of 'design-conscious' and typical firms, the main conclusion of the chapter is that 'good design' can contribute towards improved business performance but cannot guarantee success. To be effective, design must be integrated with other aspects of product development, especially marketing and manufacture.

Chapter 3 considers company strategies towards R&D, design and innovation in new and mature industries. This encompasses the decisions leading to investment in research, design and development and the relationships between company, marketing and product strategy. In this chapter comparisons are made between the 'design-conscious' British and foreign firms in our studies and the more typical British companies in terms of their strategic thinking about design.

Chapter 4 describes the historical emergence of the research and development laboratory and explains why, in Britain at least, design has generally not achieved similar status in the organizational structure. This chapter gives empirical results concerning the employment of designers in companies and discusses the rise of the design consultancy industry in the UK and Scandinavia.

Chapter 5 examines various models for organizing product development, from traditional linear and iterative approaches to the use of multidisciplinary teams. Using evidence from our surveys, it considers the suitability of the different models for firms of different sizes and in industries at different stages of maturity. The necessity for a suitable organization for radical or evolutionary product development is illustrated through three examples of British Rail's fast train projects: the failed Advanced Passenger Train and the successful InterCity 125 and InterCity 225.

Chapter 6 considers the problem in design and innovation of identifying what the customer wants. It is through the use of both formal and informal sources of market intelligence that user needs and market trends are identified or anticipated and new designs are created to meet changing market demands. In product planning, decisions are made about whether or not to develop new ideas to exploit market opportunities or to modify existing products to penetrate further a given market segment.

Chapter 7 is concerned with the design and development process itself. Evidence from our own and other studies is given regarding the need for detailed briefs and product design specifications. The way in which a product passes through the stages of conceptual design, prototype development, technical and market testing, and detailing is outlined together with evidence about good practice. One of the main issues discussed in this chapter is how to achieve a thorough and systematic approach to product development without sacrificing creativity and speed.

Chapter 8 considers the role of design and innovation beyond that of the individual firm. It shows that better design or more effective innovation does not necessarily produce economic growth unless they are part of a long-term strategy at national or industry level. Government design and innovation policies aimed at developing new industries and making changes to mature or maturing ones are discussed. The book concludes by examining the environmental, social and human consequences of conventional policies aimed at achieving rapid economic growth and considers ways in which design and innovation might be used in the 1990s to improve the quality of life and preserve the environment.

1

Perspectives on Design and Innovation

Just as the 1960s have gone down in the public consciousness as the years of protest and 'permissiveness', so the 1980s were the decade of 'style'. The market success of designer-label clothes has meant that design is more often associated with sartorial elegance than entrepreneurial flair. Nevertheless, even if it is due to the ubiquity of designer goods, public awareness of design is greater than ever before – and some of this awareness penetrates beneath the chic 'matt black' surface (Aldersley-Williams, 1989).

A glance at the dazzling and fast-changing range of goods on offer in a typical high street – consumer electronics, furniture, clothes, magazines, lighting, kitchen equipment, not to mention the styling of the shop or salesroom itself – vividly demonstrates the pervasive impact of design and of technological innovation. The creation and production of every one of these artefacts have involved numerous design decisions, and many of them incorporate innovative technologies, components or materials which have only become available in the past few years.

Design means different things to different people. It is clearly associated with symbols of a fashionable and hedonistic life-style. But it is also about the development of complex engineering components and systems. Sometimes it combines both, as in the Renault 5 car called i-D ('identity') and advertised with the slogan 'Bored with the old image? This car looks better than a new wardrobe.' A sophisticated piece of engineering is sold like a pair of shoes – or, rather, like a pair of 'designer' jeans. And the advertisement itself was designed by a graphic designer. Architects, fashion designers, graphic designers, industrial designers and engineering designers are all involved in some facets of the design activity. The different skills involved in design, and the spectrum of activities which make up design, are discussed more fully later in this chapter.

The term 'design' covers a wide range of activities. All of them, however, involve the creative visualization of concepts, plans and ideas, and the production of sketches, models and other representations of those ideas, aimed at providing the instructions for making something which did not exist before, or which did not exist in quite that form – which might be a building, a dress, a plastic bowl, a machine, a company's logo or a pair of trainers bearing a company's logo.

The purpose of design is also seen differently by different people. Designers themselves may see their work in terms of creativity, problem-solving or even art. Marketing managers may see the work of designers employed by their firm as imparting distinction from other products, so that consumers will choose those items rather than competing ones. To consumers, the function of design may be the creation of new styles, fashions and images; or the improvement of products so that they are easier to use, longer-lasting or energy-saving. Again, the multiplicity of – sometimes conflicting – functions attributed to design will be discussed later in this chapter.

Despite the now quite widespread awareness of design, however, it is surprising that many firms, especially in the UK, have not regarded it as an activity worthy of investment of much time, money or professional expertise. For example, about a third of the firms making plastics products that we surveyed for one of the studies of design management and practice which form the core of this book,* did not regard design as important enough to employ specialist design staff; and some of these firms did not even seem to be aware that design decisions were being made. Thus, one manager we interviewed said, 'We don't do design,' meaning that before making a product, someone on the shop floor would sketch the design 'on the back of a cigarette packet'. In another firm we visited, the chairman of an office furniture manufacturer was responsible for new products, but admitted, 'It's not really design – we buy in our competitors' products, strip them down, and something emerges from that.' In Britain during the 1980s it was *retailers* who adopted design in a big way, to create the atmosphere that subtly seduces customers into buying their wares – in that period 86 per cent of British retailers embarked on a design

---

* The aims and methodology of our surveys are described more fully in the section 'The Design Innovation Group Studies' later in this chapter (p. 35).

programme (Polan, 1989; Besford, 1987) – while *manufacturers* are still reluctant to invest in design.

It would be wrong, however, to suggest that British managers are universally indifferent to design and innovation. British design talent is renowned worldwide and in our studies we found many 'design-conscious' and innovative British firms that compete successfully with the best of their overseas rivals. But British manufacturing industry as a whole still has a long way to go before 'Made in Britain' is synonymous with well-designed, high-quality products in the way that the terms 'Made in Japan/Germany/Sweden/Italy' nowadays suggest (Besford, 1987). Of course, references to Japanese, German, Swedish and Italian design all convey different ideas: of high-performance consumer electronics, precision engineering, functional unfussy furniture – often in natural materials – or high fashion and elegance. But they share the high-quality image. And it is interesting that Japanese design has only achieved this reputation relatively recently as a result of considerable effort in improving quality. In the early days of portable radios, 'Made in Japan' and the names of companies like Sony – now a leading firm in innovative design and world sales – were more likely to be seen as meaning cheap and shoddy.

Definitions of Design and Innovation

So far we have referred to the terms 'design' and 'innovation' as similar activities, without making clear what the similarities and the distinctions are, or attempting to define them. Unfortunately, definition is not easy. One frequent source of confusion is that design and innovation can mean either:

An *activity* – the design process or the innovation process.

Or:

The *outcome of that activity* – 'a design' meaning an idea or a plan from which an object can be made, or the form of the object itself; 'an innovation' meaning a new product or industrial process when it first appears on the market or enters into use.

In this book it is inevitable that we slip from one use of these terms to another, but in general we will use the term 'designing' or 'design and development' to mean the part of the total innovation or new product development process that starts with a brief and ends with a product ready for manufacture, as will be discussed in chapter 7; and we will use 'design' to mean the configuration of materials, elements and components that give a product its particular attributes of performance, appearance, ease of use, method of manufacture, and so on. The sections below explain how we arrived at these definitions.

Technological innovation

The definition of industrial or technological innovation used by those economists who have attempted to examine them, is that of a 'milestone' in the process leading from invention (the first idea, sketch or model for a new or improved device, product, process or system) to diffusion (of the resultant practical product, process or system) in which an increasing proportion of a population of potential users actually adopts the innovation. Thus innovation is defined by Freeman et al. (1982) as 'the first introduction of a new device, product, process or system into the ordinary commercial or social activity of a country'.

However, innovation is frequently also used to describe the whole activity from invention (the discovery of the new device, product, process or system) to the point of first commercial or social use. Thus, for example, technological innovation is defined in the *Frascati Manual*, issued by the Organization for Economic Cooperation and Development (OECD) as a proposed standard for measuring scientific and technical activities, as follows: 'Technological innovation is the transformation of an idea into a new or improved saleable product or operational process in industry or commerce' (OECD, 1981). This definition includes all the various activities – research, design, development, market research and testing, manufacturing engineering, etc. – involved in converting a new idea, invention or discovery into a novel product or industrial process in commercial or social use (see figure 1.1).

New product development

New product development is often used, especially in management and marketing circles, to describe the process that transforms technical ideas or market needs and opportunities into a new product

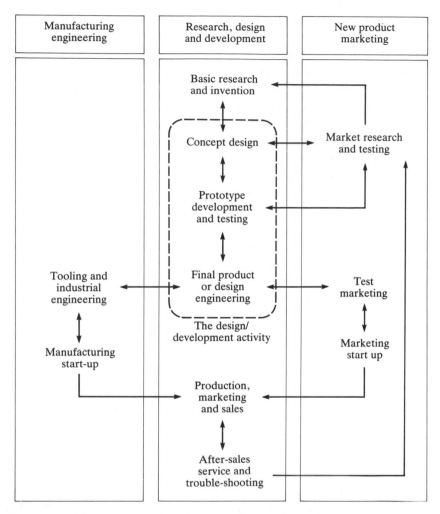

Figure 1.1 The process of technological or industrial innovation, showing the place of the design and development activity
Source: Roy and Bruce (1984)

launched on to the market. The difference from technological innovation is that the 'new product' concerned might involve only changes in form, components, materials, or even just packaging, rather than changes in operating principle or technology.

Product design and development

Product design and development may be seen from figure 1.1 as the core of the new product development or innovation process. It is the activity that transforms the brief or initial market specification into design concepts and prototypes and then into the detailed drawings, technical specifications and other instructions needed to actually manufacture a new product.

Caldecote (1979) defines design as 'the process of converting an idea into information from which a new product can be made'. Design, therefore, is the activity in which ideas and needs are given physical form, initially as solution concepts and then as a specific configuration or arrangement of elements, materials and components. Thus, 'Design is the very core of innovation, the moment when a new object is imagined, devised and shaped in prototype form' (OECD, 1982).

Development is the activity in which prototypes are tested and modified until a satisfactory pre-production version of the product has been evolved. This may then require further refinement in the process of final product or design engineering in order to meet manufacturing and marketing requirements. The term 'development' is used in conjunction with both 'research' and 'design', as in 're-search and development' and 'design and development'. The differences between them will be explored in the following two sections.

Research and development

Technological innovation, defined above, is dependent on research, design and development, although these activities may not necessarily have all been carried out by the innovating organization or in the period immediately preceding the launch of the innovation. The *Frascati Manual* defines R&D as follows: 'Research and experimental development (R&D) comprise creative work undertaken on a systematic basis in order to increase the stock of knowledge . . . and the use of this stock of knowledge to devise . . . new materials, products, or devices . . . new processes, systems and services, or . . . improving substantially those already produced or installed.' (OECD, 1981).

R&D may thus be considered to be an activity which is intended to lead, sooner or later, to innovation, but the experience of the past twenty-five years' study of the innovation process indicates two important qualifications. First of all, R&D may not lead to invention, or invention to innovation. A great deal of new knowledge is not necessarily applied to a practical end, and a majority of inventions never reach the market-place, although the generation of both the new knowledge and the inventions may have been necessary (for example, to demonstrate what will not work). Second, a successful innovation requires a great many inputs in addition to R&D, such as good communication between R&D staff and the rest of the organization, effective management, efficient production, marketing, investment and skilled personnel. Indeed, inefficient management of the whole innovation process may be an important reason why some inventions do not become innovations, and why some new knowledge may not be applied to practical ends. Technological innovation is thus absolutely, but not exclusively, dependent on R&D.

Design, the main subject of this book, is of course also of vital importance to innovation. Much of the development work in R&D involves the design, construction and testing of experimental proto-types or other activities in which the discovery or novel idea is translated into a configuration of materials and components. But it is also part of the innovation process outside the R&D function, con-tributing, for example, to the identification of user requirements and technological options before R&D gets under way, to marketing by means of packaging design, company logo and 'image', advertising material and so on, or to production in the form of layout, sequencing of tasks and plant design. Indeed, the *Frascati Manual,* which is intended as a guide to member states' contributions to OECD com-parative international statistics on science and technology, and is easily the most extensive and comprehensive set of such statistics available, has great difficulty with 'design'. It does not compile sta-tistics on design; indeed, there are no systematic statistics on design produced on a regular basis (certainly not internationally compara-ble ones). Design is a 'borderline case between R&D and other in-dustrial activities' and OECD member states are asked to divide their data on design, some to be included in R&D statistics and the rest excluded (OECD, 1981).

Differences between R&D and design

There is thus considerable overlap between R&D and design, since an important aspect of development work is design, and vice versa. However, design also differs from R&D in two important respects. First, design is more widespread throughout industry in general, and throughout any particular industry or firm, than R&D. Second, and somewhat paradoxically, design is very much the poor relation com-pared to R&D, in that the latter is a much more respected activity, even by firms that do not do it. The historical reasons for this are discussed in chapter 4.

Firms carry out a range of activities as part of the day-to-day business of surviving and possibly expanding, which may – depending on strategy – include technological innovation. Design will play an important part in both technological innovation and non-innovative activities. Similarly, design will play an important part in both R&D and other activities necessary to the innovation process. Design is thus more widespread than R&D in any particular firm or industry, and in this sense more closely resembles activities such as marketing or production. The fact that any of these activities – R&D, design, marketing or production – may be sub-contracted to another, independent firm rather than carried out within the firm, does not alter the general point.

Design is also more widespread throughout industry in general, for similar reasons. That is, although a large number of firms nowadays carry out some R&D, the resources spent on R&D indicate that it is an activity that is concentrated in only a handful of industries. In the UK in 1987, for example, the aerospace, electronics and chemicals sectors accounted for 71 per cent of all resources (that is, from government, industry and other sources, for military and civil projects) spent on R&D in the business enterprise sector. In Germany and Japan, 70 per cent and 73 per cent respectively of such resources was spent on electronics, chemicals and engineering (OECD, 1987). Some industries are thus highly research-intensive, while others are much less so. Design, however, is very important to both research-intensive industries, such as aerospace or consumer electronics, and traditional, craft-based sectors not so concerned with R&D or technological innovation, like furniture or pottery, even though the type of design input may vary, engineering design being much more important to the former, for example.

The second distinction between R&D and design concerns the attitude firms have towards both activities. Firms vary enormously in the extent of time, effort and money which they believe should be accorded to design, and the extent to which design is carried out by professional design staff (employed by the firm or retained as consultants). There are, of course, design-conscious firms, some of which we have visited in our studies. These firms employ professional design staff or retain design consultants, take design seriously throughout the firm and allocate resources accordingly (see figure 1.2). For example, one of the firms making plastics products which we visited in Study

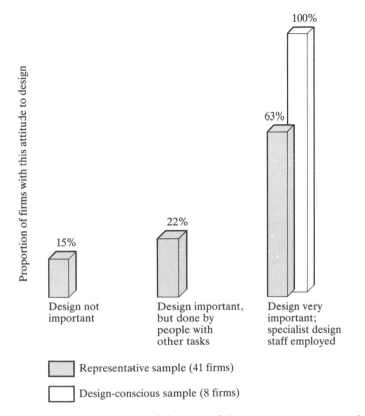

Figure 1.2 Attitude to design and the use of designers in a sample of design-conscious and typical firms making plastics products (Study A)
Source: Walsh and Roy (1983)

A (described later in this chapter) was chaired by a designer and both the sales director and marketing manager were designers. (All three were women, which was even more unusual among the firms we visited.) A well-known designer was retained as consultant, and a substantial number of staff were employed as practising designers as well. Indeed, this particular firm might have erred on the side of over-emphasis on design at the expense of financial and strategic management, since it had won a number of design awards but had been making a loss at the time of our study. Another design-conscious firm, which was both commercially successful and had won many design awards, had a design director, responsible for nothing but design, who said, 'Design is not the icing, but the first nut and bolt.'

However, we have also visited many firms which regularly design new or improved products without being fully aware of how the design process happens; they are the firms where design is done by staff whose main job is something else (what Gorb and Dumas (1987) call 'silent design'), who may have no training in design and who may not accord it much time or effort. Figure 1.2 shows that more than a third of the randomly sampled 'typical' firms visited in the plastics sector during Study A, either did not consider design important at all or produced new products without retaining outside designers as consultants or employing full-time in-house design staff. The firm we visited which said they literally did design by a 'sketch on the back of a cigarette packet' has already been mentioned. In another firm, which produced low-precision plastic components, whenever a new product was to be made, the toolmaker who was to make the mould would first decide on a suitable shape for it and, in effect, would thus design the product. Two heating equipment firms we visited in Study B (described later in this chapter) illustrate the difference in attitude to design among firms which are similar in many other respects, including size. The first had a large team of industrial designers, testing staff and combustion engineers concerned with the design of new products. The second had only the technical director doing virtually all the product design as well as playing a managerial role.

Thus, although design is carried out almost universally, while R&D is not, firms regard R&D as an activity for professional, technically qualified staff and one which must be done properly and regarded as important, if it is to be done at all. On the other hand, the image of design is far more patchy, with a substantial number of firms still not regarding it as very important in terms of resources, even though they do carry out design in some way or other.

In an attempt to distinguish design from research and development in the context of the total innovation process, Christopher Freeman (1983) has identified four kinds of design activity:

> *Experimental design*: the design of prototypes and pilot plant leading to the preparation of production drawings for the commercial introduction of a new product or process.
> *Routine design engineering*: the adaptation of existing technology to specific applications (typical of the design work done by many engineering firms when installing new plant or equipment).
> *Fashion design*: aesthetic and stylistic design of items ranging from textiles and shoes to chairs, car bodies and buildings. (This

kind of design may result in novel forms, shapes or decorations, but often involves no technical change at all.)
Design management: the planning and coordinating activity necessary to create, make and launch a new product on to the market.

Moreover, Freeman (1983) sees design as crucial to innovation in that it is the domain of creativity where ideas are devised, but also where 'coupling' occurs, that is to say, where technical possibilities are connected with market needs. The four categories of design are concerned, he writes, with 'matching techniques and markets'. Further, Freeman suggests that this integrative role of design is not limited to matching inventions and markets. It is equally important in relation to production techniques as many new products also require a new process to produce them. In the studies that form the core of this book, we identified a similar role for design, describing the role of the designer as partly that of 'gatekeeper' (Walsh and Roy, 1985). By this we meant that the designer accessed all the specialized functions within the firm, such as R&D, marketing, production, finance, materials testing, strategic management and corporate planning, and some outside the firm, such as trends in fashion and design, from which to assemble the necessary information to input to the design process.

Design Professions and Specialisms

A more usual way of classifying design is in terms of its different professions and specialisms. The Design Council's (1988) directory of design expertise gives the following categories:

- *product design*, including products ranging from ceramics and toys to scientific instruments;
- *graphic design*, covering everything from corporate identity and packaging to magazines and film;
- *interior design*, including shops, buildings and exhibitions;
- *fashion and textiles*, ranging from clothing and carpets to jewellery.

Figure 1.3 shows some of the main areas of design broadly grouped into products (three-dimensional design) and graphics (two-dimensional design).

In this book we are concerned mainly with product design, occasionally straying into other areas such as packaging and brochure

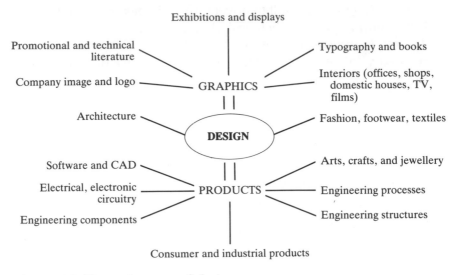

Figure 1.3 The main areas of design
Source: Shirley and Henn (1988)

design where this is relevant to a particular product or range of products.

Engineering design and industrial design

The Corfield Report (NEDO, 1979) defines product design as including 'both engineering design and industrial (aesthetic) design'. However, in manufacturing industry a distinction is frequently made between the contribution of the engineer and the industrial designer.

The Fielden Report on 'Engineering Design' (DSIR, 1963) defined mechanical engineering design as 'the use of scientific principles, technical information and imagination in the definition of a mechanical structure, machine or system to perform pre-specified functions with the maximum economy and efficiency'. This definition suggests a conception of design in which products are regarded as an assembly of components and materials, the arrangement of which is determined by the imperatives of technical function. The selection of a particular design configuration emerges through the engineering designer trying out different arrangements on the drawing-board (or CAD terminal), performing the necessary stress and other calculations, and selecting components and materials according to their performance and cost. Although many engineering products are designed in this way, such an approach does not take into account the relationship of the product to its users. Moody (1984) provides a lucid explanation for the emergence of industrial design as an activity distinguishable from engineering design:

> Industrial design seeks to rectify the omissions of engineering; a conscious attempt to bring form and visual order to engineering hardware where the technology does not of itself provide these features. There are a few instances where technology has an intrinsic elegance: the steam-turbine rotor has complex symmetry which derives from the mechanics of fluids; the exterior of the modern aircraft fuselage has a continuous organic form which derives from its aerodynamic purpose; the modern suspension bridge is the essence of structural simplicity. . .
>
> Industrial design seeks to relate the hardware to the dimensions, instinctive responses, and emotional needs of the user where these are relevant requirements. Through the conscious control of form, configuration, overall appearance and detailing, industrial design is capable of conveying to the user the abstract characteristics of a product, e.g. robustness, precision. . . . It can arrange for controls to be comfortable, pleasant, and easy to operate. It is capable of imbuing a product with a distinctive ambience, style and feeling of good quality which equates with the personal taste of the user. By these various means, industrial design is capable of bringing a rounded contribution to innovation, reaching out sensitively to the user.

In practice, the relative importance of engineering and industrial design varies considerably from product to product. There is a spectrum of product design, as illustrated by the examples given in figure 1.4, in which the contribution of engineers and industrial designers depends on the relative importance to the purchaser and user of technical, aesthetic and ergonomic factors.

Is Design more Important than Invention and Innovation?

Every innovation, from the most radical to the incremental, requires design input. But each basic technical idea, invention or principle is

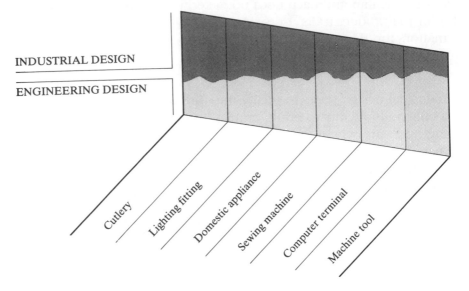

INDUSTRIAL DESIGN

ENGINEERING DESIGN

Cutlery

Lighting fitting

Domestic appliance

Sewing machine

Computer terminal

Machine tool

Figure 1.4 The design spectrum, showing the relative contributions of industrial design and engineering to the development of different types of product
Source: Design Council (1977)

likely to generate a vast array of possible design configurations and subsequent modifications, so the majority of product designs are based on past inventions and innovations.

Designing often involves no technical change at all, but may simply result in a product with a different form, style, pattern or decoration – for example, a 'new' design of chair or body styling for a car. Fashion design has been described as the creation of 'non-innovative novelties' (Piatier 1984). Often, designing involves incorporating new components, materials or manufacturing methods into an existing product – for example, a washing-machine with micro-electronic controls or a civil airliner with a head-up display originally developed for military aircraft.

Designing is thus broader than invention and innovation because, while invention and innovation involve a technical advance in the known state-of-the-art of a particular field, designing normally involves making variations on that known state-of-the-art. Designing is involved across the whole spectrum of technical innovation shown in figure 1.5. But most of it – perhaps 90 per cent – occurs towards the incremental innovation and design variant end.

Radical or breakthrough innovation	Transistor,* steam engine Hovercraft,* 'safety cycle'	Major change
Major product innovation	Advanced Passenger Train Microwriter portable word processor	
Incremental product innovation	Netlon extruded plastic mesh Raleigh Chopper 'fun' bicycle Lego plastic construction toys	
Design variants and new models	Ferranti IBM-compatible computer Gordon Russell office desks	Minor change

* Not case studies in our studies

Figure 1.5 Spectrum of innovation from technological breakthroughs to design variants with examples from our studies

Rothwell and Gardiner (1983) have distinguished between pre-production design processes, leading from a basic idea to an original innovation, and post-production design processes of successive re-design, component changes and evolution. Post-production redesigning may eventually result in further product innovations, the emergence of a standardized 'dominant' design and 'families' of design variants – for example, a range of aircraft engines or motor cars of similar basic design but with different specifications.

Several authors have captured this concept of a process in which a 'dominant design' emerges. Utterback (1979) also writes about dominant designs, Nelson and Winter (1977) about technological regimes and natural trajectories, Sahal (1981) about technological guide posts, Dosi (1982) about technological paradigms and Georgiou et al. (1986) about technological corridors. The idea common to all of them is that the beginning of the evolution of a new technology is characterized by a multiplicity of potential approaches which is gradually replaced by a convergence on one common approach. The implication is that firms do not have infinite freedom in technological decision-making, but that constraints limit their technological options except during the early stages of the evolution of a new technology. Furthermore, these constraints are common to a large number of firms operating within one technological area.

Utterback (1979) suggested that, as an industry moved into its mature phase, emphasis was shifted from a diversity of designs to undifferentiated standard products, while flexible but inefficient production processes evolved into efficient, capital-intensive but rigid ones, involving automation and the replacement of highly skilled labour by less skilled jobs of monitoring and control. While this pattern has been characteristic of a number of industry sectors, developments in Flexible Manufacturing Systems (FMS), since Utterback was writing, have now made possible capital-intensive, highly automated production processes which are capable of a high degree of flexibility and the production of products with varied specifications (see also Womach et al., 1990). At the same time, our research on design suggests that the changes in design emphasis over an industry's life cycle are much more complex than those proposed by Utterback. Product differentiation is a major strategy in the mature phase, as Utterback acknowledges when emphasizing incremental innovations. This differentiation involves a multiplicity of design changes, fashions, styles, redesigns and variations in the designs within a product range aimed at different market segments, rather than 'undifferentiated standard products'. Indeed, this is why we have chosen to examine design strategy in mature as well as newer industries.

A good example of a mature industry which has responded to consumer demand for a large variety of good designs at affordable prices is knitwear (Baden-Fuller and Stopford, 1990). The introduction of computer-controlled knitting machines in the mid-1980s, plus computer-aided design of garments, together with other organizational innovations, has enabled knitwear firms, which formerly could only produce a limited range of relatively expensive garments, to offer customers an enormous variety of designs of good quality at reasonable prices. The technical, organizational and design innovations have also enabled some firms in the industry, like Benetton, to respond very rapidly to fashion changes and to get its products into the retail shops very fast (Belussi, 1989).

However, there is a difference between the design variations involved in product differentiation, such as the difference in the shape, colour and pattern of different sweater designs, or bicycle specifications based on three-speed hub or ten-speed derailleur gears, steel or alloy components, etc., and the major variations in basic design in the early stages of an industry's life cycle, such as the variety of early bicycles based on two or three wheels of different or equal sizes and an assortment of frames and drive mechanisms (see figure 1.7 on p. 34 in the section below which discusses the evolution of cycle design). The difference is not just a quantitative one: the adoption of a dominant design involves a choice between qualitatively different concepts (such as steam, diesel or electric locomotives), while product differentiation in the mature phase involves incremental improvements of appearance and performance within the established dominant design. In this sense, our experience of design in mature and newer industries does not differ greatly from that of Utterback (1979). However, in that paper he does not fully take into account the tendency of mature industries, such as bicycles or railways, to try to break out of the constraints imposed by a dominant design by developing new radical innovations (such as recumbent and electrically assisted cycles (see figure 1.7) or magnetically levitated rail vehicles). Utterbach and Suarez (1992) explore dominant design further.

As far as design is concerned, therefore, we would describe the process in which an industry, product or a technology matures, as a shift in emphasis from designing for experimentation and technical innovation to designing for technical improvement, lower cost and ease of manufacture, and finally to designing for user needs, fashion, style and product variants, for different markets and applications.

Roy et al. (1990) argue that the economic and commercial importance of incremental innovations and design improvements has been greatly underestimated. In Britain especially, attention has tended to focus on the research, design and development work involved in transforming an idea or invention into an innovation on the market for the first time. However, as Japanese industry has so dramatically demonstrated, just as important are the processes of successive redesign, component improvement and evolution of the product to improve its performance, increase its quality and reduce its cost (see figure 1.6). The Japanese approach to design is discussed further in chapter 3.

Empirical evidence of the importance of incremental innovation and design improvements comes from a study of *Post-innovation*

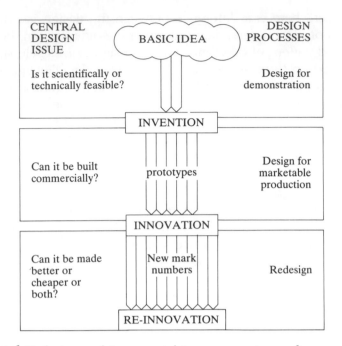

Figure 1.6 Redesign and incremental improvement are often more important economically and commercially than producing the original invention and product innovation
Source: Rothwell and Gardiner (1985)

Performance by Georgiou et al. (1986). This followed up thirty-six innovations which some fifteen years earlier had won a Queen's Award to Industry for technological innovation and which were originally reported in *Wealth from Knowledge* by Langrish et al. (1972). *Post-innovation Performance* attempts to see how companies introduce incremental innovations and design changes in order to compete. It shows that firms tend to compete within the defined 'technological corridors' mentioned above. By building up specific competences, particularly an organized knowledge base, companies are able to develop a family of designs within the technological corridor. The successful companies are those which improve their products in response to user needs and continuously modify and adapt their designs in response to new technologies and competing products.

Incremental innovations and design improvements are the 'bread and butter' of new product development for most firms, most of the time. Indeed, many firms do not even attempt to seek radical innovations, for a variety of reasons to do with their size and resources, the nature of their industry, the level of research and development necessary, or the size of risk involved. Even the firms that successfully introduce radical innovations do not do so very often (Freeman, 1982).

The reason why radical innovations have occupied such a prominent position in case studies of innovation is, first, that they are more likely than incremental innovations to be well known and therefore easily identified. Second, and more important, if they are particularly successful they can stimulate a series of related product and process innovations and give rise to new industrial sectors; and if such a series of related innovations occurs in certain infrastructural areas (for example, materials, energy, transport, communications, automation) they can have a pervasive effect throughout the economy, even making major contributions to 'long-wave' economic upswings (the periods of growth following the application through the economy of, for example, steam power; steel; electric power; plastics; electronics) (Freeman et al., 1982). Sectors experiencing rapid technological change and expansion grow faster than mature sectors. Over a period of time the result is a structural change in the economy, some sectors becoming much more important than others (see chapter 8 for further discussion).

Radical innovations may thus form the basis of technological revolutions, signalling major changes in direction in science and technology and significant economic changes as well. Incremental innovations and design improvements, on the other hand, are typical of the day-to-day work of most firms – the period of 'normal' technological activity and the working-out of Dosi's 'technological paradigms', mentioned above. Radical innovations, and incremental and design innovations, are thus equally important in economic terms, but in different ways.

New technologies and long waves

Recent work on the theory of major economic upswings and downswings has related such changes in the nature and emphasis of innovation and design to the take-off of new technologies and industrial sectors in attempting a dynamic, time-dependent theory of innovation (e.g. Freeman et al., 1982; Coombs et al., 1987; Dosi et al., 1988). The implication of such studies for design is that strategies based *primarily* on design, rather than on radical innovation (which also requires design, of course), are more appropriate than others at certain stages in the economic 'long wave'. These issues also relate to the relative importance of technology push and demand pull factors in the life cycle for an industry.

One of us (Walsh, 1984) has shown that the emergence of a 'radical' innovation or series of related innovations which provides the basis of a new industry, is likely to be more stimulated by scientific and technological developments in a relevant field than by upsurges in demand. The entrepreneur who recognizes the potential of the discovery (in the way described by Schumpeter, 1934) is likely, of course, to anticipate a future demand, or it would not be worth making the necessary investment to transform the discovery or invention into an innovation. But, as we discuss in chapter 6, it is unlikely that any kind of measurable demand for a completely new product could exist before it is available (unless the demand is for an earlier product that performed the same market function as the innovation, using entirely different technology).

As an industry or technology grows, however, there is a rise in the number of secondary innovations and competing designs (Schumpeter's 'swarming secondary innovations' competing for a share in the high, monopoly profits of the first new product), which settles down into the mature phase of a few dominant designs and a shift in emphasis from major product innovation to design modifications, incremental product innovations and (cost-cutting) process innovations. The influence of the demand-pull side becomes stronger relative to the push from technological advance, and the influence of price competition becomes more important relative to non-price competition (see chapter 2). Non-price competition in turn becomes more concerned with product differentiation, reliability and servicing than with major changes in the features or technological sophistication of the product.

As is shown later in this book, our own research supports the view that, in the sectors we studied, the evolutionary improvement of past innovations and existing designs was a more certain strategy for business success than attempts at introducing innovative products on to the market for the first time. Indeed, many of the product innovations we studied failed commercially, at least for their originators. It is rather a different matter for firms in high technology, R&D-intensive sectors such as pharmaceuticals, parts of electronics and biotechnology, where competitiveness is very heavily reliant on the ability to introduce innovative products. Nevertheless, even in these sectors, many firms deliberately choose to imitate or to be second in the market rather than first (see chapter 3).

Design clearly plays an important role in product differentiation and reliability, and also in price competition via the efficient use of materials and design for ease of manufacture (discussed further in chapter 2). But it is also important in the realization of the radical invention as an innovation and in the period of 'swarming secondary innovation' via competing designs. Thus design is important *throughout* the industry life cycle, and at different stages of the 'long wave', but plays a different role at each stage. The strategies of firms with respect to R&D, design and innovation may thus be considered in relation to the dynamics of the industry life cycle, and of economic upswings and downswings. This will be discussed further in chapter 3. Most of the remainder of this chapter and much of the book reflects our research in focusing on designing at the incremental end of the innovation spectrum, because this area of the innovation process is as important, for different reasons, as radical innovations and innovations in high technology sectors, but far more neglected. First, however, we illustrate some of the arguments about industry life cycles with an example from our own research.

Design, innovation and industry life cycles – the example of bicycles

From our Study A, bicycle technology may be used to illustrate these ideas of industry life cycle, natural trajectory and dominant design. A huge variety of cycle types developed between 1860 and 1890 before the now familiar diamond-frame 'safety bicycle' (and its women's frame variants) was universally adopted as both the most technologically efficient and the most practical machine (Roy and Cross, 1983). This dominant design has survived virtually unchanged since the turn of the century.

Manufacturers introduced many incremental improvements, including new materials (such as alloy steels for frames), components (such as gears) and accessories (such as electric lights). By 1930 these changes extended the range of cycles that manufacturers could offer from the 'roadster' (steel frame, three-speed hub gears, lever-operated brakes and 'sit-up-and-beg' handlebars) to lightweight racing bikes (alloy steel frames, ten or more derailleur gears, cable-operated brakes and aluminium alloy drop handlebars). However, essentially the same basic design was being offered in a range of specifications for different users. Inventors and designers continued

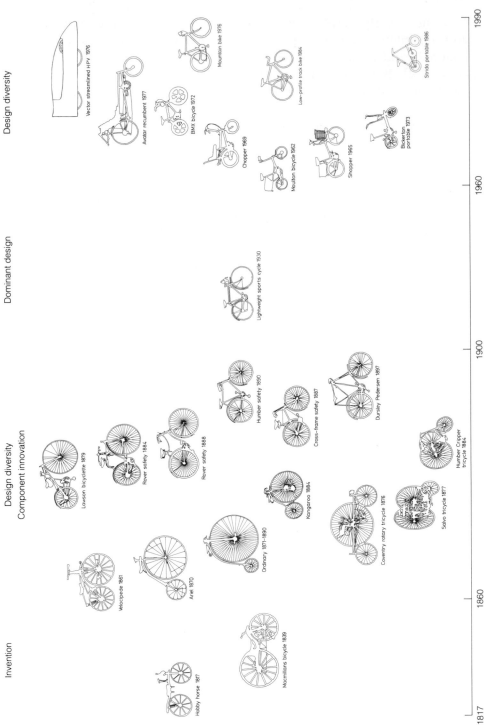

Invention

Design diversity
Component innovation

Dominant design

Design diversity

Hobby horse 1817

Macmillans bicycle 1839

Velocipede 1861

Ariel 1870

Ordinary 1871-1890

Lawson bicyclette 1879

Rover safety 1884

Rover safety 1888

Kangaroo 1884

Humber safety 1890

Cross-frame safety 1887

Coventry rotary tricycle 1876

Salvo tricycle 1877

Humber Cripper tricycle 1884

Dursley Pedersen 1897

Lightweight sports cycle 1930

Vector streamlined HPV 1976

Avatar recumbent 1977

BMX bicycle 1972

Mountain bike 1976

Chopper 1969

Moulton bicycle 1962

Shopper 1965

Low-profile track bike 1984

Bickerton portable 1973

Strida portable 1986

1817   1860   1900   1960   1990

to try to make more fundamental changes, and the flow of novel ideas after 1900 was maintained, but until the 1960s and the development of the small-wheel 'shopper' based on Moulton's innovative design, and various 'fun' bikes for children, none of the more radical innovations had any significant market impact or challenged the dominant design (see figure 1.7). Firms like the bicycle manufacturer Raleigh, visited in Study A, competing in a market in which there is an established dominant design, are faced with difficult strategic and design choices, for example whether to produce standard models at the lowest price or highest quality; or to attempt to innovate in design, materials or technology; or to adopt a combination of innovations in manufacturing technology and product design in order to offer a variety of high-quality machines at reasonable prices (on the pattern of the leading firms in the knitwear industry described earlier). This is discussed in chapters 6 and 7. Another example from our research, that of railways, also exemplifies the life cycles described above. This is discussed more fully by Potter (1987) and in chapter 5.

Before presenting any further findings from our studies it is necessary to describe them in more detail than we have done so far.

The Design Innovation Group Studies

The Design Innovation Group at the Open University and UMIST has been studying the role of product design and innovation in the business performance and international competitiveness of manufacturing companies since 1979. The studies described here were based on visits to more than 100 companies, ranging in size from fewer than twenty to more than 10,000 employees, in a number of specific industries. We focused on UK industries which had experienced a decline in relative trade performance over the previous decade, but which nevertheless included examples of British-based companies that were 'successful' when measured either in terms of commercial

---

Figure 1.7 (opposite) The evolution of bicycle design from a divergent, innovative phase at the early stages of the industry, through the convergence on a single 'dominant' design, and then to a second divergent phase as the mature industry attempts to innovate and differentiate its products to avoid declining demand
Source: Roy (1984); Roy (1992)

performance and/or in terms of their reputation for product design. The chosen industries also had both engineering and industrial design input, and included examples of traditional and more advanced technological bases. We investigated the technical and economic contexts of the chosen industries, the approach of specific firms to new product development, and case histories of particular products and innovations.

Study A was the initial phase of the research. It was a systematic examination of design and business performance in the UK plastics products industry, plus more general studies of design practice and management in two contrasting sectors – pedal cycles and motor cars. In the plastics industry, eight 'design-conscious' companies (including one Danish firm, Lego), which had won design awards of various kinds, were compared with a random selection of forty-one firms representative of the UK plastics products industry as a whole. In the pedal cycle and motor car manufacturing sectors, there were too few UK firms for this approach to be adopted, and so as many as possible of the firms that were identified via the industry trade association were visited. In total, twelve pedal cycle and cycle component firms and two UK car manufacturers (Austin Rover and Ford UK) were visited. Management and design staff were interviewed, using a check-list of questions covering the nature and strategies of the firm; the management of design and product development; factors in competitiveness; and production, quality control and marketing practice. The resulting data were analysed in the following main ways:

1 By categorizing and analysing firms according to size, type and ownership of firm; goals and strategies; planning, pricing and marketing policies; quality control; and attitude to design (plastics products only).
2 Statistical analysis of business performance against design performance, using the definitions of business success and design performance given below (plastics products only).
3 By developing case studies of successful and unsuccessful new product development. In the bicycle and motor industry studies these cases were used as the basis of Open University course material (Roy and Cross, 1983; Walker et al., 1989).
4 Some general conclusions were drawn and hypotheses made about the process, management and practice of design and innovation.

Study B was the main phase of the study, in which the hypotheses generated during the initial study were tested using an in-depth questionnaire administered during visits to companies in three further industry sectors: electronic business and computing equipment; office furniture; and domestic heating equipment. The two-part question-naire covered:

1 Company organization and strategy; product planning and marketing; expectations of future change; and factors in competitiveness.
2 Product specification; the design, development and production process; human and other resources devoted to product design and development.

Success and failure of firms were measured, using indicators of financial performance, market performance and design performance, defined more fully below. International comparisons between British firms and their leading overseas competitors were also made. The foreign firms were chosen for their reputation for good design and their success in UK and world export markets. From the three sectors, forty-two British and nine overseas firms (three Danish, two Swedish, two Japanese, one Dutch and one Canadian) were visited. The British firms were sampled randomly from trade directories as representative of their industry sectors and included eight design-conscious companies which had received various awards and citations for good design.

The firms in the survey came from sectors and countries where large firms predominate and from those where small firms play an important role. Of the British firms we visited, nineteen (47.5 per cent) were small (up to 199 employees); eleven (27.5 per cent) medium-sized (200–499 employees); and ten (25 per cent) large (over 500 employees); plus two firms which did not supply details of size (table 1.1). In the UK Business Monitors only 9 per cent of furniture firms, 15 per cent of heating equipment firms and 25 per cent of office machinery and data processing equipment firms have 200 or more employees. As Business Monitor surveys exclude firms with under twenty employees, estimated to represent at least two-thirds of the firms in these sectors, the real figures are more like 2 per cent, 5 per cent and 8 per cent respectively. The average size of the UK firms in our sample is thus larger than the average in the sectors as a whole.

The world-leading overseas firms in the sample were, on average, larger than the UK ones (table 1.1). Three (33 per cent) were small (up to 199 employees); two (22 per cent) were medium-sized (200–499 employees); and four (45 per cent) were large (all with over 2000 employees, and three were multinationals with over 10,000 employees). Given the increasing dominance, economic and political power, and share of total employment and output of very large

Table 1.1 Size of firms in Study B

| | Number of employees | | | | |
Sector (UK firms)	Not known	Up to 199 (Small)	200–499 (Medium)	Over 500 (Large)	All firms
Office furniture	1	9	6	2	18
Domestic heating equipment	1	1	1	5	8
Electronic business and computing equipment	0	9	4	3	16
Total (UK)	2	19	11	10	42
Sector (overseas firms)					
Office furniture	–	2	1	0	3
Domestic heating equipment	–	1	1	0	2
Electronic business and computing equipment	–	0	0	4	4
Total (overseas)		3	2	4	9

n = 51

firms, it is easy to forget how few of them there are relative to the thousands of small ones. About equal numbers of independent firms and subsidiaries of larger groups appeared in our sample. The size differences of the firms we have studied, and the importance of different-sized firms in the sectors in which they are located, are very important reasons for the differences in organizational structure and methods of managing the design and product development process discussed in chapters 5 and 7.

Financial and market performance

The business performance of the firms we studied was viewed as comprising financial and sales indicators, similar to those provided by Inter-Company Comparisons Ltd. Measures of *financial success* used were profit margin; return on capital; asset growth and profit growth. Measures of *market success* were turnover growth and export sales. Data were collected for the seven-year period before the interview, from Companies House returns and Annual Reports, and adjusted to constant prices. It is important to bear in mind that these indicators are only as valid as the accounts submitted by the firms, and that accounting conventions, estimates and intra-firm trade may have distorted the figures available. Furthermore, these data are measures of *firm* success or failure, rather than of product or project success or failure. The products that won design awards might be wholly or partially responsible for the recorded business performance of the firm, or responsible for a profit or loss completely at variance with the overall trend of company performance.

Design performance

Design performance is more difficult to define and measure than business performance and depends on who is doing the evaluation (see plates 1–4). Senior management may define 'good design' in terms of a product's impact on sales or profits; engineers may view good design in terms of technical performance; industrial designers in terms of ergonomics and appearance; purchasers in terms of value for money; end-users in terms of ease of use and reliability; and so on. Given the difficulty of measuring good design, we used available indicators of a firm's reputation for producing well-designed products, namely its success in gaining various awards for design, plus the views of other firms in the same industry. The following measures were used:

1 Total number of awards and prizes for design won by a firm at the time of interview, including Design Council Awards (now British Design Awards) and/or other industry awards and prizes, including overseas and international awards. (Studies A and B)
2 Net number of times a firm's products were cited on the Design Council's selection of well-designed British-made goods. (This scheme, formerly known as the Design Index, was discontinued in 1988 after being in operation for nearly thirty years.) This measure applied only to furniture and heating equipment as, at the time of Study B, electronic business equipment was not covered by the scheme. (Study B only)
3 Number of times a firm was mentioned by other firms in the survey as making the best-designed products in their industrial sector. (Study B only)

These indicators are based on expert and peer group judgements of what is 'good design', and are not entirely satisfactory. In such judgements modern aesthetics, use of materials, methods of construction and innovativeness tend to be important criteria, rather than long-term performance or consumers' views. Measures of consumer satisfaction could be derived from market demand for products, but would not give an independent variable to compare with business performance. It is possible to employ test results and user evaluations of good design, such as Consumers' Association recommended buys. It was not practical to use them in this study, however, as insufficient assessments compatible with the design award and citation data were available. However, other work by members of the Design Innovation Group (e.g. Leslie, 1984; Mole and Potter, 1991) has investigated this approach further.

The data from these two strands of work – design and business performance – were coded and analysed using a suite of computer programmes (especially developed for the project by Dr J. Towriss). This enabled within- and between-sector differences in management strategies and product development practice to be statistically related to the various business and design performance indicators. In addition to the computer-based statistical analysis a considerable amount of manual data analysis was undertaken.

Further details of the methodology used in Studies A and B, including questionnaire samples, details of design awards and business performance indicators, and statistical techniques used, are available in the following publications: Walsh and Roy, 1983; Roy and Bruce, 1984; and Roy et al., 1986.

We refer in this book to a third study conducted by the Design Innovation Group, *Study C.* It is not substantially discussed here as it is the subject of a separate detailed report (Potter et al. 1991) and has already been presented in several papers (e.g. Roy and Potter, 1990; Bruce and Roy, 1990) and other publications (e.g. Design Council, 1991; Roy et al., 1990). This study was an evaluation of the costs, benefits and risks of investment in specific product development and other projects involving inputs of professional design expertise. The study used as a data base a sample of over 200 firms in receipt of a UK government grant towards the cost of employing a design consultant, under the Funded Consultancy Scheme/Support for Design Programme described in chapter 2. Some of the findings are outlined in chapter 8.

Lastly, a study of high-speed trains is discussed at several points in this book and especially in chapter 5. It is both an extended case study and a sector study, conducted originally as the basis for Open University course material by one of the authors, Stephen Potter, separately from Studies A, B and C but concurrently with that work (see Potter and Roy, 1986; Potter, 1987).

Different Views of Design

Managers' understanding of design

Formal definitions of design, such as those given earlier, have their uses, but in reality it is the understanding of those who actually have to use and manage resources that determines attitudes, policies and practices. Indeed, one of the major barriers to the promotion of design in British industry is widespread confusion over its meaning.

The report of the NEDO Design Working Party (Fairhead, 1987) bemoans the fact that among British managers design tends to be equated with 'industrial design' and hence mainly with styling or visual appearance. The report then proposes that design is best used to mean something very similar to the whole process of new product development or innovation, namely 'the inter-disciplinary process by which products are effectively planned and brought to the market'. It is hardly surprising that managers are confused!

Evidence of this confusion is provided in a survey of British firms that had won a Queen's Award for Technology or for Exports, in which managers were asked to rank factors that represented the most important aspects of design (Ughanwa and Baker, 1989). A wide variety of factors was mentioned, ranging from 'making profitable products' and 'safety' to 'efficiency in production or use of materials', with no clear pattern emerging.

In our surveys we also asked managers or other senior staff how they defined 'design'. This too produced a wide range of answers. But in general we found that in commercially successful firms, senior staff had a broad understanding of what was involved in designing, while in less successful firms managers had a much narrower view.

In Study A of the plastics products sector, there was a contrast between the award-winning, design-conscious firms, which viewed design in terms of several factors – fitness for purpose, making products that sell or make a profit, ergonomics, production efficiency, etc. – and the randomly sampled typical firms, one-third of which

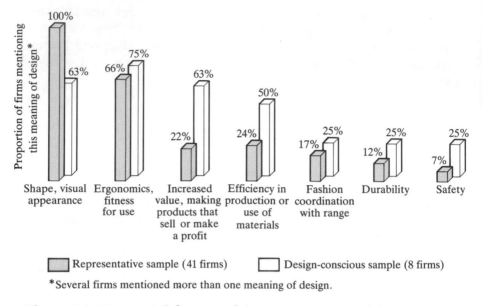

Representative sample (41 firms)   Design-conscious sample (8 firms)

*Several firms mentioned more than one meaning of design.

Figure 1.8 Managers' definitions of design in a sample of design-conscious and typical firms making plastics products (Study A)
Source: Walsh and Roy (1985)

defined design narrowly as 'shape' or 'visual appearance' alone (see figure 1.8).

Likewise in Study B of the furniture, heating and electronics sectors, there was a contrast between the firms whose managers had a broad understanding of design and firms that saw design as being concerned mainly or solely with one aspect: creating the initial concept; optimizing technical performance; or styling.

Table 1.2 shows that over 40 per cent of furniture, heating and electronics firms defined design as creating new concepts or ideas, that is, focusing on the early conceptual stage of the design process. At the same time many firms defined design in terms of several factors and clearly saw it as an activity which involved balancing multiple considerations, including those of function, market requirements, manufacturing and profitability. Over 30 per cent of firms specifically referred to a whole process or compromise between different considerations. But whether or not this process was described as 'design', 'product development' or 'innovation', it was noticeable that in all the sectors we studied, the financially most successful firms were those which realized that designing a product involved making decisions on very many factors. Such firms also realized that to take these many factors into account required some way – such as a

Table 1.2 Features mentioned by furniture, heating and electronic firms in defining design (Study B)

Factors	Firms mentioning (%)
Aesthetics,* appearance, style, looks, beauty, fashion, form, detail, packaging	53.1
Function, efficiency, quality, performance, engineering, 'technicalities'	51.9
Marketing, user requirements such as safety, reliability, ease of maintenance, ergonomics	48.9
Creativity, concept, original idea, problem solving	42.3
Ease of production	32.7
Whole process, compromise between different considerations, embodiment of idea in various ways, global role of design, 'too complex to sum up', planning	30.8
Cost, financial constraints, profit	13.5

n = 51
* Only one firm mentioned aesthetics, etc. alone. All the others linked considerations of style and appearance to other factors.

multidisciplinary project team – to coordinate the inputs of managers, design and development, marketing and production staff. The different methods of achieving this coordination are discussed in more detail in chapter 5. In addition to coordinating the inputs of staff in various departments and disciplines, some method is needed to make the different perspectives from which these staff view design, complementary rather than contradictory or conflicting. The different perspectives from which design may be viewed are analysed in the following sections. In particular, the potential conflict between the marketing view and that of designers themselves is considered.

Design from a marketing perspective

To most managers and marketing staff, design is primarily a resource. If used properly it can add value to products, thus improving profits, and can tailor products to particular markets, so improving sales. Just like money spent on new equipment or on advertising, investment in design can contribute to profits and growth. Kotler and Rath (1984) argue that 'design is a strategic tool' enabling marketers to match customer requirements to a product's performance, 'fitness for purpose', quality, durability, appearance and price. Thus Archer (1976) has described designing as 'the trick of discovering which set of attributes prospective purchasers would value and of discovering a product configuration embodying them at the right price'. For each market segment the mix of attributes and the price the customer is prepared to pay will differ. Thus, for example, in the bicycle industry, one of the sectors surveyed in Study A, price is the key factor in the lower 'utility' end of the market, fashionable styling and image are crucial for children's and teenage bikes, while technical specification and choice of components and materials are of importance to buyers of up-market sports and mountain bikes.

The argument of Kotler and Rath is that consumers' perceptions of the product are shaped by its configuration and ability to convey 'value for money' in comparison with alternatives. Our survey of the plastics industry in Study A found many examples of the importance of 'value for money' in determining customer choices and of products that failed commercially because they did not offer enough value for the price. This issue is discussed further in chapter 2.

Putting effort into design is one way in which companies can add value to their products and hence command higher prices. But in mature industries in which many products are competing for the same market, value for money alone is not enough. Where many products represent good value for money, design is also regarded by marketers as the ingredient needed to make their company's product distinctive, or to 'differentiate' it from the competition.

Kotler and Rath (1984) say that well-managed design offers a company several benefits:

> It can create corporate distinctiveness in an otherwise product- and image-surfeited marketplace. It can create a personality for a newly launched product so it stands out from its more prosaic competitors. It can be used to reinvigorate interest for products in the mature stage of its life cycle. It communicates value to the customer, makes selection easier, informs and entertains.

This role for design is not only understood by marketers. PA Design, a leading British design consultancy, says in its company brochure:

> The fundamental purpose of design is to differentiate a product or service from its competitors . . . that is what designers have always done. They have done it through aesthetics, they have

done it through function, they have done it in many ways. But invariably the purpose is the same: differentiation. (PA Design, 1988)

Some designers would go further in describing the marketing-oriented role in which design is often employed. In designing a product, and even more in designing the environment in which it is seen by potential customers, and the promotional material used to draw it to the attention of those customers, the designer stimulates their imaginations, projects an image of desirable life-style by 'symbolizing meanings beyond the ones that are obvious' (Woudhuysen, 1989) and turns a 'need into a want' (Conran, 1989). People buy products not only for what they can do but also for what they mean. Design thus provides an 'elusive psychological bridge between people as they are and people as they would like to be' (Seymour, 1989).

The use of market-oriented design for product differentiation has its dangers and limitations. It may mean missed opportunities for leading the market with novel design concepts or major technical innovations. Traditional marketing research is unlikely to reveal demands for something really new. Radically new designs and, even more so, radical innovations, are far less likely to be stimulated by 'demand pull' than incremental changes. A shrewd or experienced entrepreneur may anticipate a future demand on seeing or hearing about a radical new design or invention; but the stimulus in that case is essentially a 'push' from the new discovery or idea (Mowery and Rosenberg, 1979), and in such cases the inventors, designers and entrepreneurs must usually overcome many obstacles, including conservatism within the organization and/or the firm's reluctance to adopt a more 'creative' approach to marketing (Alexander, 1985).

Traditional and creative approaches to the identification of customer needs and requirements are discussed in chapter 6. That is why we have included in our studies some examples of products which are innovative in design and/or in technology. These examples indicate that creating an innovation is not usually enough to produce a commercial success. Subsequent technical and design improvements, and the existence – or creation – of substantial demand, stimulated by a major promotional effort and, for radical changes, the re-education of potential users by means of training programmes and technical services, are usually needed before the product is accepted widely on the market. As will be shown in chapter 7, such improvements are often made by firms other than the original innovator.

Designers' views of design

Designers may resist attempts to quantify their efforts in financial terms or to view themselves as 'a strategic tool' of managers and marketers. They often stress other priorities in their work, such as achieving technical excellence or visual harmony in a product, or keeping up with the latest technical or design ideas. Or they may have wider objectives such as wishing to improve the environment or seeking to elevate public taste. It is perhaps not surprising that designers and architects are in the forefront of the movement (briefly discussed in chapter 8) to develop 'environmentally friendly' products as a response to growing environmental problems such as global warming.

The various awards, exhibitions and competitions by which the design community gives recognition to 'good design' have generally rewarded those designs displaying excellence in performance and quality, elegant appearance, originality and, sometimes, social responsibility. Inevitably attempts to judge design in terms of its impact on sales and profits, such as the Design Effectiveness Awards introduced in 1989 by the Design Business Association, have drawn criticisms from some designers that this runs counter to their main objectives and core values. As one consultant industrial designer observed, 'It [the Design Effectiveness Award] means that as a designer you must pursue different objectives. It then becomes pure marketing and is not a design function. . . . Design is being driven by marketing and managerial imperatives. People are just copying each other and design is becoming stagnant' (quoted in Myerson, 1989).

There is bound to be a certain element of subjectivity in the concept of 'good design' – like notions of art or beauty, it is partly a function of each person's own taste, though clearly influenced by (as well as influencing) fashion. There is always the danger that 'good design' is simply what designers like at that moment. And yet there is a strong feeling that good design should not be defined simply as 'what appeals to the market', which is in danger of leading to what might be called the 'coal-effect fire syndrome'. Most designers, and many other people who like to think they have good taste, deplore the design of fake wood and fake coal electric fires. Yet many thousands, if not millions, of members of the public choose such designs in preference to others on offer. Does this fact make it a good design? Someone viewing design from a marketing perspective might say 'Yes', whereas a designer would probably say 'No' (with a shudder). This example poses the potential contradictions between marketing and design perspectives at their most extreme. Nevertheless such tensions are always present in some, possibly more limited, degree. Buhl (1990) has also discussed this point and several examples are illustrated in plates 1–4.

Designers often see themselves primarily as creative people, generating ideas and embodying them in products, buildings, shop interiors or corporate identities. The buildings, products and so on thus represent the realization of their self-expression. This image is emphasized by the way some industrial designers described themselves and their work, which reinforces, and is reinforced by, images other people have of them – as 'arty', idealistic and possibly difficult to manage. A well-known product and engineering designer said, 'It's the job of designers to delight and surprise consumers, specifically not to churn out the same old stuff that everybody expects' (Dyson, 1987). Some designers we interviewed agreed and talked about conceiving new concepts, forms and configurations. Others talked about their work in terms of art, and the creation of excitement or beauty. They also obtained satisfaction from the technical problem-solving required to produce a design that functions efficiently, is economical with materials, looks good, is easy to use, and so on.

Some designers inevitably felt a tension between creating original ideas or technically satisfying solutions and the marketing or commercial constraints imposed by management, for example the need to meet given cost targets or to avoid designs that would not be accepted by the mass market. In one of the bicycle firms visited in Study A, for example, the design department had developed a new type of foam-filled saddle against the wishes of the marketing department which considered that it would not sell. It was not surprising that a common demand from managers and marketers was that designers needed to understand market requirements better and develop skills such as costing design proposals.

Some designers may also experience a conflict between their own expectations of creativity and problem-solving and the firm's expectations of balancing many requirements and coordinating with many other functions within the firm. On the other hand, other designers have found that they can express their creativity precisely by attempting to satisfy multiple requirements and liaising between departments.

The social utility of design

The views expressed by designers and by marketing and other staff in manufacturing firms are essentially concerned with design as they experience it, as practitioners, managers and users of design activities.

Recently, however, particularly since design has received a great deal of media and popular attention, attempts have been made to analyse, and criticize, design from the point of view of its function in society more generally.

Following radical critiques of the idea that science and technology are 'neutral' (e.g. Young, 1977), Thackara (1988) argues against the idea that design is just a 'neutral planning tool' providing tasteful goods and possibly cleaning up the urban landscape. He is emphatic that design is neither neutral nor apolitical, but is a planning activity dictated by commercial and political interests, and responsible for products and environments that sometimes fail to meet even basic human needs.

Similarly, Papanek's (1982) radical critique of industrial design is that it is concerned mainly with providing unnecessary 'toys for adults' (like rhinestone-covered pill-boxes or electric hairbrushes) to make profits, while ignoring the 'real world' problems of environmental pollution, disabled people, Third World poverty, and so on. Papanek suggests that the onus is on members of the design profession to take moral responsibility and to work only on projects which are justifiable in terms of their social utility and value.

Some designers might counter this by maintaining that what they are doing is enriching the quality of human life, or at least the choices available to consumers, and bringing about constant improvement and changes to the material world. But is it possible for designers to act, as individuals, to bring about fundamental social changes? Forty (1984) suggests that the main intention of professions like industrial design in market economies is to make a profit for the manufacturers.

Objects are devised by designers who are subject to the ideas and influences of the society in which they live. For Forty, design activities are so enmeshed with the economics and culture of capitalist society that it cannot be the responsibility only of designers to change the nature of their work. It requires a more fundamental change in the values and structure of society. The same argument might be applied to technology – to alter the rate, and especially the direction, of technological change may require political change.

Design, therefore, is not only a subjective concept, the judgement that it is 'good' or not being a function of individual taste. It also has an important objective economic and social role. For the firm, de-signing products means combining function with materials so that they can be produced efficiently; it also means combining style and appearance with function so that they appeal to potential customers.

Together they mean imparting to the product features that will make it profitable. Design also acts as a mechanism for translating broad concepts of invention into a commercially viable commodity which will become an innovation once it reaches the market-place.

Through design, an idea is embodied in the product in such a way that it will sell; but in order to sell it the designers must also have created ideas, fantasies and so on in the potential consumer, via the product's image. In the course of imparting an image – of a desirable life-style, for example – the designer makes a great many assumptions which reflect his or her own values and which are not necessarily the result of market research by the firm. For example, assumptions are made about the desirability of a middle-class life-style, about certain attitudes to property, about what working-class people want, about styles that are appropriate for women rather than men, or for girls rather than boys. In this way design reflects and reinforces many social values and prejudices about people's roles and relationships (even while it may also set trends and fashions in other respects). It is also very easy to ignore the wider consequences of design, for example environmental consequences, unless these are explicitly specified in the brief and therefore required by the firm. We return to this question in chapter 8.

Design Skills

The 'tacit knowledge' of the designer is one way of expressing an aspect of the conceptual processes making up creativity. A distinction can be made between 'knowing what' and 'knowing how'. The former refers to the explicit and stated rules of going about a task, like the recipes in a cookery book or the Highway Code's rules for driving. The latter refers to the implicit and internalized knowledge and individual way of doing something. 'Tacit knowledge' is 'knowledge we know but cannot tell'; it is non-verbal and derived from experience: for example, the skill of the Cordon Bleu chef which goes well beyond the simple following of instructions in a recipe book and which it may not be possible to articulate in the form of a recipe; or the ability many drivers experience from time to time, of driving on 'auto-pilot' – doing everything necessary to proceed safely to a known destination without being conscious of the individual actions required to control the car.

Working-class people often have a vast array of craft and organizational skills and understanding of practical aspects of otherwise quite theoretical and academic subjects which is tacit and not easily passed on by explanation; hence 'learning by doing' and 'sitting by Nellie'; and hence also the fact that such skills are easily given less than their due recognition by people with more formal educational backgrounds (Cooley, 1987).

Tacit knowledge is regarded as an essential component of the skills and quality of designers. Often it is difficult for designers to convey which factors have contributed to the devising and shaping of an idea and the criteria governing the choice between one or more solutions – once all the constraints and requirements are specified, sometimes they just 'know' what will work.

As we have seen, designers think of themselves as being creative. But designers are not the only creative individuals in a firm. Design skill involves a particular type of creativity, namely, the ability to visualize something that has not existed before and to manipulate and represent that idea through sketching, drawing and modelling. Figure 7.1 in chapter 7 (pp. 193–5) shows some examples of design sketches and drawings from different stages of the design process.

Visual imagination is crucial in design because, in Theodore Levitt's (1984) words, it enables mental pictures to be constructed of 'what is not actually present, what has never been experienced'. And drawing and modelling are key design skills because they enable alternative ideas, forms and details to be explored before actually making the object. So while a manager or marketing expert might have a clear idea of the market for a product and the requirements and constraints it has to satisfy, he or she does not usually have the ability to picture the design. It is the designer's task to visualize new possibilities, to manipulate forms and geometries and to communicate his or her ideas in a way that can easily be understood. As a result designers tend to be very solution-focused; they leap quickly from a problem to produce convincing-looking solutions.

The act of visualization, as well as helping the designer explore possible solutions, also helps others to clarify and assess ideas. Dreyfuss wrote in 1955 that the industrial designer can 'listen to executives, engineers, production and advertising [people] . . . throw off suggestions and . . . incorporate them into a sketch that crystallizes their ideas – or shows their impracticality'. The value of multidisciplinary brainstorming sessions to generate new product concepts, which we found in some innovative and design-conscious firms, were greatly enhanced if the group included one or more designers. The designers could provide sketches, or even simple mock-ups, of promising concepts for the group to evaluate before approving the idea for further development.

While most design involves drawing and modelling, the specific skills and knowledge required of different types of designer, and their ways of working, vary widely. Conway (1983) points out that, whereas a mechanical engineering designer needs the ability to visualize objects in three dimensions, and to use and understand the properties of materials and structures, an electronic designer works essentially in two dimensions and needs to know the logical consequences of arranging a particular set of components into a circuit design. And neither type of engineer tends to work in the same way as an industrial designer. As we discussed earlier, engineers normally design something from the 'inside out', starting with the component parts, internal mechanisms, and so on, industrial designers tend to work from the 'outside in', starting with the product concept, its overall form and relationship to its users.

New roles for industrial design

This concern of industrial designers with the whole product and the user has resulted in moves to broaden their traditional role beyond that of dealing with styling and ergonomics. It has been suggested, for example by Lorenz (1986) in his influential book *The Design Dimension*, that designers can play a key integrating role in product development teams, bringing together the many requirements that have to be met in a new product. As described earlier in this chapter, our own research supports the idea of industrial designers acting in a 'gatekeeper' role in multidisciplinary product development teams to coordinate the inputs of marketers, production engineers and other specialists (Walsh and Roy, 1985).

There is also evidence of industrial design consultants becoming increasingly involved with top management in determining product and marketing strategy. The reason is that designers are seen as being in close touch with technical and market trends and opportunities across a wide range of products and cultural fields. As one senior design consultant observed: 'We hold structured brainstorming sessions about the future with our clients. . . . The designer is a radar scanner, probing out architecture, technology, fashion, the market place, pop, everywhere, and subliminally translating that into design' (quoted in Chung, 1989).

For the same reason some firms, especially world-leading, design-conscious firms like Olivetti, Fiat and Sony, take care to find out about the latest ideas being produced in the design community by attending student design shows, sponsoring design competitions and commissioning design consultants to explore new possibilities in their particular products and markets (see chapter 4).

The Design and Product Development Process

Having discussed some of the ways in which different people view design, we are now able to distinguish some common features that apply across different design specialisms.

The '4 Cs' of design

The design activity, which we have described from various perspectives, has four essential characteristics. These might be described as the '4 Cs' of design (by analogy with the familiar '4 Ps' of marketing: Product, Price, Place, Promotion).

Creativity: design requires the creation of something that has not existed before (ranging from a variation on an existing design to a completely new concept).

Complexity: design involves decisions on large numbers of parameters and variables (ranging from overall configuration and performance to components, materials, appearance and method of manufacture).

Compromise: design requires balancing multiple and sometimes conflicting requirements (such as performance and cost; appearance and ease of use; materials and durability).

Choice: design requires making choices between many possible solutions to a problem at all levels from basic concept to the smallest detail of colour or form.

It is now recognized (e.g. Jones, 1970; Pugh, 1986b) that there is a common pattern to the design and development process across a broad range of industries and types of product. For example, design and development is usually an iterative process involving repeated activities of problem exploration, solution generation and selection that transform the brief via many possible solutions to a particular design specified in sufficient detail to enable it to be manufactured.

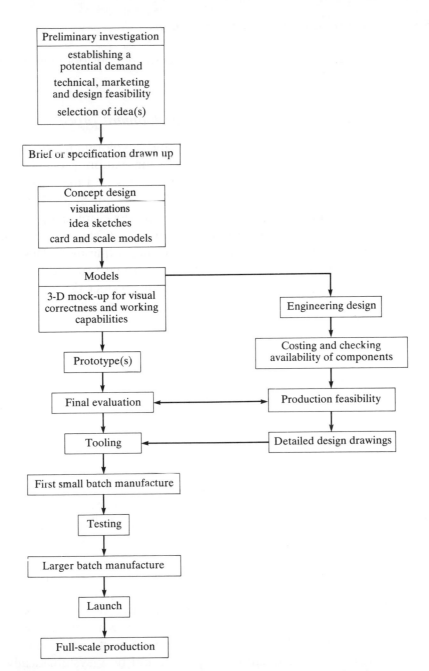

Figure 1.9 Schematic model of the product design and development process used by a manufacturer of electronic business equipment in Study B.

Note that prototype development, component costing and testing for production feasibility are undertaken in parallel. To speed the process further, a greater overlap between stages would be required.
Source: Bruce (1986)

In chapter 7 the various stages of this process are considered in more detail (see also Womack et al., 1990).

Design within the product development process

Earlier in this chapter we saw that design and development are at the centre of the new product development, or innovation, process providing the bridge between ideas, customer needs and manufacture. To check how this accords with reality, firms in our Study B were asked for a description of a typical new product development process from initial concept to final production. Figure 1.9 shows a typical example from a firm that made electronic business equipment. Despite many differences in the details of what individual firms did, what was striking was the similarity in the overall product development process between firms and across sectors. In virtually all cases a familiar pattern of stages was found:

Planning, which includes development of the initial idea; analysis of potential demand; feasibility assessment and briefing.
Design and development, which include market and technical specification; concept design; prototype development and testing; detail design and production engineering.
Manufacture and sales, which include production planning, tooling, test manufacture, full-scale production and market launch.

While this model describes the various stages we observed in a schematic way, it is important to emphasize the non-linearity of the process. At every stage there could be bugs, problems to be solved and new information required, which produced feedback loops, so that the whole design and development process was something of an iterative one, as suggested above. At the same time firms are having to carry out the various stages in parallel to speed the process (so-called concurrent engineering). The business performance of a firm did not appear to be related to the sequence of stages it went through when undertaking product development. What was far more important was the way in which product development was organized, as is discussed in more detail in chapter 5, and how systematically, as well as rapidly, the process was carried out, as is discussed in chapter 7.

2

Design, Innovation and Competitiveness

We began the research described in this book in response to increased concern, expressed in media, political and academic contributions, about the competitiveness of British industry. This chapter examines Britain's competitive position in international markets and explores the theoretical and empirical studies that have attempted to explain the British economy's relative decline. In particular, we focus on arguments about the key factors in international competitiveness: notably the price of goods, and their design, quality and technological sophistication, examining in particular the role of design. We also give some of the findings of Studies A and B, outlined in chapter 1, on the relationships between good design and business performance.

British International Competitiveness

The decline in Britain's competitiveness

The international competitiveness of British manufacturing industry has been declining or stagnant for many years. The UK share of world manufacturing exports was 25 per cent in 1950. In 1970 it was only 11 per cent, while it had fallen below 8 per cent by 1983, and has not risen much above this level since (see figure 2.1).

Most of the lost market share went to (then West) Germany and Japan. From 1950 to 1988 West Germany increased its share of manufacturing exports from 7 per cent to 20 per cent, with a peak of 22 per cent in 1973. Japan's share increased from 3 per cent to 18 per cent over the same period, with a peak of 20 per cent in 1984 (NEDC, 1989; Roy et al., 1990), see figure 2.1.

While British goods have been taking a declining share of exports, they have also been failing to maintain their share of the home

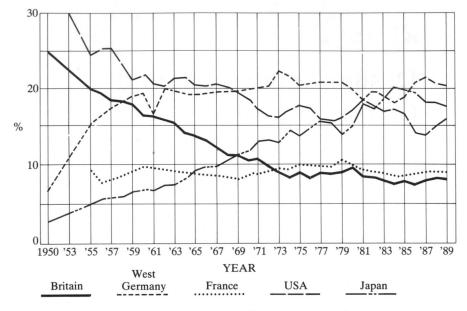

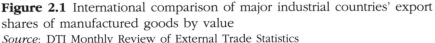

Figure 2.1 International comparison of major industrial countries' export shares of manufactured goods by value
Source: DTI Monthly Review of External Trade Statistics

market. Import penetration of manufactured goods in the UK has seen a long-term and accelerating growth rate (see figure 2.2). In 1955 only 6 per cent of manufactured goods sold in Britain were imports. By 1970 it was 20 per cent, and by 1989 over 35 per cent. Table 2.1 shows some examples of sectors in which import penetration was particularly high.

Britain is not alone in experiencing increased import penetration. The United States also experienced rapid import penetration during the 1980s, while commentators in France have observed that country's poor position in some international markets (Chesnais, 1990). In fact, Japan is one of the few advanced industrialized countries which has not had a substantial increase in import penetration (see figure 2.2). Britain and the United States, however, not only have the problem of sustained increases in imports as a percentage of home market sales, but also the failure of exports to keep pace. Many countries, especially the smaller advanced ones, have higher rates of import penetration than Britain – but they have higher levels of exports too, so that goods produced in those countries have a substantial share of the home markets of other countries (Walsh, 1987).

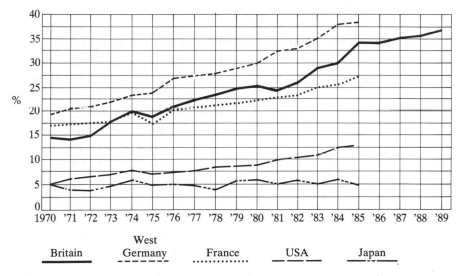

Figure 2.2 International comparison of import penetration of manufactured goods by value, with imports as a ratio of home demand
Source: NEDC (1989), Central Statistical Office Monthly Digest of Statistics

Table 2.1 Percentage and value of manufactured goods sold in the UK which are imports (1988)

Sector	(%)	Value (£bn)
Motor vehicles and parts	48	11.3
Electronic data processing equipment	87	5.5
Footwear and clothing	39	3.4
Electronic consumer goods	72	1.4
Domestic electrical appliances	42	1.1
Toys and sports goods	75	0.6

Source: Business Monitors (1989); quoted in Roy et al. (1990)

By 1983, Britain's imports of manufactured goods overtook exports for the first time since the industrial revolution. By 1988, the trade deficit in manufactured goods was £14.4 billion, nearly half of which was due to the deficit in cars, clothes, textiles and consumer electronics, all sectors with a high technological and/or design content (NEDO, 1989). During the 1980s, the United States experienced a rapid deterioration of its trade balance in the same sectors (Berger et al., 1989). UK sectors like chemicals, aerospace and construction and earth-moving equipment, on the other hand, had a positive trade balance, with 46 per cent, 64 per cent and 76 per cent of sales exported, respectively (Roy et al., 1990), although their contribution was not enough to offset the overall deficit.

This analysis is given further support by an international study of the performance of five key industries – mechanical engineering, chemicals, electronics, motor vehicles and textiles – in four major industrial economies – the UK, West Germany, the United States and Japan – carried out by the Policy Studies Institute (Cox and Kriegbaum, 1989). This study showed that between 1972 and 1985 in all these five sectors UK industry grew slower and, with the exception of chemicals and electronics, fared worse in export performance than the same industries in the other three countries studied. US industry also declined relative to West Germany and Japan. And, with the exception of textiles, Japanese industries out-performed those in all the other countries.

The example of the car industry

The car industry is characteristic of many of the arguments we advance in this book, as its competitive position is heavily dependent on design and innovation. Since the major product innovation of the motor car and its key components, the establishment of a dominant design (see chapter 1) based on the internal combustion engine, and the major process innovation of the production line, the car has changed over the years by an evolutionary process of incremental technological and design innovations. The competitiveness of the car industry today is therefore very highly dependent on technical and design input, which incorporates innovations in fuel efficiency and use of new materials with design changes, improving aerodynamic effficiency, safety, comfort, internal space and other features. Some of these issues are discussed in more detail by Walker (1986).

The car industry is also often taken to be symbolic of UK manufacturing industry in general and, for a number of reasons (Stubbs, 1979; Jones, 1981, 1983), a key indicator of the country's economic health. A healthy motor industry is seen to be linked to economic growth and a rise in real incomes; at various times the motor industry has been very 'visible' in the media; the car industry is still a major employer of labour, especially when its supplier industries are

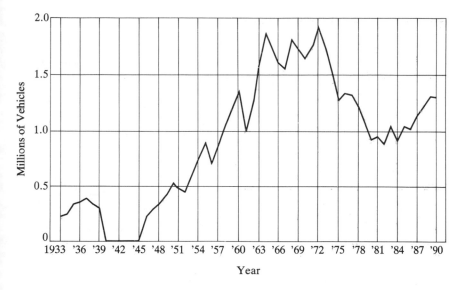

Figure 2.3 UK annual output of cars by volume: 1933–1990
Source: DTI Business Monitors, Society of Motor Manufacturers and Traders

considered; and at various times the industry has been used as an instrument of macroeconomic policy, for example by being encouraged to locate in areas of high unemployment.

Figure 2.3 shows the number of passenger cars produced in the UK from 1933 to 1989. The overall growth during the 1950s and 1960s represents a general increase in demand as a result of increases in real incomes during the post-war boom. The decline during the 1970s, however, was not the result of a corresponding decline in demand, but of the increased competitiveness of imported cars in the British home market.

During the 1980s, production began to increase again, but, as figure 2.4 shows, imports grew in number as much as total UK production, and by about twice as much as exports. Figure 2.4 shows that imports exceeded exports during 1975, and that the gap was greater than ever in 1989.

Although a variety of political and industrial factors is involved in the declining competitiveness of the UK motor industry relative to that of other countries such as Germany and Japan, much of the problem is due to a relative lack of investment in design and technical innovation. Cox and Kriegbaum (1989) have shown that throughout the 1970s and early 1980s the UK motor industry invested a lower

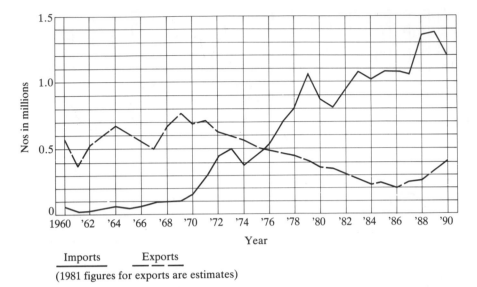

Imports _____   Exports _____
(1981 figures for exports are estimates)

Figure 2.4 UK car imports and exports by volume: 1960–1990
Source: DTI Business Monitors PQ 381, PQ3510

proportion of its sales on R&D, design and product development, market intelligence and manufacturing engineering than did its more successful competitors in Germany and Japan. While the British motor industry's investment in research, design and development as a proportion of sales caught up with German and Japanese levels by the mid-1980s, the British motor industry had by then shrunk in size compared to its equivalents in Germany and Japan. The latter were able to invest larger amounts in absolute terms, in order to maintain and improve their competitive position (see also Womack et al., 1990).

Competitiveness, economic performance and the quality of life

So far we have examined the case for concern about Britain's economic performance, using data on output, exports and imports for various countries. Aggregate figures used as proxies for economic performance do not, however, indicate the 'quality of life', the share of the national wealth spent on such items as health, education and so on, or the way in which the national income is divided among social classes, geographical regions, ethnic groups, etc. The limitations of economic indicators such as GNP (gross national product) are discussed much more fully by Miles (1985). It may be argued that countries with, for example, high rates of literacy, low rates of infant mortality, low levels of pollution or relatively small income differentials are at least as 'successful' as those with higher absolute levels of output or GDP (gross domestic product), or higher rates of growth in output or GDP, but with substantial sections of the population suffering from poverty, bad housing, ill health, pollution and so on, and small numbers of people earning high salaries and being responsible for a large share of consumer spending.

We will explore some of these issues more fully in chapter 8, together with the contributions design effort may make to goals of improving the quality of the environment and meeting human needs in the widest possible sense. For the purpose of this chapter, however, we will focus attention on the contribution of design to economic 'performance' at the national level and business performance at the company level. For, despite the limitations mentioned, these indicators are still the most commonly used, especially for comparative purposes, as reasonably up-to-date information is available for most countries, and it gives some indication of the potential, at least, for investment in improvements to the quality of life as well as the overall productive wealth of a nation. And most of the arguments which emphasize the importance of either design or innovation, and which we review in this chapter, are concerned primarily with their potential to stimulate economic growth.

For the purposes of the argument in this chapter, we are also making the assumption that improved economic and business performance is a goal that may be achieved by increasing competitiveness, which in turn may be achieved by improving innovativeness and increasing investment in design. This, too, is a question to which we will return in chapter 8.

Reasons for Britain's Competitive Decline

A great number of reasons have been advanced at various times for the decline in Britain's economic health. Serious and tabloid newspapers, television programmes, political manifestos and speeches and both theoretical and empirical studies by academics, have all addressed the issue. The reasons advanced have been as varied as those advancing them, and have included the relatively high prices of British goods, the exchange rate of sterling, the number of strikes, the lack of commitment by the workforce, aggressive trade unions, bad management, absenteeism, long holidays and many other factors. Essentially, the factors mentioned are all variants on *price* factors – and the argument that British goods *cost* more than competing products for a variety of reasons that amount to inefficient production, low productivity and high manufacturing costs.

Theories of competitiveness and trade

An important theoretical source of this argument is the conventional, neo-classical economic theory of trade which is based on the concept of 'comparative advantage'. That is, because some countries have certain natural resources, cheap labour, particular skills, easily available capital or prevailing weather, we would expect to find that those countries have a comparative advantage in production and export of goods taking advantage of such endowments. Essentially, the comparative advantage amounts to an opportunity to produce certain goods more *cheaply* than other countries. The comparative advantage theory of international trade gained prominence in the nineteenth century. It is still quite widely accepted, although it has been modified to take into account other factors, such as exchange rates (e.g. Meade, 1951; Edwards, 1985) and multinational operations, oligopolistic competition, strategic behaviour and industrial structures (Caves, 1971, 1974).

In more recent years, however, a number of theoretical and empirical studies raised more fundamental questions about the validity of the comparative advantage theory (e.g. Leontieff, 1953), leading to a series of 'new technology' theories of trade. International trade theory underwent a profound change in the 1960s (Freeman, 1979), beginning with Posner's (1961) development of a set of concepts that explained a large part of foreign trade from the starting-point that a country which first introduces a *new product* may export it at least until imitators come into the market, and may then maintain the 'technology gap' by continued innovation. It was Posner who first spoke of 'non-price' factors, including innovation, the product cycle, the operations of multinational enterprises, delivery dates and sales efforts, in competitiveness, in contrast to the price and cost factors which had previously tended to dominate trade theory. Vernon's (1966) product cycle theory provided a plausible resolution to the inconsistencies between conventional trade theory and the pattern of US trade observed by Leontieff.

By 1979, the National Institute of Economic and Social Research had compiled a book (Blackaby, 1979) addressed to the problem of British 'de-industrialization', the majority of leading economists and policy-makers who contributed concluded that a variety of 'non-price' factors were the major cause of lack of competitiveness and consequent slow growth in output and declining share of world manufacturing exports.

Further developments of trade theory were made by Vernon (1970), Hufbauer (1970), Wells (1972), Soete (1985), Dosi et al. (1990) and others, all exploring the importance not of a comparative advantage that allowed a country to produce certain goods more *cheaply*, but a comparative advantage that allowed it to produce goods that were *qualitatively* different – more technically sophisticated, better designed and so on. As Dosi et al. (1990) and Dosi and Soete (1988) point out, however, what appears to be a 'comparative advantage' is not the result of any 'endowment', but the result of what is essentially a learning process: innovative advantages are established by the gradual accumulation of capital and technology, which are not freely available but firm-specific, and which are both the result and cause of technological specialization in certain areas. A similar argument is developed by Cantwell (1989) in relation to the competitiveness of multinational corporations in particular.

During the same period, empirical evidence was also accumulating, showing that more expensive products sometimes outsell cheaper alternatives (Stout, 1977; Posner and Steer, 1979; Pavitt, 1980), and that, in general, there is a correlation between economic growth and growth of national technological activities (Pavitt and Soete, 1980; Fagerberg, 1985, 1988). An empirical study focusing on the Nordic Countries led Fagerberg (1985) to conclude not only that technological innovativeness made an important contribution to economic performance, but that 'contrary to popular belief, neither growth of relative unit labour costs nor differences in welfare state activity seem to have strong effects on the balance of payments constraint and growth.' Some more recent case studies and sector studies illustrating these points are discussed below. While design was not included as a factor in these new technology theories of trade, except in so far as it could be assumed to be part of innovation and technological change, some of the case and sector studies discussed in the next section do focus specifically on design.

Price and non-price competition

We now turn from macroeconomic analysis of competitiveness and international trade to micro-level consideration of particular products. Customers decide to buy products for a great variety of reasons. Apart from deciding that they need or want to buy something in the first place, and have some degree of purchasing power, they must make a choice between different items. Some products are obviously competing for roughly the same market – like different manufacturers' washing-machines or TVs. In other cases, quite different products are competing to provide a solution to a given problem, need, demand or desire. For example, demand for home entertainment may be met by a TV, board-game, book or the necessary items to follow a hobby. The demand for equipment to prepare food may pose a choice between a single expensive item like a food processor, or a variety of cheaper ones, such as sharp knives, a chopping-board, a grater, a lemon-squeezer, etc. There are endless examples and, of course, there will be purchasers who do not have to make a choice but will buy more than one of the potential alternatives.

Customers also make a choice between products and services: buying a washing-machine rather than using the laundry or launderette or, for the upper classes, employing servants; buying a TV and/or a VCR rather than going to the cinema; or buying a car rather than using public transport. Gershuny (1983, 1988) and Gershuny and Miles (1985) point out that the trend in households over many years has been an increase in purchases of manufactured goods (such as washing-machines, cars, TVs, vacuum cleaners, etc. – 'consumer capital') to fulfil various service needs or demands (for domestic work, transport, entertainment) by providing the service themselves, unpaid, rather than in the purchase of final services. Gershuny (1983) points out that there are in fact five classes of input to this new mode of provision of services: domestic machinery, for example cars, washing-machines, TVs; infrastructure, for example electricity generation and distribution, road networks, broadcasting networks; raw or semi-finished materials, such as petrol, washing powder, electricity; software and other intermediate services, for example equipment maintenance, TV programmes; and informal (unpaid) labour to combine and organize the other factors into final service functions. This innovation in the provision of services is what Gershuny calls the 'self service economy', which he has contrasted with the forecasts by Bell (1974) and others of a service economy (Gershuny, 1978).

The increased output of such 'consumer capital' goods and the competition between the firms that supply them, have represented an important growth in demand for design. Yorke (1988), however, shows that British design is world-famous in the fields of graphics and communications, but less important in the design of the products that use them: 'The British do not make video-recorders; they make what goes into the tape. These are post-industrial skills used in value-added inspirations.'

There is thus a vast array of reasons for making any given choice, related to the cost, convenience and quality of the alternatives, even before the influence of advertising, media images, brand loyalty and even ideology is taken into account.

The previous section introduced the distinction between 'price' and 'non-price' factors in competitiveness. The non-price factors are those related to the quality and design of a product, such as performance, reliability, appearance, safety, durability, ergonomics or ease of use and maintenance ('intrinsic' non-price factors); and those related to the quality of the service offered by its manufacturer or supplier, such as delivery time, user training, technical services, after-sales service or availability of spare parts ('associative' non-price factors) (Saviotti et al., 1980; Gibbons et al., 1982). Increasingly, as we note in chapter 8, non-price factors such as environmental impact or the political acceptability of the firm making the product or of the country where it is made, are also influencing consumers. While these might be described as associative non-price factors, they are only very indirectly concerned with the service offered to the consumer by the manufacturer. Price factors include financial arrangements for purchase or hire, trade-in allowances, depreciation, running costs, servicing and parts costs as well as the sales price after discount (see table 2.2 for a summary).

If two products of similar quality and design are on sale at different prices, the theory is that a rational purchaser will choose the cheaper product. Similarly, a rational purchaser will choose the better-designed, higher-quality product if two products of different design and quality are available at similar prices. These choices, in practice, will be influenced by advertising, company image and brand loyalty, which affect the purchaser's perception of quality, design and price. Ughanwa and Baker (1989) point out, for example, that purchasers generally regard price as an indication of quality rather than an independent factor, as captured by the saying 'You get what you pay for'. But, in any case, decisions are usually complicated by the fact

Table 2.2 Factors influencing competition

Factor	Example
Price	Sales price, discount, financial arrangements for purchase, trade-in allowances, depreciation, running costs, servicing costs, parts costs
'Intrinsic' non-price (embodied in the product)	Quality, appearance, innovativeness, technological sophistication, ease of use and maintenance, reliability, durability, compatibility with other products, ergonomics, portability, safety, comfort
'Associative' non-price (dependent on organizational arrangements of production and distribution)	Delivery time, after-sales service, packaging, distribution networks, availability of spare parts, technical back-up, good user-friendly manuals, advertising

that a variety of different price and non-price factors is usually associated with every choice between alternative products. The additional option of choosing a service rather than a product adds a further complication.

Several empirical studies have investigated purchasers' decisions, in order to assess the relative importance of price and non-price factors. Pavitt (1980) collected several studies of a variety of UK manufacturing sectors, and concluded that innovativeness or technical sophistication were the 'non-price' factors most strongly associated with competitive success in international markets. Other empirical studies have been based on statistical comparisons of technological and commercial performance (e.g. Patel and Pavitt, 1987).

The study by Cox and Kriegbaum (1989) mentioned earlier provided statistics from the early 1970s to the mid-1980s to show that British and, to a lesser extent, American industries, have invested less than their competitors in Germany and Japan on the research, design and development of new products. It is to this 'non-price' investment in R&D and innovation (in which they include design, product development and marketing) to produce high-quality, technically sophisticated products – more than 'price' investment in new plant and machinery to increase productivity and lower costs – that the authors attribute competitive success, especially that of German and Japanese industry. This is the case in established industries such as motor vehicles and textiles as well as in new technology industries such as electronics. The amounts invested in R&D and innovation that are necessary to achieve international competitiveness vary from sector to sector, but the key factor is to keep up with the 'going rate' for a particular technology. Germany and Japan in fact recognized in their post-war reconstruction programmes the need for advanced industries capable of supplying products of high quality and good design, incorporating the latest technology and materials. In post-war Japan, there was actually an explicit struggle between the traditional economists who argued that Japan should concentrate on sectors like textiles, where it had a comparative advantage (cheap labour), and the majority of economists in the Ministry of International Trade and Industry who argued for the identification of key 'leading edge' technologies and strategies for Japan to achieve in them an internationally competitive position in the medium term (Freeman, 1987).

Other studies have emphasized the importance of design, although probably the largest number of research projects, and certainly of theoretical explanations, have concentrated on innovation and technical change, rather than design, as factors in competitiveness.

The recognition of the importance of design as a non-price factor was stimulated in Britain by two official reports, the Corfield Report on *Product Design* (NEDO, 1979) and the Finniston Report, *Engineering Our Future* (Committee of Inquiry into the Engineering Profession, 1980). Both reports emphasized the importance of design in adding to the value of products, in particular to their technical performance and overall quality, as reflected in their appearance, finish, reliability, durability, safety, ease of use and maintenance. The Corfield Report concluded:

> The difference between the apparently more successful companies and countries and those less so is not in the *quantity* of work performed, but rather the *quality*. Not in the volume of final output, but in the value added to basic raw materials. This value is determined more by the *quality of design* and the way it is made to meet customers' requirements, than by other factors.

Table 2.3 Three ways of improving competitiveness

Product Innovation

The commercial introduction of novel products based on new technologies, materials, inventions and design ideas that offer unique features or performance to the user.

Good product design

The creation and development of product forms and configurations that may or may not be technically novel, but which offer enhanced value to the purchaser in terms of performance, appearance, reliability, ergonomics, etc., while at the same time permitting economic manufacture.

Process innovation

The introduction or adoption of new or improved methods of manufacture to allow high-value goods to be made at a competitive cost.

In addition, the Finniston Report emphasized the point that the innovation, design and price aspects of a product's competitiveness are closely related:

> The strengths of the advanced countries lie in inventing and exploiting new products and processes, incorporating high levels of human skill and knowledge, most of it at the leading edge of technology, and in continual incremental improvements to current products and processes through reducing production costs.

Table 2.3 illustrates the same point in another way.

Neither the British government nor the tabloid press has abandoned concern about price factors – used to legitimate policies to restrict trade union power and attempts to control inflation and rises in wages greater than the cost of living. But recent attempts to focus attention on design and innovation clearly indicate a change in emphasis to include 'non-price' factors.

Government Support for Design and Innovation

Support for design

British governments have recognized the importance of design to the competitiveness of manufacturing industry at least since the establishment of the Council of Industrial Design (now the Design

Council) in 1944 (Stewart, 1987). The recent upsurge of official interest in design came in January 1982, when the Conservative Prime Minister, Margaret Thatcher, held a seminar on 'Product Design and Market Success' at 10 Downing Street to which a wide range of personalities from the design world were invited – from Zandra Rhodes, the fashion designer, and Terence Conran, founder of Habitat, to the chairman of British Aerospace. In the May 1982 issues of the Design Council's sister journals *Design* and *Engineering* Thatcher wrote:

> There are many ingredients for success in the market-place. But I am convinced that British industry will never compete if it forgets the importance of good design. By 'design' I do not just mean 'appearance'. I mean all the engineering and industrial design that goes into a product from the idea stage to the production stage, and which is so important in ensuring that it works, that it is reliable, that it is good value and that it looks good. In short it is good design which makes people buy products and which gives products a good name. It is essential to the future of our industry.

One of the outcomes of this prime ministerial concern was a modest government-sponsored campaign called 'Design for Profit', launched in 1983, which aimed to make industrialists aware of the benefits of paying attention to design. Further promotion of design followed with the publication of the Department of Trade and Industry's *Design Policy* in 1984. That policy was to increase awareness of the benefits of good design in industry and commerce; to achieve a greater consciousness of good design among customers in the public and private sector; and to strengthen design education and training at all levels. This was reinforced by a new campaign to increase industry's awareness of design in 1986.

The publicity campaigns to improve industrial competitiveness by encouraging good design may have been slightly at variance with governmental emphasis on price competition, but did not seriously conflict with their well-publicized *laissez-faire* approach of relying on market forces and opposing public spending, since industrialists were being encouraged to invest their own money – or money obtained via the financial markets – in design activity. The significant departure from Conservative philosophy was the more substantial programme of government intervention called the 'Funded Consultancy Scheme' (FCS), which provided small and medium-sized firms with subsidies to employ a professional design consultant to help with the design of new or improved products, components, packaging, graphics or technical literature. This scheme ran from June 1982 to March 1985 and was succeeded by the 'Support for Design' (SFD) scheme, which ran until it was replaced by the Design Initiative, part of the wider Enterprise Initiative, in January 1988. (Firms receiving subsidies for design under these schemes were surveyed by our Study C (described in chapters 1 and 8 and by Potter et al., 1991).)

The FCS provided funds to enable manufacturing firms (including subsidiaries of larger groups) of thirty to 1000 employees to employ a design consultant for fifteen days at zero cost and for a further fifteen days at half cost. The SFD programme had similar aims, but the individual level of subsidy was reduced, while opening up eligibility to firms with one to 500 employees from all sections of British Industry (services as well as manufacturing). Under the Design Initiative, the size of firm remained restricted to under 500 employees and it had to be an independent firm or group. The subsidy amounted to half the cost of five to fifteen days' consultancy, with a two-thirds subsidy in Assisted Areas and Urban Programme Areas. In 1989, packaging and graphics design projects were deleted from the scheme.

The government has thus been spending public money in support of design. Government policies such as these, aimed at encouraging design and innovation, are the result of three important realizations. First, that the international competitiveness of manufacturing industry is closely linked to success in design and innovation; second, that left to themselves, market forces cannot – or do not – ensure an adequate level of activity in these areas; and third, as a consequence, that although Britain has perhaps the strongest design consultancy industry in the world (McAlhone, 1987), British industry is not viewed as making proper use of this major national resource.

The role of design and innovation in competitiveness has been the subject of a number of academic studies over the past few years, reviewed in this chapter. The failure of market forces (e.g. Pickering and Jones, 1984) explains why governments which are convinced that design effort and innovativeness contribute to competitiveness, feel obliged to stimulate, and even pay for, some of this activity themselves, even though their general philosophy may be to reduce government intervention and public spending in the way that the British Conservative government did in the 1980s and 1990s.

During the five years of the FCS/SFD programme, £22.5 million of public money was allocated to support some 5000 projects (Shirley and Henn, 1988). This sum of money is, in fact, very small. The average sum paid to a company was only about £4500. These subsidies undoubtedly encouraged small and medium-sized businesses to increase their use of professional design expertise, but to set them in context, it should be noted that sums up to three times as great are routinely written off by large corporations as a result of accounting errors (see Woolf and Tanna, 1988).

British governments have been notoriously slow to promote either design or innovation. The FCS/SFD programme was the first instance of government intervention to promote design with public funds, apart from the establishment of the Council of Industrial Design in 1944, with the specific remit of promoting good design in British-made consumer goods. It became the Design Council in 1970, with responsibility for engineering products as well as consumer goods, partly in response to the Fielden Report, *Engineering Design* (DSIR, 1963), which stressed the importance of design in engineering.

Innovation policies

Government promotion of technological innovation has had a longer history in Britain than promotion of design, but has still lagged well behind that of its competitors. Before and after the First World War, in steel, machinery and especially in precision engineering and other new technologies, the superior position of industry in the United States and continental Europe, compared with the UK, was in large part due to the much stronger policy of government in promoting innovation in those countries. Those governments used a variety of policy instruments, including the allocation of major resources for the education and training of skilled workers, scientists, technologists and management; differential taxes; patent law; and the encouragement of financial institutions that would invest in high-risk, innovative activities (Walker, 1980; Coombs et al., 1987). Even earlier, the decline of the British, and rise of the German dye and chemical industry after 1870, has been attributed in part to the strong policies used to promote technology in Germany, and the absence of any such policy in Britain in the name of *laissez-faire* ideology (Beer, 1959; Coombs et al., 1987; Walsh, 1984).

Although the Department of Scientific and Industrial Research (DSIR) was establishment in 1917, and campaigns to promote economic planning, including the promotion of science and technology, gathered momentum during the 1930s, serious government promotion of technology on any scale in Britain was essentially a post-Second World War – indeed, post-1964 – phenomenon (Williams et al., 1982). However, the Board of Trade did sponsor extensive studies in the 1950s of how science might be harnessed to industry (Carter and Williams, 1957). The Ministry of Technology, established in 1964 by the new Labour government, was responsible initially for four key sectors: computers, electronics, telecommunications and machine tools. It later merged with the Ministries of Power and Aviation, and eventually took on the rest of manufacturing, including the less glamorous industries. But even the (Labour) government, committed to the 'Britain that is going to be forged in the white heat of this technological revolution', limited its promoting policies to certain strategic industries, like aerospace. Support for the car industry, for example, was avoided even by Labour governments until the threat of both British Leyland and Chrysler going bankrupt in 1975 obliged the government to rescue both (Williams et al., 1982; Stubbs, 1979).

Conservative governments have been philosophically more opposed to intervention, despite the 1971 nationalization of Rolls Royce (aeroengines). Intervention is justified by the failure of the market mechanism to ensure the allocation of resources considered by the government as necessary for the benefit of society (Pickering and Jones, 1984). In practice this means that Conservative governments are willing to support research and development in defence-related fields, civil aerospace, nuclear energy, health, agriculture, basic research and certain other areas of potential competitive or strategic importance where the private sector is not prepared to finance a level of R&D the government considers desirable. Clearly, the Thatcher government's support for design, albeit on a limited scale, was seen to fall within this category. Despite the small amount involved, this expenditure of public money clearly underlined the government's realization that *laissez-faire* was not sufficient, especially in view of the magnitude of Britain's decline in international competitiveness discussed in the first section of this chapter.

The Economic and Commercial Role of Design

Design in manufacturing and service industries

During the 1980s it was popular to contrast the decline of British manufacturing industry with the growth of the service sector. It was argued that the relative success of the service sector – especially financial services, retailing, telecommunications services, property development and design consultancy – would make up for Britain's poor performance in automobile, machine tool, electrical appliance, electronic office and consumer product manufacture. Indeed, it was often seen as an inevitable and desirable shift in the economy (see, for example, Robertson et al., 1985). The British government's opinion was expressed by a former chancellor, Nigel Lawson (1985), as follows: 'If we are relatively more efficient at providing services than at producing goods, then our national interest lies in a surplus on services and a deficit on goods.'

However, it is clear that many service industries, ranging from electricity supply to financial services and design consultants, are far more dependent on manufacturing firms as major customers than they are on final consumers. Gershuny (1983) demonstrated that the fastest-growing part of the service sector in Britain was in 'producer services' or services like business or design consultancy, telecommunications and financial services, which are purchased by other firms, while 'marketed final services', such as transport and entertainment, bought by final consumers (households), had declined. Gershuny and Miles (1983) showed a similar pattern in other EEC countries.

In the early 1990s it is generally accepted that the service sector, however successful, is no substitute for a thriving manufacturing base. Furthermore, the stock market crash of 1987, the rise in interest rates in the late 1980s and early 1990s, the end of the consumer boom and the decline in the housing market, have underlined in practical terms the vulnerability of some of these service industries. In the past few years, the growing gap between exports and imports of manufactured goods has been offset by a surplus in 'invisible trade' such as financial and other services, including design consultancy. The reason why the London stock market was 'sent into shock' in early 1990 (Elliott, 1990) was that even invisible trade had gone into deficit.

Gershuny and Miles (1985) show that the greatest proportional growth in service jobs was not in any case the result of a shift from manufacturing to service industry, but the result of increasing service employment within each industry. Meanwhile, growth has taken place in the provision of a variety of services on a sub-contracting basis, rather than by the firm's or institution's own salaried employees, adding to the growth of 'producer services' mentioned above. That is, the growth of the service sector in the 1980s was not by any means entirely due to real growth, but partly to a reclassification of activities from 'manufacturing' to 'services'.

Gershuny and Miles (1985) were critically examining the 'three-sector model of economic development' in which economies are first dominated by primary production (mining, farming), then by secondary (manufacturing) activities and finally by the tertiary (service) sector, and Bell's (1974) influential *The Coming of Post-Industrial Society*, with its forecast of a mainly service economy. Their more flexible alternative to the 'three-sector' classification (based on a matrix of two horizontal categories – service and non-service, and four vertical categories – industry, occupation, product and function) may be applied to an analysis of design in terms of institution, occupation and 'product'.

In-house design, on the one hand, is carried out by manufacturing firms and is the central subject of this book. On the other hand, design is also provided by design consultancy firms as a service for sale both to manufacturing firms and to retailing and other service businesses. This growing 'design industry' is the subject of a new research study by the authors of this book. It is also an example of Gershuny and Miles's observation that tasks are increasingly being sub-contracted, rather than being carried out in-house. The design function, however, is rather more complex than even Gershuny and Miles's more sophisticated classification. Not only is it a 'service' occupation carried out by manufacturing or service firms, it is also a job done part-time by staff with other main occupations; and these, in turn, may be 'manual' or 'white-collar' staff (for example, tool-makers or managers). This point has already been noted in chapter 1 and we return to it in chapter 4 in the discussion of 'silent design'.

Although the design industry has been growing rapidly, as we noted in chapter 1 and discuss in greater detail in chapter 4, much of the growth in the 1980s was in design work for retailers rather than manufacturers (Besford, 1987). Manufacturers are increasingly using design consultants, as we found in Study C, but the major growth in sub-contracting has been in the supply of components and intermediate goods, rather than design, to manufacturers. In the plastics products industry (Study A) we found that sub-contracting of tool-making (producing the mould for the injection moulding of plastics) was also growing. Indeed, Leadbeater (1989) forecast that 'manufacturing expertise will increasingly lie in designing, sourcing and assembling components' rather than in making products by transforming raw materials. If this is so, design – and management of design – will acquire an even more pivotal position for manufacturers/assemblers as the quality of the final product will depend on designers' abilities to communicate with a variety of outside firms as well as with the many functional departments of their own organizations. This represents a further development of the role of the 'designer as gatekeeper' (Walsh and Roy, 1985).

As a result of design's position in both service and manufacturing industry, it contributes to the economy in two ways. First of all, design consultancy firms generate profits and turnover, pay taxes, rent or purchase equipment, premises and other services, and employ staff whose wages buy products and services. Second, the design function, whether carried out in-house by other (manufacturing *or* service) firms, or by consultants, contributes indirectly to the economy by affecting the performance of those manufacturing and service sector firms. It contributes to manufacturing firms' performance by improving the quality of products, and by improving the efficiency of production methods and the use of materials and energy and hence the price of products. It also affects their performance by improving the marketing of both product and company image via the design of packaging, publicity material, logo and so on. Design contributes to service sector firms' performance by providing an environment that encourages customers to value, and buy, their service (or, in the case of retailing, the products of manufacturing firms), as well as making a contribution to marketing the service or company image and to prices via the efficient use of materials and energy.

However, the success of design as carried out by design consultancy firms, does not automatically benefit the national economy of the country where the design firms are located. If the manufacturing sector is doing badly in any national economy, but the service sector is doing well, the design firms may have difficulty finding an adequate market among manufacturers at home, but may export their services very successfully. They may thus contribute directly to export revenue, but indirectly to imports by improving the competitiveness of overseas firms. In 1987, the top ten British design consultancies all had a substantial overseas customer-base, representing 10–30 per cent of their business (McAlhone, 1987). Glancey (1990), for example, gave the case of the car industry in arguing that Britain's overseas competitors were 'benefiting from exploiting the design talent that is here in Britain', citing Martin Smith's design of the 'classic Audi Quattro four-wheel-drive sports coupé'. Several successful Danish firms (for example, Bang & Olufsen) employ British designers. In fact, some of these designers have now exported their whole consultancy businesses as well as some of their services, and are now located in Denmark (Bernsen, 1990).

Of course, this point is not peculiar to the design industry. Similar points may be developed for other branches of the service sector, such as financial services. In manufacturing industry, too, multinational operation, transfer pricing and so on can ensure that the success of the firm may contribute to the economic growth or exports of a country other than the one where the headquarters or parent is based. Around one-third of world trade in goods is in intra-firm transfers (Edwards, 1985), where transfer pricing allows profit earned to be recorded in the country where tax rates are most favourable.

We have attempted to show that exporting services such as design, while contributing directly to a positive balance of trade, can also contribute indirectly to a deficit in trade in manufactured goods. The House of Lords Select Committee on Overseas Trade (1984–5) found that a 1 per cent drop in manufacturing exports required a 3 per cent rise in services exports to maintain the same level of economic activity, because value added in manufacturing is higher. The CBI (1984) found that 75 per cent of value added in exports was in manufactures. Godley and Cripps (1983) predicted that, at best, the UK could expect an overseas trade surplus of only £10 billion from services and £3 billion from overseas investment, to offset a £20 billion deficit in manufactures. Clearly, manufactured goods still have the major role to play in Britain's economic performance, especially now the service sector is no longer growing rapidly as in the 1980s. We now turn to the position of design in contributing to this performance, arguing that it is more than a 'non-price' factor.

Design as a non-price factor

As we show in later chapters, what most designers do is first in the area of evolutionary improvement or 'incremental' innovation of existing products. Second, designing products so that they can be manufactured economically, and introducing process innovations (such as robots and computer-controlled machine tools) are two ways in which high-quality goods can be made and sold at a competitive price. The design effort put into innovative new products is a major factor in their ability to meet customer needs, appeal to completely new customers, be produced at acceptable prices and solve a whole range of problems that are always involved when first combining new technological principles, materials, style, anticipated customer requirements and so on, but which by its very nature is not the kind of activity that occupies most designers most of the time.

Many researchers have used sector studies to link design and profit or competitive success. For example, the UK agricultural implements industry was the subject of an empirical study of price and non-price factors. This industry began losing markets abroad and suffering import penetration at home in the late 1960s. Between 1979 and 1988 import penetration increased from 43 per cent to 68 per cent and was particularly severe at the sophisticated end of the market. By 1988 there was a £75 million trade deficit in agricultural machinery (Roy et al., 1990). Rothwell (1981) investigated the reasons why a sample of British farmers purchased certain kinds of machinery. The study showed that British farmers chose foreign-built machinery for a variety of reasons related to better engineering design and greater technical sophistication, mainly as a result of incremental design changes, even though competing British-made products were often cheaper. On the other hand, purchases of British equipment, mostly small items of relatively unsophisticated machinery, were made on the basis of price and the convenience of a close relationship with local suppliers.

A study by Moody (1984) of purchasers of professional ophthalmic equipment found that they decided mainly on the basis of design and quality factors such as appearance, ease of use, handling, finish and technical performance, rather than lowest price. *Value for money* was an important secondary consideration to the purchasers Moody investigated. Swann and Taghavi (1988) investigated international competition in fridge–freezers, and showed that British designs were competing in the moderate-quality section of the market, while West German, Danish and Swedish products competed on high quality. They argued that British decline in market share was due to British manufacturers being squeezed out by low-priced basic designs from Eastern Europe and higher-priced, high-quality designs from Germany and Scandinavia. Robinson (1989) found 'a new pressure to deliver quality' in studying the increased sub-contracting activities of large motor, electronics and textiles companies, whereas in the past 'the purchasing officer would have picked the supplier which quoted the bottom price'.

A survey of scientific instrument users by Ng (1986) shows that the key factor influencing consumer purchase behaviour was the design and quality of the instruments rather than price. A study of consumer purchase behaviour in a quite different market, that of home interiors, showed that perceived quality, aesthetics and comfort for a given price were the primary elements in the consumer's decision to purchase (Bruce and Whitehead, 1988). Publications by Clipson et al. (1984), Lorenz (1986) and Pilditch (1987c) have also reinforced the links between design and competitiveness or profit.

Does good design pay?

Most of the other accounts of design as an important factor in competitiveness have relied on anecdotal evidence and individual case study accounts. (The advantages and disadvantages of case study accounts are discussed more fully in chapter 3.) The Design Innovation Group's programme of a series of research projects (described in chapter 1), was one of the first to attempt a more systematic study of representative samples of firms in various sectors of manufacturing industry. In our Study A, we found that 'design-conscious' plastics firms, which had one or more products included in the Design Council's Selection of well-designed British goods and/or had won various awards or prizes for good design, performed significantly better, in terms of turnover growth, capital growth and return on capital, than the randomly selected 'representative' firms without such accolades (see figure 2.5). The differences were statistically significant – in other words, the better business performance of the design-conscious firms was not just a matter of chance.

In Study B, where design performance indicators were further refined as described in chapter 1, there was a significant positive statistical association between a firm's design performance – measured by the number of citations on Design Centre Selection or the number of awards and prizes for design – and its subsequent average profit margin, supporting the view that design effort adds to value and hence to profits per unit sale. Firms with a large number of citations by the Design Centre Selection also exported a significantly higher proportion of their total sales, supporting the link between good design and export success identified by other studies. The six UK furniture, heating and electronics firms which did best overall in design terms (measured by a combined indicator of citations, awards and peer evaluation) had significantly higher profit margins and return on capital than the remaining UK firms sampled in these sectors (see figure 2.6). But, unlike the plastics sample, no statistically significant differences in rates of turnover growth or capital growth between the design leaders and the rest were found.

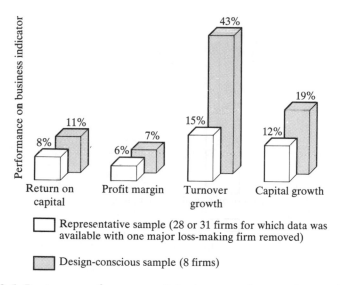

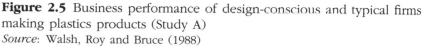

Figure 2.5 Business performance of design-conscious and typical firms making plastics products (Study A)
Source: Walsh, Roy and Bruce (1988)

Figure 2.7 shows how British furniture, heating and electronic business equipment firms and their leading overseas competitors responded to the question 'What gives your products the edge over your competitors?' Only 16 per cent of British managers and 11 per cent of their overseas competitors cited price as the key factor. The main difference between the British firms and their major competitors in other countries was that the latter tended to attribute product competitiveness to *more* factors. In particular, technical performance was crucial to all the foreign firms, with a high proportion also citing product quality, delivery and after-sales service.

Design, innovation and value for money

The studies cited in this section, as well as our own work, show fairly conclusively that design (and innovativeness) were, and were perceived to be, important factors in a firm's competitiveness in home and export markets, and important factors in customers' decisions to buy in some sectors of the market. But most of these studies showed that price was also important, and more important than design in some market sectors. Two vital points emerge from this.

The first, which we have emphasized from the beginning of our

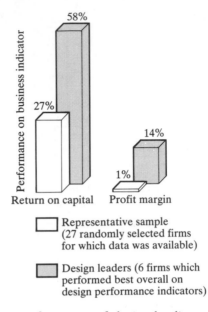

Figure 2.6 Business performance of design-leading and typical British firms making office furniture, domestic heating and electronic business equipment (study B)
Source: Walsh, Roy and Bruce (1988)

research (e.g. Walsh and Roy, 1983), is that design and innovation are not just non-price factors. Both innovation and design contribute to the price as well as to the quality of a product or the service associated with it. Designing for economic manufacture, process innovations and design of the processing equipment and its layout, optimize energy and material consumption, increase labour productivity and thus reduce the costs of manufactured products. Design for durability and ease of maintenance reduces the service and repair costs. Design of fuel or power-efficient products, such as cars made with a higher proportion of lightweight materials like plastics, or well-insulated fridges and freezers, reduces the running costs.

Design and innovation thus contribute to both price *and* non-price competitiveness (see table 2.4). In all the debates about price and non-price factors in competitiveness, and all the earlier studies which emphasized the importance of innovativeness in economic performance, it is very unusual to find this point made. While it is important to counter the argument or the assumption that competitiveness is primarily about the price of goods, and to emphasize the

Proportion of firms mentioning factor in competitiveness

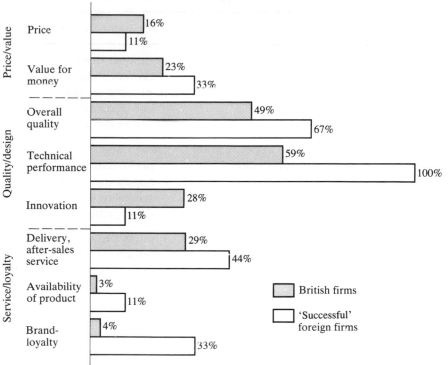

Figure 2.7 What British and foreign firms said gave their products a competitive edge. The sample included forty-two typical British firms and nine successful overseas firms in the office furniture, domestic heating and electronic business equipment and computing industries (Study B)
Source: Roy (1990)

importance of design, quality and innovation, it is a mistake to go too far in the other direction and ignore, or even deny the validity of, price factors altogether. It is also important to emphasize the resulting policy implications: both the need for an expansion of science, technology and design education and of publicly funded research and development on the one hand, and the need to question the existing concern with wages and hours of work on the other. More recently, research on industrial strategy has begun to recognize that design and technological innovation make the choice between price and non-price competition less valid. Studies of some industries, such as the knitwear industry mentioned in chapter 1 (Baden-Fuller

Table 2.4 The role of product design in competitiveness

Factor in competitiveness		Influence of design
Price	Sales price	Is product designed for economic manufacture?
	Life-cycle costs	Is product designed taking into account costs of use and maintenance?
Non-price (product-related)	Product specification and quality	Design affects product performance, uniqueness, appearance, finish, reliability, durability, safety, ease of use, etc.
Non-price (service-related)	Company image and sales promotion	Product presentation, packaging and display design affects image and promotion
	Delivery to time	Is the product designed for ease of development and to meet delivery schedules?
	After-sales service	Is product designed for ease of service and repair?

Source: Walsh, Roy and Bruce (1988)

and Stopford, 1990), and parts of the computer and consumer electronics industries, indicate that some companies and some countries, by utilizing the latest manufacturing technologies and computer-aided design and communications systems, have become extremely successful internationally by offering a wide variety of well-designed, high-quality products at relatively low prices (Dodgson, 1989).

The second, related point is that design and innovation on the one hand, and price on the other, have an importance relative to each other. Neither design nor innovativeness is of absolute significance, independent of price. There may be exceptions in very specialist areas, such as defence, where the most technically sophisticated, most efficiently designed product is demanded, regardless of its price (McLean and Rowland, 1985), although even here governments are becoming more cost-conscious. But, in general, it is value for money that is a key consideration. Customers will pay more for a better-designed, more technically sophisticated product if it represents, in their perception, better value for money. And, furthermore, the balance between quality and price, or the line between what is and what is not perceived to be value for money, will be closer to price in some market segments than others, a point to which we return later in this section.

Hart et al. (1988), reporting on the 'Design for Profit' programme at Strathclyde University, also found that firms' 'policies were to try to achieve an optimum balance between the fulfilment of purpose, the market requirement for appearance and the product's costs', although most of their work concentrates on design as essentially a non-price factor.

In our own Study A, we found that the most successful plastics products firms offered well-designed, high-quality products, not at the lowest or highest prices, but at a price that consumers felt provided value for money, a point that was echoed in the international comparisons of several sectors we made in Study B. One-third of overseas firms mentioned 'value for money' as a key factor in giving their products a competitive edge, though fewer than a quarter of British firms did so (see figure 2.7).

In the toy industry (Study A), for example, companies like Lego (Danish) and Fisher Price (American), both of which manufacture as well as sell in the UK, are concerned with value for money. Fisher Price used the term 'play value' to describe the balance between price and the hours of concentration children put into playing with a particular toy, or the variety of uses they found for the toy. Parents and other adults appear to be prepared to pay high prices for toys that keep children amused for a long time. Both firms have discovered this, and invest heavily in design to achieve it. Both firms also used high-quality, expensive plastic (ABS in the case of Lego) and more material than their competitors in the case of Fisher Price. The quantity and quality of materials enhance the reputation of both firms' toys for durability, another aspect of value for money.

In contrast, the (wrong) balance between price and design quality – poor value for money – has contributed to the commercial failure of some of the firms in our studies. Thus in the toy industry, Airfix Industries, makers of plastic model aeroplane and other kits, collapsed financially not long after its subsidiary, Meccano, makers of construction toys, had also closed down. Another firm bought the rights to the trade names Airfix and Meccano. This firm's strategy was to 'keep prices to a minimum. Improved quality comes second.' Both Airfix and Meccano were seen as too expensive for what they offered, and despite a world-wide following of enthusiasts and a listing on the Design Index, Meccano was seen as outdated compared with competing products like Lego.

At a more aggregate level, Kravis and Lipsey (1971) attempted to attribute the performance of US exporters to West Germany to definite percentages of price and various non-price factors. In their study, relative price advantage accounted for only 28 per cent of trade success, while 47 per cent was attributed to product superiority or uniqueness, both factors in which design and innovation are crucial. A study by Schott and Pick (1983) of British trade performance showed that non-price factors accounted for 45 per cent of British export behaviour, and were responsible for 80 per cent of British exports. More recent research by Cronshaw et al. (1990) examined the relationships between the price/quality mix and the business performance of a large number of firms included in the PIMS database containing information on some 7500 businesses. This showed that the highest proportion (average 47 per cent) of successful companies (measured by return on investment) produced products or services rated as being of high quality. However, as many successful companies were offering high-quality goods or services at low or medium prices as at high prices.

However, while it is very attractive to be able to put percentages on various factors in this way, and these studies certainly underline the importance of non-price factors, the contribution of design or innovation as such cannot be so easily calculated. This is, first, because design and innovation, as we have argued, are both price and non-price factors, and second, because computing the share of various price and non-price factors in export or import behaviour needs to take into account such features as differences over time and between industry sector. Mixes of price, design, quality and other factors also differ for particular firms and sectors, when selling in different national markets or to different segments of the market.

For example, two design-conscious firms visited in Study A, one making furniture and the other making building components and flooring, observed that price was more important in Britain than other countries where they marketed their products. The manufacturer of plastic netting we visited found that price was crucial in selling mesh for packaging purposes (for example, for fruit and vegetable supermarket pre-packs), but less important for gardening uses, and fairly insignificant for selling kidney machine filters.

Why Good Design is Not Enough

Earlier in this chapter we reported our findings that firms which were recognized as being good at design by a variety of awards, citations and the opinion of other firms in their industry, were in general significantly more successful in business than the sample of firms which had not won such accolades. However, there were also cases of firms we visited which were recognized for their design excellence, but which were not doing very well commercially. One well-known British furniture-maker, for example, consistently won design awards, but was reporting losses in the period when we collected data. A manufacturer of plastics dark-room equipment had many of its products included in the Design Council Index, had won several design awards and had many years of business success. But colour photography almost completely replaced black and white among amateurs as the price of colour film dropped, while for the amateur, colour developing and printing is more difficult and expensive. The mail-order firms, using automatic equipment, provided a faster, cheaper and more efficient service, undercutting 'do-it-yourself' as well as the local chemist. The dark-room equipment manufacturer lost sales and profits, showing that even the best-designed products cannot maintain commercial success in a sector whose technology is changing.

The construction toy company, Meccano, mentioned above, had a following among generations of budding engineers, and was listed on the Design Index, but went bankrupt for a variety of reasons, including (in addition to poor value for money) failure to reinvest in more efficient production equipment, failure to keep up with trends in the market and failure to explore the possibility of potentially doubling their market by appealing specifically to girls (see chapter 6).

Logica VTS developed an award-winning, innovative special-purpose word-processing system for the business market. It was not a commercial success, however, because it was launched just before a (short-term) slump in the market for personal computers, and then the (long-term) demise of special-purpose word-processing systems for business use, with the advent of low-cost personal computers and standard word-processing packages.

There were also some quite successful businesses which paid more attention to marketing or to manufacturing technology than to design. Having a strategy which puts emphasis on producing good design can yield commercial benefits, but cannot guarantee them. It is one route to business success; there are also other routes. Similarly, firms in some industries can survive and even do quite well for a relatively long time without innovation, while firms in high-tech sectors must innovate or die. The really successful firms we visited, such as Lego and Netlon, were good at many aspects of business, in particular marketing, innovation and manufacturing, as well as design.

While good design is not alone sufficient to ensure business success, there is evidence to suggest that firms who pay particular attention to design, also invest in other activities that maintain or improve their product quality. In the plastics industry, for example, concern with quality control correlated with design effort. In the past, plastics products had a cheap, shoddy, *ersatz* image. This was due not only to the more limited properties then available from the raw materials, but to the reliance on operators and packers noticing unsatisfactory mouldings, and the firms' tendency to wait for customers to complain. From the mid-1970s some firms, at least, began to introduce more full-time quality-control staff and a wider range of quality tests, at the same time as they started to aim at the top end of the market with well-designed, high-value products.

In chapter 6 we discuss the link between both design and business success, and firms paying particular attention to user needs. For example, commercially successful firms would gather market intelligence from several sources, and would be more likely to have established good, long-term contact with customers, to use customer feedback in product planning and prototype evaluation, and to be more aware of what their competitors were offering than a random selection of firms in the same industries. In chapter 7 we discuss the provision of a brief by management or marketing to design and development staff. The rapidly expanding and profitable firms were significantly more likely to provide designers with a comprehensive written brief or initial specification, containing several elements, such as target market, guidance on appearance, image and style, evidence of demand, relevant national and international standards and ergonomics and to include sketches as well as descriptions. The most successful firms were also more likely to have a group of people responsible for drawing up this specification.

Chapter 5 discusses the different ways in which the whole design and development process is organized and managed by successful and representative firms, and chapter 7 indicates that successful firms are also more likely to ensure that production needs are 'designed in' at an early stage in order to avoid either costly delays at a later stage and/or having to sacrifice some design feature or element of quality to ensure efficient manufacture. The key characteristic associated with the financially most successful firms was not just 'design for economic manufacture' (the importance of this was quite widely recognized), but the use of a 'systems' approach in which various aspects, including production, were either considered by a multi-disciplinary team or by a product development committee where decisions were regularly reviewed, and where considerable attention was paid to the firms' acquisition or development of a variety of management skills for this coordination of design activities with the various other tasks in the firm.

In short, the most successful firms were those that placed a high priority on multiple (but achievable) objectives in corporate strategy, notably excellence in design, satisfaction of customers and a systems approach to planning, incorporating these and other elements. We now turn to the question of corporate strategy in chapter 3.

3

Innovation, Design and Corporate Strategy

In the last chapter we argued that design was an important factor in the competitiveness of firms, affecting both the quality and the price of products. We also argued that paying attention to good design and investment in professional designers were not, however, sufficient by themselves to ensure commercial success. In this chapter we explore these ideas further, considering whether commercial success can be ensured at all; what strategies firms adopt to improve their chances of commercial success; and how design is incorporated into company strategy with other functions and foci considered to be important by the firm.

Innovation Theory and Design Management

In discussing these issues we draw both on our own surveys, and on empirical results and theory from the literature. This literature includes publications about the management of innovation as well as those specifically concerned with design. The reason for including some of the innovation literature is that the analysis of the design process and its management is a much newer field than the innovation area, and its literature less substantial, while there is now a considerable body of literature dealing specifically with innovation in relation to corporate strategy.

Given the important overlap between the activities of design and innovation, described in chapter 1, whereby the novel system, process or device is embodied in the form of a drawing, model or prototype, some of the findings reported in the innovation literature are directly relevant to the management of design. And some of the theoretical achievements in understanding innovation may, if care is taken to distinguish the differences between innovation and design as well as to exploit their similarities, act as a starting-point for a theoretical understanding of firm behaviour with respect to design.

Some of the writings on management of design are very clearly a development of the innovation literature (e.g. Rothwell and Gardiner, 1984). Some, on the other hand, are an extension of the marketing literature (e.g. Kotler and Rath, 1984) and only marginally (or not at all) concerned with technological change. The innovation literature itself has developed from two traditions. One is part of the management literature and typically has a prescriptive or even exhortative style. The other is in the social science tradition of economic or sociological analysis of firm behaviour.

In some senses, current work analysing the design process and its management is at the stage which the innovation discipline had reached about twenty years ago: with a focus on the natural history or case study approach on the social sciences side, a 'how to do it' approach in the management literature, and very few attempts to develop a framework to incorporate innovation into theories of the firm. Indeed, if it was the case in the 1960s and early 1970s that economic theory of the firm either ignored innovation and technical change or classified it as the 'residual' left when measurable variables such as labour, capital and quantity of output had been calculated, it is even more the case today that design has hardly any place in the thinking of economists, particularly those in the established neo-classical tradition (see Swann, 1987; Swann and Taghavi, 1988 for some of the few exceptions to this). The analysis of design, however, does have one advantage over the budding innovation discipline of twenty or thirty years ago. A great deal of analytical work on innovation has been carried out in the meantime, much of which challenges conventional thinking about theories of firm behaviour and of economic growth; and which offers guidelines for the development of theory concerning the innovation process, some of which may fairly readily be directly extended to design.

The case study approach to design, as to innovation, has identified a wealth of useful information about the detailed and day-to-day activities which culminate in new products and processes. It is thus a necessary and important step in the development of our understanding of these processes and, potentially at least, a better management of them. The disadvantages of the approach are first, that it tends to present a 'snapshot' of design (or innovation) over a relatively short period in the life of a firm or an industry, and thus does not capture the rather different circumstances, external influences, management 'styles' and so on, that are relevant to other periods in the firm's or industry's evolution. Chapter 1 discussed different design strategies appropriate to different stages of an industry life cycle. Second, the approach is very rarely able to give a generalized picture of innovation or design, locked as it is into specific cases, and often gives a false impression of general validity, because the number of cases examined may be large, but not statistically representative. Our Studies A and B, described in this book, attempted to avoid this problem by focusing on *industries* rather than individual cases, while Study C was based on a *statistical* sample of design projects that received government funding.

The main problem with the managerial, prescriptive approach is that, while providing useful insights into the process of managing design (or innovation) and helpful advice about all the factors that need to be taken into consideration (such as liaison between all departments at an early stage, specific and detailed design briefs, and so on (discussed in chapters 5–7)), there is a danger of suggesting that 'following the recipe' will guarantee success. However valid any set of recommendations, and however successfully they may be applied, the process of designing and introducing a new product (or process) involves a certain level of risk that cannot be 'managed out', a level that is higher the more technologically novel the new product or process is.

Technical, economic and market uncertainty

Firms are faced with several kinds of uncertainty. First of all, the general economic climate causes uncertainty. In periods of economic upturn, there is an increased level of confidence in the likelihood of business, and personal, success. Financial institutions are more likely to provide investment funds, managers are more willing to take risks and customers are more willing to buy. Each of these is influenced by interest rates, inflation, rates of economic growth and other factors outside the immediate control of the firm.

Second, firms are affected by market uncertainty, which interacts to some extent with economic uncertainty. Changing consumer needs or levels and patterns of demand and the introduction of new products by competitors, as well as increased prosperity and the ease and cost to consumers of obtaining credit, will alter demand for a firm's new or redesigned product or may make it redundant. Despite the best attempts at market research and other means of forecasting trends, some unforeseen changes in the market between the decision being taken to introduce a new product and market launch are inevitable. Firms may adopt pricing policies to compensate for changes in the market, but these will only have a marginal impact where there are major changes. Changes in supply of raw materials and components and in distribution are another source of uncertainty. These issues are discussed further in chapter 6.

These two kinds of economic and market uncertainty affect all firms to some extent. In addition, firms which attempt any kind of technical change face a third type of uncertainty, technical uncertainty. The three types of uncertainty are described by Freeman (1982), who further disaggregates various degrees of technical uncertainty. A radical product innovation involving an input from basic research is associated with the highest degree of uncertainty, while the design of a new model of an existing product with minor technical improvements involves far less uncertainty (see figure 1.5). The design of new packaging or the redesign of a product involving no technical changes at all (for example, resiting the controls or changing dimensions to meet user needs better) will mean hardly any technical uncertainty, although the firm will still be faced with market and economic un-certainties. Radical product innovation is a high-risk venture because it combines the greatest degree of market *and* technical uncertainty. Part of the uncertainty is due to the magnitude of the change and the fact that the outcome of research and development is unknown (to a greater or lesser extent) in advance. Part is due to the *time* taken. The longer the time needed for the project, the more difficult it is to calculate costs and benefits and the more chance there is for changes in the market or the economy to affect the commercial outcome, or for new technical developments made elsewhere to affect the tech-nical outcome. This is particularly clear in the case of the Advanced Passenger Train, discussed more fully in chapter 5.

Design is probably associated with less uncertainty than techno-logical innovation. First, although all innovations are embodied as products and processes via design, as shown in chapter 1, there are also large areas of design work which do not involve technological innovation. Second, by the time even the most radically innovative project reaches the product design stage, a great deal of the uncertainty will usually have been eliminated. However, technical uncertainties do persist throughout the design process, as shown by the appearance of 'bugs' in a new product during the design process, and sometimes after market launch. 'Bugs' can cause delays and expensive development work ('debugging') and can undermine the firm's reputation for quality. One design manager we interviewed took the view that one of the purposes of design was precisely 'to make sure there were no bugs'. Some degree of uncertainty still persists at the production stage. Chapter 7 discusses ways in which successful firms attempt to take the requirements of production into account in the early stages of the design process in order to minimize costly changes later; but even some of the firms who did this still had to modify designs when they reached the production stage.

The purpose of this discussion has been to show that a firm can use all the most highly recommended and sophisticated management techniques, adopt all the procedures identified in case studies, have a history of successful product design and of technological innovation, and still produce a failure. It is one thing to identify the factors making for success and failure after the event, and quite another to find a recipe that will guarantee success in advance.

In the 1992 Olympics, the athletes who failed to win any medals nevertheless performed better than the gold medallists of 1936. Partly this was a result of innovations in training and partly a result of innovations in materials and hence in clothes and equipment in the intervening fifty-two years. The general level of performance has improved, but there are still winners and losers. This may not be the case with new product designs, but it very often is. Many firms today are able to benefit from the insights obtained over the past thirty years into the process of new product development and innovation, but some are still going to introduce their new product into the market-place before their competitors, and some are still going to produce market failures from time to time.

Market and technical uncertainties identified by firms visited in our Study B are discussed more fully later in the chapter (see the section 'The Return on Investment in R&D and Design' and table 3.6). It is important to bear in mind that all the activities associated with commercial success identified in this book, or elsewhere in the design and innovation literature (including management texts advising 'how to do it') can only *improve* the firm's or the managers' *chances* of success. They cannot guarantee success.

Technological opportunity

In the theory of conventional industrial economics, the behaviour of a firm is described by the structure–conduct–performance paradigm. In other words, the primary variable is the market *structure* in which a firm finds itself, that is, the degree of monopolization or competition in the market. This in turn influences the firm to adopt a particular pricing policy, R&D strategy, product differentiation and so on – in other words, it influences the firm's *conduct*. This then determines the *performance* of the firm in terms of profit. So external factors primarily give rise to the behaviour of a firm including its strategy towards new product design and development and towards technological innovation. Some of the popular management literature, in contrast, is concerned less with attempts at objective explanation of firm behaviour but rather with advice to firms about how they *should* behave in order to plan and implement their strategies more effectively.

Neither approach is very effective at explaining why there is often a very similar share of resources (such as percentage of turnover or profit) allocated to research, design and development by firms *within* a particular industry, but a very different pattern *between* industries. Some recent work reported in the innovation literature suggests that *technological opportunity* is a much more significant variable than industry structure in determining company conduct and performance. Firms in industries with greater technological opportunities are likely to invest more, proportionately, in R&D and therefore have a higher R&D intensity. These firms, as a result, will experience more rapid technological progress and a higher rate of innovation and economic growth. Those firms which are first in a new sector of high-technological opportunity may be able as a result to establish an oligopoly in that sector. In other words, a reversal of the direction of causation described in conventional economics (from market structure to innovation) can be proposed (Momigliano and Dosi, 1983). The balance of opinion in the innovation literature is that causality runs both ways (Chesnais, 1986).

While industries with strength in R&D may be correlated with those with high levels of technological opportunity, the same will not necessarily be true of strength in design. Chapter 1 showed the way in which types of innovative activity, competitive behaviour and design activity change over the life cycle of an industry. Design of radically new products is an important component of competitive strategies based on the exploitation of technological opportunities in newer, more R&D-intensive, more innovative sectors. But design is equally important, though qualitatively different in nature, to mature industries and those with relatively few technological opportunities. In those sectors design strength is oriented to improvements in established products and in company image, but can play a major part in competitive strategy.

Although it is difficult to test empirically, innovation theory suggests that technological opportunity is more important than market structure in determining company strategy, especially strategy towards R&D (Coombs et al., 1987). However, technological opportunity operates in a different manner on design strategy than on R&D strategy. R&D intensity may be assumed to be fairly simply correlated with technological opportunity (Kay, 1979; Freeman, 1982; Stoneman, 1983). Design effort, however, varies *qualitatively* rather than *quantitatively* with technological opportunity.

Thus, for example, investment in engineering design is likely to be high where R&D intensity and technological opportunity are great; but investment in industrial design, graphics and, in some sectors, fashion design are likely to be high where technological opportunity is quite low, and where competitive strategy is based mainly on product differentiation and effective marketing rather than on fairly radical technological innovation. Thus firms in high-tech sectors, like electronic business equipment, for example – one of the sectors in Study B – have considerable technological opportunities. They also have to pay close attention to both engineering and product design, to ensure efficient performance, ease of use and customer acceptance. Firms in mature industries, such as the furniture sector, also investigated in Study B, have fewer technological opportunities. They may introduce new materials, new manufacturing processes or apply ergonomics to product design, but otherwise there is not a lot of scope for technological changes. However, there is considerable opportunity for new designs, in principle at least. In practice, revival of older design styles (for example, Art Deco) may be as popular as innovative modern design, although both require commitment of design effort.

Thus, while the innovation literature has challenged an explanation of company behaviour and strategy based mainly on market structure, the alternative explanation, based on technological opportunity, needs some modification to take account of design strategies. While R&D intensity may vary in quantity with technological opportunity, design effort may vary not in quantity but in nature and emphasis.

Innovation Strategies and Firm Culture

Technological opportunity, together with levels of R&D expertise and managerial expertise and favourable or unfavourable market opportunities, may also contribute to an explanation of the differences in strategy between firms in the same industry, as well as explaining the relatively greater differences between industries. Freeman (1982), for example, has advanced a typology of innovation strategies, elaborated with reference to a vast array of empirical data. He describes 'offensive', 'defensive', 'imitative', 'dependent', 'traditional' and 'opportunist' strategies defined in table 3.1 and relates them to the character of R&D, the relative strength of R&D, production and marketing capabilities, the product cycle and other factors.

Table 3.2 compares the strengths necessary in research, development, design, quality control, patenting, technical services, forecasting and training between firms adopting different innovation strategies. Offensive and defensive innovators must be very strong in design engineering as well as in R&D to produce an innovative product. Firms following an imitative strategy also need to be quite strong in design in order to take advantage of cheaper raw materials or energy, tariff protection or other advantages in their particular market, and to compete with the offensive and defensive innovators. Traditional and opportunist strategies also call for design strength, but in the area of product, graphics and fashion, rather than engineering design, while successful marketing of products from such firms is also often heavily reliant on interior and packaging design.

However, the adoption of one of these strategies may be the result not only of strengths in R&D, production, marketing and design, or of technological opportunity, but of cost, political or market advantages. The strategies are also a consequence of something less easily defined, which Keynes (1936) called 'animal spirits'. 'Animal spirits' support and supplement 'reasonable calculation . . . so that the thought of ultimate loss which often overtakes pioneers . . . is put aside as a healthy man puts aside the expectation of death'. This 'something', less easily defined, could equally well be called the 'culture' of the firm, which is the product of influences from its foundation and includes its philosophy and attitude towards business in the widest possible sense, and may be essentially a matter of collective optimism about taking risks, the likelihood of making a profit, and so on.

The concept of culture in an organization has been discussed at some length by industrial sociologists (e.g. Knights and Willmott,

Table 3.1 Freeman's innovation strategies

Strategy	Definition
Offensive	Aims at technical and market leadership: being ahead of competitors by introduction of new products
Defensive	Aims at market launch shortly after offensive innovator, to profit from their mistakes and their opening up of a market, but not to be 'left behind'. (May also be an intended offensive innovator that did not quite make it)
Imitative	Follows a long way behind the technological leaders, possibly licensing from them, taking advantage of cost advantages, captive markets or geographical location
Dependent	Satellite of other firms, reliant on customer or parent for technical and design specifications, often a sub-contractor
Traditional	Produces a product that changes very little technically – if at all – and is often based on craft skills (e.g. hand-thrown pottery). Design may change in response to fashion but not technology
Opportunist	Realizes new opportunity in changing market, not based on in-house R&D or complex design input, but on finding an important niche, providing something no one else thought of (e.g. Sock Shop, Tie Rack and Knickerbox in the 1980s)

1987; Filby and Willmott, 1988) as an attempt to study organizations in a more qualitative way, taking into account unfolding processes, and not just analysing in terms of measurable quantities and static structures. Parsons (1988) notes that there is a danger of treating 'culture' as a 'residual' or 'repository for what is not immediately obvious'. However, to define 'culture' first and then proceed to relate it to observed behaviour is outside the scope of this book, so we must simply note that culture may be used to explain those aspects of firm behaviour that cannot simply be explained by the calculation of future benefit, cost and degree of risk.

Table 3.2 Strategies of the firm

Strategy	In-house scientific and technical functions within the firm									
	Fundamental research	Applied research	Experimental development	Design engineering	Production engineering – quality control	Technical services	Patents	Scientific and technical information	Education and training	Long-range forecasting and product planning
Offensive	4	5	5	5	4	5	5	4	5	5
Defensive	2	3	5	5	4	3	4	5	4	4
Imitative	1	2	3	4	5	2	2	5	3	3
Dependent	1	1	2	3	5	1	1	3	3	2
Traditional	1	1	1	1	5	1	1	1	1	1
Opportunist	1	1	1	1	1	1	1	5	1	5

Note: Range 1–5 indicates weak (or non-existent) to very strong.
Source: Freeman (1982)

The role of design in a firm is strongly related to the firm's culture. The adoption of a design-conscious attitude throughout the firm (or alternatively an indifference to design) is not just a matter of commitment of resources to design activities, though that is clearly important. It is also a question of a culture in which design is emphasized in every aspect of work and which ensures that new members of staff absorb the idea of the firm's commitment to design without necessarily being explicitly told of this. The culture of a firm also influences a collective optimism or a propensity to take risks. In a major report for the National Economic Development Council, Fairhead (1987) has argued that successful firms have a 'culture' of innovation and good design and that without this culture procedures for managing the product development process more effectively are likely to be 'no more than paper tigers'.

The now fairly well-known Japanese strategy of 'reverse engineering' of imported technology has some interesting implications for the design process, and illustrates the importance of a 'design culture' throughout the firm. For many years a major source of competitive success among Japanese firms was their strategy of importing the best available foreign technology and improving upon it. The intention was to 'take apart' the products, production equipment, user manuals, etc., and redesign them, so as to produce a product similar to one on the world market without any foreign direct investment, 'turn-key' operations or direct transfer of foreign blue-prints. The redesign adapted the products and processes to Japanese culture, consumer needs and patterns of working, to improve productivity and to raise quality. It developed a systems approach towards the whole production process among management, engineers and workers, product and process design being treated as an integrated whole. This is a point to which we return in the section on coordination, later in this chapter. Freeman (1987) describes the system as follows:

> The whole enterprise was involved in a learning and development process and many ideas for improvement came from the shopfloor. The horizontal flow of information became a characteristic feature of the Japanese style of management. Research and development were reintegrated . . . with engineering design, procurement, production and marketing even in the largest organisations. This meant that Japanese firms often seemed to take a relatively long time taking the first decisions about design and development, because it involved a great deal of internal

debate, discussion, experiment and training. . . . But . . . as development, production and marketing went ahead, the whole organization was committed to the new products and processes in a way that was relatively unknown in other countries. Moreover, once development work began, lead times were often very short, especially in the electronic industry.

Fairhead (1987) has also given a number of Japanese examples, while we found in our own Study B that the two Japanese business equipment firms we visited had an elaborate system of product planning and new product development in which marketing, design and engineering staff were involved. This is discussed further in chapters 6 and 7 where we analyse the product development process.

Design and Firm Strategy in the Nordic Countries

The previous two sections have attempted to relate strategies for design to technological opportunity and firm culture. We concluded that firms with offensive and defensive innovation strategies in sectors with considerable technological opportunities have emphasized engineering design, and to a lesser extent industrial design, in generating new products. Meanwhile, firms with less offensive strategies for innovation, in mature, medium or low technology sectors, have emphasized industrial, graphic and sometimes fashion design in product development, and interior and packaging design in retailing.

However, we have also identified an intermediate category of firms which have managed to extract the last drop of opportunity out of a relatively unpromising technology, and at the same time have placed a great deal of emphasis on product design, producing high-quality modern goods and a 'good design' image in marketing them. The result is that they have successfully penetrated export markets in competition with larger firms which are operating in their own home markets. These are firms in 'medium-tech sectors' in the Nordic countries.

The small advanced countries of Scandinavia and Finland have not always managed to keep up with the 'leading edge' of high technology – apart from a few high-tech niches, such as robot applications (Sweden) or microelectronics applied to forestry equipment (Finland) (Lemola and Lovio, 1988) – but have had very favourable conditions for technological advance in the medium-technology sectors, such as heating equipment (part of Study B) and consumer durables, where they have in some cases performed better than large countries (Walsh, 1988). In these sectors, the Nordic countries have had higher R&D intensities than larger countries, and have also paid particular attention to design effort and design-based image. Even some fairly 'low-tech' or craft-based sectors (such as furniture, part of Study B) have 'moved up' into the medium-tech area by means of advanced manufacturing processes, while plastics products (Study A), once seen as cheap and shoddy substitutes for goods made in natural materials, have also moved into the medium-tech area by means of process innovations and the adoption of engineering and other high-grade plastics materials. Furniture and plastics products are also among the sectors in Nordic countries most concerned to promote 'good design'. Qualified, professional designers are always used, usually as consultants rather than in house; design is taken seriously at all levels of the firm; it is a very important aspect of competitive strategy; and a design 'image' is strongly promoted as part of marketing strategy.

In these medium- and low-tech sectors, the technological opportunities are more limited than, for example, in microelectronics, new materials, or biotechnology. However, Nordic firms in these sectors have made the most of the technological opportunities on offer, while at the same time committing considerable resources to design, and to promoting their image. Some of them have become leading firms in world terms on the basis of this strategy. Out of the firms we studied, Lego, the manufacturer of construction toys, is the most striking example of this, with its estimated £500 million turnover (*The Economist*, 1988). Lego's strategy involves considerable effort in product development (about a third of its product range is replaced each year) based on both creative design staff (see chapter 4) and extensive market research and consumer testing (see chapter 7). This is combined with high levels of investment in manufacturing equipment to improve quality and reduce costs. It has even seen off the local manufacturer in Japan (a country often cited as impenetrable to imports), despite the 25 per cent higher cost of Lego kits (see plate 5).

Scandinavian designers we interviewed in furniture, heating equipment and plastics firms defined design in a broad way – indeed, they have two words to capture the fullness of the idea of design, one referring to engineering design and one (literally 'form-giving') to appearance/ergonomics/industrial design – but they made it clear that appearance or 'art' is as important as all the others. Many of the people we interviewed in Sweden and Denmark took for granted the multifaceted nature of design including ergonomics, function, performance, reliability, etc., and were promoting, in addition, an idea of 'art': that is, more beautiful things for everyday use (see plate 6). They had had a dual marketing strategy for decades: promoting beautiful things for workers' homes as well as for the rich (Annerstedt, 1986). Thus, where we emphasized in chapter 1 that design is not just about appearance, Scandinavian designers and marketers were saying that everyone knows design is not just about appearance, but that appearance is vital too, and needs to be promoted. It is an indication of the extent to which design is a part of Danish culture that the appearance of badly designed parking meters in Copenhagen's streets caused something of a scandal, reported in the daily papers in August 1990, and the public embarrassment of the city engineer who approved them.

Dalum and Fagerberg (1986) have shown that the proportion of manufactured goods exported by the Nordic countries to other advanced countries increased substantially relative to goods based on natural resources over the 1960s and early 1970s. (The proportion has declined slightly since then, due to the big growth of North Sea oil and gas.) While design has contributed to the export success of some of these manufactured goods sectors, we would not claim that design alone (or the strategies of individual firms alone) was responsible for the complete transformation in trade pattern. Dalum and Fagerberg (1986) argue that the Nordic countries together were able to operate as an extended home market, establishing a 'virtuous circle' in the transformation of the Nordic area to a set of highly industrialized economies, while Lego treats Europe as a single domestic market. Annerstedt (1986) advances the view that the construction of a welfare state – very early on compared to other European countries – provided a stable and sophisticated home market to stimulate the design-based sectors of furniture, glassware, textiles, lighting and household equipment in particular. (See also (Walsh 1988) for a fuller discussion of competitiveness and the small advanced countries.)

Company Goals, Plans and Strategies

Goals

According to conventional, neo-classical economic theory, firms have a goal of profit maximization, which explains behaviour such as the amounts of their labour and capital input, or their choice of techno-logy (see, for example, Coombs et al. (1987) for a fuller discussion). This theory has been criticized as unsatisfactory for describing ob-served firm behaviour in conditions of uncertainty, and alternative analyses, drawing on other social science disciplines, have been advanced. Cyert and March (1963), for example, in developing a theory of firm behaviour, identified five major goals of firms: levels of production, market share, profit, sales and inventory control. The various managers have different relationships to these goals, and the way in which decisions are made in the firm gives rise to potential conflicts between the goals. For example, increased market share will not be compatible with maximum profit if extra investment in marketing, packaging, or redesign is necessary to compete more effectively.

Firms do not, of course, aim to make a loss, although they may be prepared to do so for temporary periods of time in order to invest in longer-term goals. What usually happens is that *goals* of profit, market share, growth, diversification, sales and so on are established by various processes (rather than maximum possible profit), and strategies for achieving them developed. The processes by which these goals are achieved are iterative ones involving discussions, negotiations and trade-offs between the managers of the various departments.

In Study A we found that the plastics firms surveyed defined their goals in terms of 'survival' or 'expansion' rather than in terms of profits. Table 3.3 shows that only a minority of firms in Study B expressed their goals in terms of profits, and that most of those firms had specific goals for profits rather than the aim of maximizing profits as such (which no firm at all mentioned in so many words) or 'mak-ing money'. The largest numbers of firms expressed their goals in terms of market share, exports or profit targets, usually having two or more goals. In the electronic business equipment sector, however, small and medium-sized electronics firms competing with multi-nationals were planning mainly in terms of financial survival in the short term. A leading Canadian word-processor manufacturer in our study had been forced by the pressure of competition to change its objective from 'technology leadership' to 'making the company profitable by the end of next year'.

While all the firms defined their *goals* in terms of growth (for example, in profit, market share or turnover) or survival, their *strategies* for achieving those goals were more wide-ranging. Producing high-

Table 3.3 Goals of furniture, heating and electronics firms (Study B)

Goal	Only goal (%)	One of two or more goals (%)	Total (%)
	Percentage of firms with this goal		
Increase profits, make a profit, 'make money'	7.8	9.8	17.6
Specific goal for profits	3.9	21.6	25.5
Expand market share, become market leader, achieve specific goal for market share	13.7	15.7	29.4
Increase exports or market share overseas	2.0	21.6	23.6
Reduce costs	0	5.9	5.9
Increase, or achieve specific goal for turnover or output	2.0	15.7	17.7
Survive, get product accepted	5.9	2.0	7.9
Protect employment	0	5.9	5.9
No answer or don't know	2.0	0	3.9

n = 51

quality, competitive products by investing in design was an aspect of strategy rather than a goal in itself. Table 3.5 (discussed in the section below) classifies these strategies. A majority of firms had strategies that would involve deferring profits for a greater or lesser period of time as a result of investment in new product development or redesign. Even many of the cost-reducing strategies were medium- rather than short-term, involving investment in new plant and machinery. Only just over a quarter of firms had adopted cost-reducing strategies, those most closely related to profit-maximizing or short-term profit goals.

Plans

The evolution of the firm from the small single-product, owner-managed or family firm, possibly established by an inventor/entre-preneur, to the multidivisional, decentralized establishment has involved a gradual specialization of administrative and other functions and thus has given rise to increasingly complex communication and coordination problems, as Chandler (1962) pointed out thirty years ago. The coordination of these functions, and the definition of goals and strategies, may be achieved in part by corporate planning.

Corporate planning, and the philosophy and strategy which are implied, or made explicit, in the plans have a decisive influence over the design process. Even if design is not explicitly mentioned in a firm's strategy and plans, this itself has implications for the way in which design is likely to be regarded, the way in which resources are allocated to it and the management of the design process.

Planning is partly a function of size, since many small firms are concerned primarily with day-to-day survival rather than future plans; other small firms do plan, but do not see the need to draw up lengthy documents. Their plans may be in the owner/manager's head or in minutes of meetings between managers who are anyway in constant contact (Mintzberg, 1987).

Planning is also a function of conservatism (or lack of conservatism) in outlook. All the award-winning, design-conscious plastics firms in Study A had formal plans (figure 3.1), while the randomly sampled 'representative' firms were less likely to engage in formal planning, especially if they had under 100 employees. The UK heating equipment firms in Study B all had at least 100 employees, but were the most old-fashioned. Corporate planning simply had not reached many of them yet, or had not been seen to be an organizational innovation worthy of support. Only half of them had formal plans while one in four did not plan at all (table 3.4). Electronic equipment firms, on the other hand, were the most modern in outlook, and, faced with expensive projects and rapidly changing technology and markets, were the most likely to plan ahead.

Surprisingly, the successful foreign firms (Study B), while generally committed to planning, were more likely than the other firms to have informal or shorter-term plans (table 3.4). They also had relatively large numbers of failures (tables 3.6 and 3.7, discussed in the section 'The Return on Investment in R&D and Design') while still being very successful with their remaining designs and innovations. This could mean they were over-confident as a result of success and not stimulated by their failures to adopt organizational innovations; or it could mean that they were very flexible and adaptable, learning from failures rather than being locked into a long-term plan. This requires further investigation.

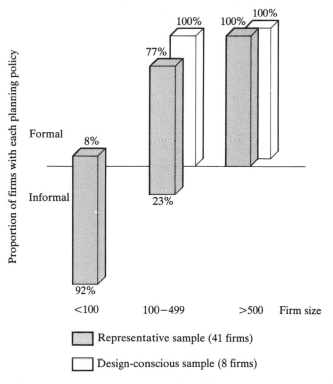

Figure 3.1 Planning policies in a sample of design-conscious and typical plastics firms of different sizes (Study A)
Source: Walsh and Roy (1983)

Strategy and investment decisions

Firms carry out a great many functions, some of which are concerned with the day-to-day business of producing and selling products in order to stay alive and some of which are more concerned with future activities – future survival, expansion, new product development, diversification and so on. All these functions involve the consumption of resources – and therefore some kind of decision-making process about the allocation of these resources.

In many ways, what is involved is an investment decision, with resources allocated on the basis of expected rates of return in the short or longer term. Concentration of effort and resources on production improvements and more efficient marketing of existing products are expected to lead to benefits in the short term. The updating and redesign of existing products to incorporate more

Table 3.4 Company plans (Study B)

	Office furniture (%)	Domestic heating equipment (%)	Electronic business and computing equipment (%)	'Successful' foreign firms (%)	All firms (%)
A Firms which do not draw up future plans	11.8	25.0	5.9	11.1	11.8
B Firms which do draw up future plans	88.2	62.5	94.1	88.9	86.2
Of B:					
(i) Those which use a formal plan	64.7	50.0	88.2	55.6	68.6
(ii) Those which use only informal plans	23.5	12.5	5.9	33.3	17.6
(i + ii = B)					
Of B:					
(iii) Those which plan over three years ahead	52.9	25.0	52.9	33.3	45.0
(iv) Those which plan up to three years ahead	35.3	37.5	41.2	55.6	41.2
(iii + iv = B)					
Don't know or no answer	0	12.5	0	0	2.0
Total	100	100	100	100	100

n = 51

sophisticated functions or to meet user requirements in a more effective way, or the improvement of processes for making such products, means deferring the return by some period of time; while research, development and design leading to entirely new products involve an even longer delay before the benefits are felt.

Despite the greater uncertainty and the deferment of profits involved, the value of investment in generating and making novel products is clearly well established, since many firms do invest in research, design and development, anticipating greater profits, increased competitiveness and improved market share in the longer term. Among the firms interviewed in Study B, half (51 per cent) had adopted longer-term strategies of expanding their product range, moving their products 'up-market' or developing new or improved products (see table 3.5). These strategies would all involve product design and some would involve R&D.

Meanwhile, table 3.5 also shows that about a quarter (27.5 per cent) of firms interviewed expressed their strategies in terms of improved manufacturing technology, reorganization or other cost-reducing activities, generally expecting a return in the medium term. Some of these options involve process redesign and/or innovation by the firm, while others are more concerned with the adoption of innovations or redesigns made by other firms. Lastly, table 3.5 shows that about a third (37.3 per cent) of firms had shorter-term marketing-based strategies of improving their ability to sell in existing markets or of expanding into new markets. Even though expressed in terms of marketing and understanding of user needs, however, many of these strategies would in fact be implemented by designing improved if not new products (see chapter 6). Market-based strategies can, of course, be quite long-term and may involve diversification or identification of 'niches' to exploit, requiring innovation and design activities. We have used the term 'short-term marketing-based' strategies here to mean just those strategies concerned with increasing the sales of existing products by expanding current markets and finding new ones.

Figure 3.2 illustrates the strategies adopted by plastics firms visited in Study A. The most striking feature is that the design-conscious firms were much more likely than the representative firms to adopt long-term strategies of moving up-market, or diversification by means of increased design effort and use of better-quality materials (which also often involves redesign). Design-conscious firms are slightly *less* likely than the representative sample to focus on medium-term

Table 3.5 Company strategies of furniture, heating and electronics firms (Study B)

Strategy	Firms pursuing (%)
1 New products, innovation, diversification, 'being technological leader' in market	47.0
2 Good design, move up-market, redesign products for new market segment	23.5
3 Improved marketing, better identification of market, more advertising and exhibitions	23.5
4 Joint ventures, buy up another firm, merge or cooperate to gain technological or market know-how	9.8
5 Increased investment in production, automation, new machinery, increased capacity, new processes	17.6
6 More financial control and efficiency in production	7.8
7 Meet user needs, liaise with customers, study design 'style' in target market to see what people want	19.6
8 Improve reliability of products and reputation of company for reliability, value, etc. (could be factor of 1 or 2)	3.9
9 Reorganize and specialize in certain market niches	9.8
10 Don't know, no answer or question not asked	13.7
A Cost-reducing strategies (5 and 6 and 9)	27.5
B New, improved or redesigned products (1 and 2)	51.0
C Improved marketing-based strategies (3 and 7)	37.3
D Information-gathering strategies to improve production of new or redesigned products (4 and 7)	31.4

n = 51
Note: Firms expressed more than one strategy, so 1–10 do not add up to 100%, and 5, 6 and 9 do not add up to 'A'. A–D were calculated separately to allow for this.

cost-cutting activities based on process automation as a major strategy for expansion. As many as 42 per cent of the representative sample, all concerned primarily with short-term survival, had no particular strategy – at least none they were able to define.

Thus the firms we visited had a range of long-, medium- and short-term strategies, with over half prepared to invest in the long term in expectation of greater benefits. However, as discussed in chapter 1,

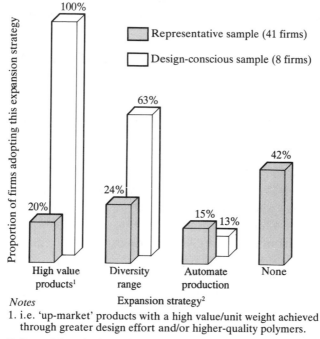

Figure 3.2 Strategies for expansion adopted by a sample of design-conscious and typical plastics firms (Study A)
Source: Walsh and Roy (1983)

all three kinds of strategy, short-, medium- and long-term, may be based at least partly on design, since design inputs are made to packaging, brochures, process improvements and new or improved products. The most financially successful firms had strategies that derived from a combination of objectives (such as 'meet user needs', 'lead in design' *and* 'increase profits') and involved increased efforts in marketing, sales, manufacturing *and* product development (Roy et al., 1986). Not all firms have the resources for such a total approach, and for smaller firms a set of narrower objectives plus a clear-cut strategy can also lead to success. For example, a profitable and fast-growing UK office furniture firm had the objective of 30 per cent growth/year to be achieved by 10 per cent more sales to existing customers, 10 per cent new customer sales and 10 per cent sales of new products specifically designed to fill unmet 'niches' in the market. Chapter 6 discusses in more detail the decisions involved in new product development and marketing planning, and the choices between the different types of investment decision involved.

The Return on Investment in R&D and Design

The uncertainties involved in innovation and design, especially of radically new products, make it extremely difficult to calculate the likely rate of return on investment in the necessary R&D, design, marketing and production facilities. It is difficult to calculate with accuracy even after the new product has been launched, but far more so in advance. The cost and time over-runs that have been much publicized in connection with major publicly funded projects, like Concorde, and more recently the Nimrod Airborne Warning System and the Channel Tunnel, bear this out. Likewise, British Rail's Advanced Passenger Train (APT) project, which is the subject of a detailed case study in chapter 5, took much longer to produce a reliable prototype than was originally anticipated. Apart from unforeseen technical problems that are impossible to allow for in advance in terms of time and cost, the actions of competitors and the preferences of customers may change the nature of demand over the time period of the project, as discussed earlier in the section 'Innovation Theory and Design Management'. Furthermore, the success in solving technical problems and designing a product that works, looks good, is convenient to use and reliable, may only be achieved at an unacceptably high price. These problems were experienced with the APT project but, in addition, the organization and management of the project, which are much more under the control of the strategic management of the organization, was a major factor in the ultimate failure of the APT (see chapter 5).

In our Study B, only just over a third of the firms had gone on to launch all the products they had developed. During the development process, the other two-thirds of firms had at least once cancelled a project at some stage before market launch (see table 3.6). Overall, technical and market uncertainties plus the difficulty of accurately forecasting costs and benefits, were the main reasons for projects to be cancelled before market launch. Technical uncertainty had most impact in the office furniture sector; unexpectedly high costs in the heating equipment sector; and market uncertainty in the case of foreign firms. Electronic business equipment firms were far more likely to cancel projects as a result of organizational changes or problems than for any other reason.

Table 3.6 Project failures before launch (Study B)

Reasons	Office furniture (%)	Domestic heating equipment (%)	Electronic business and computing equipment (%)	'Successful' foreign firms (%)	All firms (%)
All projects in past seven years led to a marketed product	47.1	37.5	25.0	22.2	34.8
Project cancelled due to poor planning or coordination by the firm at an earlier stage, or change in management	5.9	0	25.0	0	8.7
Project cancelled for cost reasons – profit margin too low: production too costly	17.6	25.0	8.3	11.1	15.2
Project cancelled due to changes in or misjudgement of the market	5.9	12.5	8.3	33.3	13.0
Project cancelled for technical reasons – failure or obsolescence	23.5	12.5	8.3	0	13.0
Parallel projects deliberate – only one chosen	0	0	0	11.1	2.2
Don't know or not asked	0	12.5	25.0	22.2	13.0
Total	100	100	100	100	100

n = 47

The technical uncertainty facing the office furniture firms was the rapid change in electronic office equipment with which furniture had to be compatible in terms of managing cabling, height adjustment and so on. The rapidly changing technology and market of the electronic business equipment firms might have been expected to generate more uncertainty for them, as well as for the furniture-makers, leading to projects being cancelled before market launch, but such office equipment firms put a lot of effort into monitoring technical and market changes because they knew how important they were. The foreign firms, which were chosen partly for their competitive success in the British firms' home markets, might be expected to be less at the mercy of market uncertainties than their competitors. The fact that market changes or misjudgements were responsible for the largest proportion of cancelled projects for foreign firms underlines the extra degree of uncertainty in export markets, as a result of different languages, standards, regulations, cultural patterns and so on.

Taking the total figure for firms which developed products that failed before market launch, the electronic business equipment firms were more likely to have failures than the heating equipment firms which, in turn, were more likely to have failures than the furniture firms. The foreign firms were the most likely of all to cancel projects before market launch.

Some of the uncertainties involved in a project may be reduced if not entirely eliminated by effective management, for example, by various methods of project selection, monitoring and control and by organizational measures to ensure the most effective interactions between people with different skills and experience and from different functional departments in the firm. Twiss, for example, discusses these measures in some detail (1980), and we take up some of them in chapter 5.

Absence of these measures contributed to project failures in our Study B (table 3.6), though fewer than 10 per cent of firms overall had cancelled projects due to organizational failures or changes. It was really only the electronic business equipment sector which experienced this as a significant cause of project failure. However, even where every care is taken to maximize the control and monitoring of projects, technical and market uncertainties still persist to some degree. Table 3.7 shows that two-thirds of the firms we visited had at some time developed products to the stage of market launch and then experienced commercial failures after launch. The most

Table 3.7 Market failures after launch (Study B)

Reasons	Office furniture (%)	Domestic heating equipment (%)	Electronic business and computing equipment (%)	'Successful' foreign firms (%)	All firms (%)
No post-launch failure	23.5	62.5	33.3	22.2	32.6
Problem with suppliers	5.9	0	0	0	2.2
Too expensive	29.4	12.5	0	11.1	15.2
Technologically obsolescent or 'bugs'	5.9	0	8.3	11.1	6.5
Not profitable enough	0	0	0	11.1	2.2
Poor sales/marketing	0	0	16.7	0	4.3
Poor design	11.8	0	0	11.1	6.5
'Didn't sell', 'didn't appeal'	23.5	12.5	8.3	0	13.0
Don't know if there were any failures, or no answer, or question not asked	0	12.5	33.3	33.3	17.4
Total	100	100	100	100	100

n = 46

common reasons for commercial failure of a product were either insufficient value for money, or just that it 'didn't sell' for no reason that the firm was able to identify (see also chapter 6). In the latter case, the actual reason for not selling could have been uncertainties in technology, the market or the economy as a whole, or lack of knowledge or poor performance on the part of the firm. The point, however, is that the *firm* did not appear to know the reason. It could not, therefore, adopt any procedure for either improving its performance, reducing risk or reducing the impact of unavoidable uncertainty, for example, by means of a portfolio of more and less risky projects.

A higher percentage of the successful foreign firms had post-launch failures than did the British firms. This was in addition to the projects cancelled before launch (table 3.6), where again the foreign firms had the highest proportion. Either the successful foreign firms had higher standards by which they judged commercial success or failure (for example, failure to meet a target rather than actually making a loss) or their successful products were more successful than those of their UK competitors, thus easily compensating for their failures. In other words, they were more prepared to take risks, balancing more failures against higher benefits from their successes.

The Problem of Coordination

One of the most important strategies of the firm, and one of the most important tasks of management, is to coordinate the functions of all the departments in the firm and the relationships between them. The different departments are likely to have different perspectives on the firm's business and immediate tasks as a result of their different functions.

For example, as chapter 6 discusses, the marketing department is concerned with prices and market shares of its own and competing products and the monitoring of customer preferences and purchasing power. Information gathered by the marketing department is used to modify strategies for selling the firm's existing products, to alert the production department to implement short-term increases or decreases in production, and to provide a crucial input into decisions about the firm's product range, and new or modified products that might be possible or necessary.

Meanwhile, R&D staff also have a view of potential changes in the firm's products and product range as a result of their own research and development and their interaction with the broader world of science and technology. It will be a view that is a compromise between what is technically possible and the demands of the market, but by the nature of their orientation, it is likely to be a compromise which emphasizes the former more than the latter. The marketing department's compromise, on the other hand, is likely to reflect a greater concern with competition, market size and share, demand and customer needs (however perceived).

A third perspective, described more fully in chapter 7, comes from the production department. Production staff stimulate ideas for new or improved products and processes as a result of their experience and their efforts to improve efficiency. Chapter 7 also describes the importance of input to the early stages of product design, of the production department's knowledge of the (possibly major) consequences for machinery, materials, working practices and order of operations of even trivial changes to a product.

The function of company strategy, and of management in implementing it, is to make these perspectives *complementary* rather than *conflicting*. Table 3.6 shows that 25 per cent of business equipment firms suffered project failures because they failed to carry out this coordination. The role of the designer can sometimes be one of coordinating various functions and inputs, by gathering information about technical market and production possibilities and optimizing them in the design of the product – what we have described elsewhere as 'the designer as gatekeeper' (Walsh and Roy, 1985).

Of the firms we visited in Study B, 38 per cent saw design as an integrating activity to which all departments should contribute. As one manager said, 'The design department is the place where everything has to be considered. Its operation depends on the company pulling together.' However, since design is not necessarily carried out in a design department, the designer may be influenced by at least two factors: the perspective derived from the function of designer and that of the department of which he or she is a member, which could be R&D, production or marketing. This is discussed in chapter 4 and we return to the question of coordination in more detail in chapter 5. The success of foreign firms may well be related to their attention to management of design and of the *whole* product development process, rather than just the quality of their designs. Responsibility for design in such firms is not located in other functional departments, but either in a separate design and development department, in an interdisciplinary project team established for the purpose, or with the firm's chief executive. One of the most important findings of Study B was that, in UK and foreign firms, the financially most successful firms were those which employed a *systems* approach to design. That is, the different aspects of new product development, including market requirements, price, production considerations, technological opportunities, materials and so on, were considered throughout the process – not added on at the end – and considered by a team. We return to this point in chapter 7.

This chapter has attempted to draw together some of the theoretical and empirical work on firm strategy in relation to both the design and innovation process, in order to analyse the findings of our empirical research in this area. We turn now to a more detailed examination of some of the functions of the firm. Chapter 4 discusses in more detail the employment of research, design and development staff. Chapter 5 is concerned with the organization of the innovation and design process in the firms we have studied. Chapter 6 considers marketing and new product planning and Chapter 7 discusses the product development process itself in some detail, from brief to manufacture.

Lessons and Conclusions

1 There is a level of risk, which is higher for firms developing, designing and introducing more technological products, which cannot be 'managed out', even by the most thorough application of the best management recommendations available. Two-thirds of firms had at least once cancelled a project at some stage before market launch. However, some of the uncertainties in product development may be reduced by effective management.

2 The allocation of resources to new product design and innovation is in some senses an investment decision, where the firm is prepared to defer a return on that investment in the interests of making a higher return in the long run.

3 Technological opportunity has an important influence on company strategy in general, and on design strategy by affecting the relative emphasis on the type of design (engineering, industrial, graphic and fashion design) that is done. Some firms in the Nordic countries have extracted the last drop of opportunity out of relatively unpromising (that is, mature) technologies by emphasis on product design and quality, thereby increasing substantially their exports of manufactured products to other advanced countries.

4 The adoption of 'offensive', 'defensive', 'imitative' or other strategies for innovation are a result of firm culture as well as careful balancing of strengths and weaknesses in R&D, production, marketing, design and opportunities and threats in technology markets and the regulatory environment.

5 Companies rarely have the goal of *maximizing* profits. They usually have goals of expansion (of profit, market share, turnover, etc.) or of survival. Firms adopt various strategies to achieve their goals, from improving their ability to sell existing products to producing high-quality products which meet customer needs. The most financially successful firms *combined* strategies, such as leading in design and meeting user needs, with goals of increasing profits.

6 The various functional departments in a firm have different perspectives on the firm's development of new products. An important function of strategy, and of management in proposing and implementing it, is to coordinate these functions so that the perspectives become complementary, not conflicting. This point is explored and expanded in chapter 5.

4

Human Resources for Design

This chapter discusses the human resources devoted to design and development – who does design, what status they have within the firm, and where they are located. These, in turn, reflect the firm's strategy towards design, its management of the design process and the importance which is given to design within the firm, all of which will influence the firm's design, and business, performance. At the same time, a firm's management is often in the position of having inherited an organizational structure and a set of conventions about 'how things are done' from the past. This means that, however strongly committed management is to design (or capital investment, modernization, innovation, financial control, a strong marketing effort, and so on), it will not be able just to conjure up the ideal organizational structure, set of working relationships and best practices, and commitment throughout the firm to the pursuit of its goals. Any necessary changes must be introduced to the firm as it actually is, having evolved historically in response to what might have been vastly different circumstances.

As a result, as we have observed in our various studies, design is an activity carried out by people with a range of skills, from different backgrounds, and located in a variety of departments in manufacturing firms, as well as by consultants outside those firms. This chapter will argue that this very variety of activities and locations that define 'design' in practice is the result of the historical evolution of the structure of firms, and in turn has very far-reaching consequences for the design function and its impact on the commercial success, or failure, of the firm.

Where Does Design Fit into Company Structure?

The evolution of functional departments

Firms come in all sizes, from the small owner-managed, single-product enterprise to the vast multinational. But all medium and large firms started as one or more small firms, and evolved into their present size as a result of growth, merger and acquisition, in various combinations at various stages.

The evolution of firms with a structure of specialized functional departments for sales, production, finance and so on (Chandler's unitary or 'U-form' organization (1962)), was an organizational innovation introduced, first in the United States, in response to the growth of the firm to a size where the original owner/entrepreneur, or a small number of closely but informally cooperating directors, could no longer handle all the information and decisions alone. They needed to recruit, or promote, staff to specialize in particular tasks.

The problem of achieving an efficient administration had become as important as the firm's main production activity, and was solved by the establishment of some kind of management structure. Some of the plastics firms we visited in Study A had recently experienced a change of this kind, but as an innovation in organization, the 'U-form' dates back to the end of the nineteenth century. The industries which first adopted it were chemicals, electrical engineering, food and drink and mass production of machinery; these industries were those where vertical integration was favoured and the volume of trade was growing, encouraged in turn by a combination of technical and market factors, such as the adoption of electric power and mass production techniques, a rise in real incomes and improved communication systems (Chandler, 1962; Williamson, 1970, 1975).

In-house research and development

The larger firms in some of these industries were also beginning to adopt their own research and development (R&D) activities, and it was fairly logical for the new in-house R&D laboratory to be a functional department in the new U-form structure. The pioneers of this second organizational innovation, however, were not the American electrical engineering companies, although they adopted it early on. It was the German chemical industry in the 1870s which first introduced the industrial R&D laboratory, internalizing and hence increasing control over the rate and direction of technical change, reducing its inherent risks and uncertainties, appropriating new areas of knowledge and hence negotiating and controlling some aspects of the environment rather than simply responding to it (Coombs et al., 1987). It also revolutionized the way in which firms compete and change their technological bases (Freeman, 1982).

It was not accidental that this development took place first in the chemical industry (or that it took place first in Germany). And because it did take place in the chemical industry, design did not have a clear-cut place in the order of things, in the way that scientific research did.

Industrial firms introduced technological innovations and redesigned products and machinery before any of them did their own R&D. Technological advances and new designs, following the industrial revolution, were mostly engineering based and were largely the result of improvements made by people working directly with the production process or closely associated with it. Mechanical ingenuity and experience enabled engineers and crafts-people to make improvements as a result of observation, imagination and trial and error (Freeman, 1982). Meanwhile, scientific research was separate – carried out in universities or privately. Pulleys, levers, pistons and so on can easily be visualized. Indeed, the development of machinery based on steam technology, which raised questions of power, energy and efficiency, gave rise to a new branch of science – thermodynamics – rather than vice versa (Lilley, 1949).

Imagining new machinery is one thing. Imagining certain other new products, like chemicals, is an entirely different matter. Some methodological understanding and theoretical ideas from the science of organic chemistry were necessary prerequisites to chemical innovation. It was not something that could be developed from an imaginative 'design' of new arrangements of atoms by production workers, as a result of their ingenuity and day-to-day experience. While the introduction of innovations in engineering stimulated the development of a new branch of science, innovations in the chemical industry were themselves stimulated by advances in the science of organic chemistry. And the rate of early chemical innovations (in dyes) began to decline again until a new development in academic chemistry (the structure of benzene) opened up a further range of opportunities. After a period of close collaboration with academic research, chemists had established the need for an input from science and stimulated a desire for more direct control over the science that was being done (Walsh, 1984; Beer, 1959). German chemical firms therefore established their own R&D laboratories, long before the same kind of pressure was felt by engineering firms.

This development took place in Germany as a result of deliberate policies in that country to stimulate science, technology and industry, to develop technical education, to provide a financial system appropriate to the needs of investment in risky innovation, to provide a legal framework (for example, on patents), to encourage innovation and to provide an infrastructure of transport and communications to encourage industrial development. As noted in chapter 2, this conscious promotion of industry and technology contrasted with the absence of such policies in Britain in the name of *laissez-faire* (Beer, 1959; Walker, 1980; Walsh, 1984).

But the chemical industry is one of the sectors where design has been of more peripheral concern – relating mainly to the design of packaging, logo and end-use applications – and so the establishment of corporate R&D departments did not at first provide design with a well-defined role or location within the firm, as might have been the case if the engineering industry, for example, had pioneered in-house R&D. As the institutional innovation diffused to other industries, it could be argued that this precedent was usually modified, as an afterthought, by 'adding on' a design function in a rather *ad hoc* way, wherever it seemed appropriate: attaching it to R&D, marketing or production, and only in some cases according it the status of a department in its own right.

In recent years, the Japanese firms following the strategy of 'reverse engineering', discussed in chapter 3, could in some senses be seen to be moving away again from a separate, specialist R&D activity. Although the incorporation of R&D within the firm represented a major advance in industries' innovative and competitive capacities, it also introduced the disadvantage of separate departments: barriers (or potential barriers) to communication between the different specialist staff. This was overcome to some extent in large Japanese firms by the approach of 'using the factory as a laboratory' in which the work of R&D staff and that of production and process control engineers became almost indistinguishable (Baba, 1985; Freeman, 1987).

The institutionalization of design

In-house R&D spread to the US electrical industry in the 1890s, but was still quite limited before the First World War (Sanderson, 1972).

Large firms in the chemical, electrical and a few other sectors in other advanced countries adopted R&D in the 1920s and 1930s, but it was after the Second World War that the real take-off in organized industrial R&D took place. At the same time, a further organizational innovation was taking place in firms, with the introduction of the multidivisional (or 'M-form') structure. The M-form has a number of divisions based on product groups or geographical areas, which operate almost as autonomous firms on a day-to-day basis (some are established as legally separate companies), but depend on the main board and top management for the allocation of investment funds.

Each division then has its own set of functional departments, appropriately specialized for the division. The take-off of R&D as a specialist, integrated function in the firm was complementary to the widespread adoption of the highly structured and functionally differentiated M-form (Kay, 1979). Some mutidivisional firms have specialist R&D laboratories in each division, while some have a central R&D activity for the whole enterprise, and others make some kind of hybrid arrangement with elements of both.

During this process, design – a function which overlaps with R&D but is different from it in several respects (see chapter 1) – never became institutionalized as a separate function within the firm in quite the same way that R&D did. There are many firms which have a specialist design activity and are very committed to design in terms of resources devoted to it, awareness of its importance throughout the firm, and promotion of design as a marketing feature to potential customers. But even these firms do not necessarily have a separate design department in the same way as they have marketing, production, finance or R&D departments. Some do, certainly, but many place design under the heading of one of these other departments.

In some firms, design may be part of R&D as captured by the term 'research, design and development'. It may be defined as the function of the drawing office, which may be part of the production department and not R&D. In yet other firms, design is the responsibility of the marketing department, in which case it is likely to focus on industrial design, with style, image and packaging design emphasized. In some firms the design function is even split up between departments. Some electronic business equipment manufacturers (in Study B), for example, have electronics engineers designing the combination of components and printed circuits which together provide the functions of the machine, while industrial designers in a separate department will design the casing and the arrangement of

Table 4.1 Responsibilty for design and development (Study B)

Department of person responsible for product design and development	Office furniture (%)	Domestic heating equipment (%)	Electronic business and computing equipment (%)	'Successful' foreign firms (%)	All firms (%)
MD or chair-person	29.4	0	31.3	22.2	24.0
Marketing/sales	11.8	12.5	6.3	0	8.0
R&D/technical	17.6	37.5	18.8	0	18.0
Production/ engineering/ Works	0	0	6.3	0	2.0
Design/design and development	29.4	50.0	12.5	22.2	26.0
Consultancy, or consultant liaising with someone in-house	11.8	0	0	0	4.0
Interdisciplinary, interdepart-mental group	0	0	25.0	55.6	18.0
Total	100	100	100	100	100

n = 50

controls. One type of designer is concerned with technology, reliability and function, the other with appearance and ease of use, but they are not seen as representing the different skills of a single design department, although the industrial designers may indeed be located in a department called 'design'.

Table 4.1 illustrates the separation of design throughout the firm. It shows that in nearly a quarter of all firms in Study B, the head of the firm took responsibility for design. In some cases this was an indication of the importance given to design in those firms, but in others it indicated the absence of specialist designers, or the firm's small size. Just over a quarter of firms had a design and development department, and the person responsible for design was in this department, usually the manager of it. In 4 per cent of firms, all in the furniture sector, an outside consultant took all or part of the *responsibility* for design. In 18 per cent of firms, design was a *group* responsibility, where some form of interdisciplinary group, usually a different one for each project, would be in charge of the design function. Over half of the successful foreign firms made design a group responsibility, and a quarter of the electronic business equipment firms did, but none of the heating and furniture firms followed this pattern. The significance of the difference is discussed further in chapter 5. The remaining 28 per cent of firms placed responsibility for design with one of the functional departments: marketing and sales, R&D/technical, or production/engineering. Being responsible for design, however, is not the same as doing it, as we discuss below.

In-house design

Who are the designers?

The Corfield Report (NEDO, 1979) advised industrial firms to devote more and better-qualified human resources to product design and development, a recommendation given further support by the Finniston Inquiry into the Engineering Profession (1980). All the UK heating and electronics firms did design and development work in house, but only 76 per cent of the UK furniture firms had in-house research, design and development staff (see table 4.2). Those without their own designers usually used consultants, but some firms neither used consultants nor employed full-time designers: 81.3 per cent of furniture firms did in-house design, even though only 76 per cent employed full-time professional designers and development staff. The difference is due to design and development being undertaken as a part-time activity by individuals with other main jobs, as discussed in detail below.

A striking fact was how few women were employed in research design and development. Sixty-four per cent of firms had no women technical staff in any role; only the electronics firms and the overseas firms employed women design and development staff in any numbers, mainly in software engineering and (in Japan) for draughting. Despite this dearth of female staff, many firms believed that women

Table 4.2 In-house design and development (Study B)

	Office furniture (%)	Heating equipment (%)	Electronic business and computing equipment (%)	'Successful' foreign firms (%)	All firms (%)
Do you employ full-time, in-house professional research, design and development staff?					
Yes	76	100	100	78	90.5
No	24	0	0	22	9.5
Do you do in-house design and development?					
Yes	81.3	100	93.7	66.7	86.0
No	18.7	0	6.3	33.3	14.0
Total	100	100	100	100	100

n = 50

could bring different and useful skills to design, for example, a better appreciation of user needs. This is taken up again in chapter 8 and discussed in more detail by Bruce and Lewis (1989).

There were significant differences in the mean percentage of a firm's staff employed in research, design and development, ranging in UK firms from 3 per cent in furniture and 5 per cent in heating to 20 per cent in electronics. In the Japanese electronics companies the proportion was even higher – one such company employed 5000 scientists, engineers and designers: 25 per cent of its total staff. Another important difference was in the level of qualifications: in the UK heating sector fewer than 10 per cent of R,D&D staff had a degree equivalent or higher qualification, compared to 50 per cent in UK furniture, 90 per cent in UK electronics and 95 per cent in overseas firms. The lower average level of qualifications in British firms compared with their overseas competitors, especially in management jobs, was noted in 1980 by the Finniston Inquiry and again in 1987 by Freeman.

Lego, a highly successful company in both business and design terms (see chapter 3), has shown that it values highly qualified and specialized people on its staff, but can also be flexible when it comes to the recruitment of people whose main contribution will be their creativity. In addition to a similar number of mostly highly qualified specialists in quality testing, materials technology, engineering, child psychology and other disciplines, Lego employs in house about 100 people with talent as designers. About two-thirds of these are qualified in design or architecture, but the rest are not; they recruited a baker and a former salesman, for example, who showed creative ability with Lego bricks and components and new play ideas. Once, when eighty people applied for one design job, Lego held a competition: the best and most original builder of a model using Lego pieces got the job. The company had advertised for creative people regardless of qualifications, age, sex or background.

The differences in the human resources available for undertaking design and development work in different firms could therefore be very great, even among firms making competing products. In chapter 1, for instance, we mentioned one heating firm where the technical director would undertake virtually all design and development work, while in others similar products were developed by large teams of combustion engineers, testing staff and industrial engineers.

Types of design staff and 'silent design'

Table 4.2 showed the proportions of firms doing their own research, design and development. Table 4.3 and figure. 4.1 expand this information, indicating the percentages of firms with different kinds of research, design and development staff, and further illustrating the argument in the previous section about the location of design. Nearly 30 per cent of firms have some production staff who spend some of their time on design and development, while over 40 per cent have full-time draughtsmen and -women, probably also located in the production department, although only 2 per cent of firms located responsibility for design in this area. Surprisingly, there are even some firms where staff in the finance area do part-time design and development work. More than a quarter of firms have marketing and sales staff involved in design and development some of the time, though only 8 per cent of firms place responsibility for design with this department. In nearly two-thirds of firms, engineering designers are employed, many of whom would be in the R&D department and some in a design department. In nearly a quarter of firms industrial designers are employed, again some in a design department, some

Table 4.3 Staff involved in design and development (Study B)

Percentage of firms which employed the following:	Office furniture (%)	Domestic heating equipment (%)	Electronic business and computing equipment (%)	'Successful' foreign firms (%)	All firms (%)
Industrial, product, interior or graphic designers (full-time)	23.5	25.0	17.6	33.3	23.5
Design, development or test engineers (full-time)	47.1	50.0	82.4	66.7	62.7
Software engineers or designers (full-time)	0	0	70.6	22.2	27.5
Draughtsmen and -women (full-time)	29.4	75.0	41.2	33.3	41.2
Draughtsmen and -women (part-time)	17.6	0	0	11.1	7.8
Marketing or sales staff who design part of the time	17.6	37.5	35.3	11.1	25.5
Production or engineering staff who do design part of the time	41.2	12.5	23.5	33.3	29.4
Purchasing or finance staff who do design part of the time	0	12.5	5.9	0	3.9

n = 51

in marketing. Table 4.3 and figure 4.1 also reveal important differences in the employment of research, design and development staff in the British and foreign firms. This is discussed below in the section concerning the employment of design consultants.

These tables illustrate not only some of the many facets of the activity called design, but also the many functions of the firm which

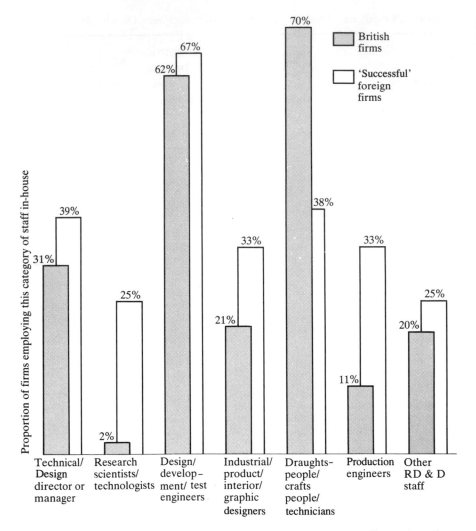

Figure 4.1 Full-time research, design and development staff employed by a sample of forty-two typical British and nine successful foreign firms in the office furniture, domestic heating, electronic business equipment and computing industries (Study B)

may be deemed to include design and development activities. Table 4.3 also illustrates what Gorb and Dumas (1987) call 'silent design' – the marketing, production and other staff who contribute to design decisions, or who do design and development part-time. These statistics do not indicate whether the part-time staff are qualified designers who have taken on other responsibilities in the firm, or are not qualified in design but are doing it because the firm is unable, or does not see the need, to get professional design and development staff or to retain consultants. In some of these firms they are the only designers.

In smaller firms, even where testing and quality control are full-time jobs, design is often done on a part-time basis. In addition to marketing and production staff doing part-time design, there are many firms where the technical director is also the chief designer. They may be highly qualified in, and committed to, design, but their managerial responsibilities make it impossible to devote much time to design. At the other extreme, they may be neither qualified designers nor talented amateurs, but the firm does not think design important enough to deserve better.

Such a variety of qualified and unqualified, manual and non-manual workers, who do design and development part-time or full-time, not only reflects a great variety of attitudes to the importance of design in manufacturing industry (discussed in chapter 3), but also complicates the classification of design work, even using the flexible approach developed by Gershuny and Miles discussed in chapter 2.

There is a strong correlation between the way design is defined and the department responsible for carrying it out. Thus design seen mainly in terms of engineering and function is likely to be the responsibility of development staff (in an R&D department) or of production engineers, while 'industrial design', which is concerned more directly with 'customer appeal', might be the responsibility of marketing.

Whether it is the location of the design function which influences the way in which it is defined, or the aspect of design emphasized by the firm which causes it to be located in a particular department, is a matter for debate. Probably the plethora of ideas about design, what it is and what its function is, that exists among the firms that use design and in society at large, is both a cause and a consequence of the *ad hoc* and rather muddled growth of the specialism. It is a cause in that the very different views of design keep it divided up in separate departments (or 'balkanized' to borrow Nelson and Winter's (1977) concept), reinforcing the career pattern of separate professional sub-groups with limited contact with other sub-groups. It is a consequence in that the different outlooks of the various departments where design is located, and their possible prejudice towards other such departments, reinforces the separation.

Table 4.4 Status of design in the firm

	Office furniture (%)	Domestic heating (%)	Electronic business and computing equipment (%)
Is someone qualified in design or technology on the company board?			
Yes	58	50	91
No	42	50	9
Is a board member responsible for product design and development?			
Yes	47	37	55
No	53	63	45
Total	100	100	100

n = 42 UK firms

Designers on the company board

The Corfield Report (NEDO, 1979) recommended that to improve the performance of British manufacturing there should be a qualified design director on company boards. In our sample three-quarters (74 per cent) of British firms in Study B already had someone qualified in design or technology on the board, ranging from 90 per cent in electronics firms to 50 per cent in the heating firms (see table 4.4). However, only 22 per cent of British Study B firms had a director responsible for design alone, and in 26 per cent the managing director was responsible for design and development as one of many tasks.

When we analysed the status of design in the Study B firms against their business performance, we found a significant statistical association between high profit growth and the presence of a designer or technologist on the company board, but there was no evidence of improved business performance on other financial indicators (described in chapter 1). The links between having a formal design director and these indicators require further investigation, but we noticed that the firms with the highest reputations for design (in terms of citations, awards and peer evaluation) were all founded by designers or had designers in very senior positions in the firm. In some cases this was associated with great financial success, but as we show in chapter 2 and throughout the book, a high reputation for design does not by itself guarantee success in business.

The Design Consultancy Industry

We have argued above that there is no clear-cut institutionalization of the design function within manufacturing industry in the same way that there is of the R&D function, such that design is *typically* the function of a separate design department. It is not even the case that design is normally the function of any *particular other* department, since it can be located in R&D, production or marketing. In the successful foreign firms, however, not only were they more likely to employ specialist research, design and development staff, but responsibility for design *was* located either in a separate design department, with an interdisciplinary project team established for that purpose, or with the firm's chief executive (see table 4.1).

Growth of the design consultancy industry

The institutionalization of the design function in some countries, particularly in Scandinavia, took on a form quite different from that of R&D, with the evolution and growth of a separate design consultancy industry doing work for manufacturing industry. More recently, design consultancies have developed in other countries, including Britain. Thus manufacturing industry, which could in principle manage the design function administratively within the hierarchy of the firm, typically in Scandinavia and increasingly elsewhere, acquires design expertise by sub-contracting, that is, by means of an 'arm's-length' transaction via the market-place. Williamson (1975) discussed the factors most likely to shift the boundaries between firms and markets. It is outside the scope of this book to review the now fairly substantial literature that has since developed from Williamson's work, on the factors that influence the selection of in-house or sub-contracted production or services. The point, however, is that for whatever reason, the historic trend in R&D has been for it to be increasingly incorporated within the firm (although some firms do sell R&D to others as a service), while the trend in design has been the growth of arm's-length transactions with separate consultancy firms.

Lewis (1988) has described the growth of the design industry and the increased sub-contracting of design by manufacturing firms as the 'distancing of design'. Although this trend was well established in Scandinavia in the 1930s (Annerstedt, 1986), consultant designers hardly existed in Britain until after the Second World War (Heskett, 1980), the first of the new generation of consultancies being founded in the late 1950s and early 1960s. Consultancies grew in the 1970s and many new ones emerged; by the 1980s they had become a 'billion-pound business' (McAlhone, 1987), employing nearly 30,000 people in over 2700 firms. While the largest number of consultancies were involved in interior, exhibition and graphic design work, often for the retail business (Olins, 1986), there was also a large number of engineering and product design consultants as well as those involved in fashion and textiles. Francis and Winstanley (1987) describe the increasing trend towards employing outside *engineering* designers in the mechanical engineering industries as well as sub-contracting draughting work, which has been common for longer.

Some firms do not fit easily into either the category of design consultancy or employer of in-house and/or consultant designers. For example, the Storehouse Group is a large service sector empire which, until Terence Conran left in May 1990 taking some of the subsidiary businesses with him, included retailing firms (Habitat, BHS, Mothercare, Debenhams), property development (Butler's Wharf), publishing (Conran Octopus), financial services (Storecard), catering (Bibendum restaurant), all employing designers, and the Conran Design Group which includes separate firms specializing in, for example, architecture (Conran Roche) and product and graphic design (Conran Associates). Design was the basis of the whole business group, since Conran was originally a furniture designer who felt obliged to open his own shop because of lack of interest from established stores (Sudjic, 1990).

Table 4.5 shows that about three-quarters of firms in Study B use consultants for design and development work, a figure which rises to over 90 per cent in the office furniture sector but is as low as 50 per cent in domestic heating. The main reason for employing a consultant is either a general lack of in-house skill, or lack of a particular skill, for example, designing in plastics, graphic design for a brochure, or software development. The foreign firms were more likely to employ consultants for design and development as a matter of principle or company strategy, in order to maintain a flow of fresh ideas. An example from Study B is the highly design-conscious US-owned office furniture firm, Herman Miller, which since the 1930s

Table 4.5 Use of consultants (Study B)

	Office furniture %	Domestic heating equipment %	Electronic business and computing equipment %	'Successful' foreign firms %	All firms %
Have you used a consultant for product design and development in the last seven years?					
Yes	94.1	50.0	70.6	77.8	76.5
No	5.9	50.0	17.6	11.1	17.6
Did not say or n/a*	–	–	11.8	11.1	5.9
Main reason for using a consultant					
Lack of in-house skill in general	17.6	37.5	47.1	11.1	29.4
To gain a wider perspective or to prevent 'staleness'	17.6	0	5.9	33.3	13.7
For speed	17.6	0	0	11.1	7.8
For specialist work	23.5	12.5	11.8	11.1	15.7
To save money	5.9	0	0	0	2.0
Did not say	11.8	0	5.9	11.1	7.8

n = 51
* Two firms were consultancies themselves.

has retained eminent consultant designers on a long-term basis to do most of its product design. Another well-known example, although not included in our survey, is the Italian multinational, Olivetti. Olivetti's reputation for design is based on the company's long-established policy of using 'in-house independent designers' for product design. These are teams of independent designers, led by internationally known designers like Ettore Sottsass, employed on a long-term consultancy basis and provided with offices, administrative support and full access to the company's operations (Kicherer,

1990). On a much more modest scale, the success of Plaspugs, the British manufacturer of do-it-yourself products, is based on a similar design policy (see plate 7). On the other hand, the Dutch electronics giant Philips, visited for Study B, relies more on in-house than external design resources. Apart from its many thousands of R&D staff, Philips employs world-wide some 300 in-house product, industrial and graphic designers, most of whom are based at the company's Corporate Industrial Design centre at Einhoven. In addition, the company often uses external design consultants for specific projects.

In our studies, the foreign firms were generally larger than the UK ones, so the use of consultants was less likely to have been due to the lack of sufficient resources to employ a range of professional design skills in-house, as it would have been with some of the smaller UK firms. Several of the overseas firms specifically stated their preference for outside designers. Although the foreign firms were not the group most likely to use consultants, comparison with table 4.2 suggests that they were the most likely to use consultants instead of, rather than in addition to, in-house designers, at least in the areas of product, industrial and graphic design.

Use of design consultants in Scandinavia

Both Studies A and B have indicated the widespread importance of a separate design industry in Sweden and Denmark in particular. All the firms we visited in those countries used industrial design consultants regularly and a majority did little or no in-house industrial design themselves, relying almost entirely on the design industry. Lego is one of the few Danish firms, for example, to employ a substantial in-house design team. In 1980 it employed consultants only for packaging design but now regularly employs them for product design too.

The Scandinavian heating equipment firms employed their own *engineering* designers and used consultants as industrial designers, but the furniture firms surveyed did not do any in-house design. Some firms were positively opposed to employing in-house designers. They expected the consultant designer to liaise directly with the firm's model builders, production and marketing managers and others responsible for the design brief. In-house designers, they believed, would get in the way of this interaction (Bernsen, 1990).

However, even Nordic firms which relied entirely on consultants to *do* their design, still employed qualified designers in other jobs, often responsible positions on the company board, for example as product development director. It may be seen from figure 4.1, in fact, that more foreign firms than UK firms employed full-time, in-house research, development and design staff in all categories except draughtsmen and -women. In contrast, many of the smaller or less design-conscious UK firms' *only* full-time designers were draughtsmen and -women. Only one in five UK firms employed industrial, product, interior or graphic designers, compared with one in three foreign firms, even though the foreign firms were more likely to have their products, packaging and graphics designed by consultants.

In Denmark, especially for major projects, it is common for firms, public corporations and government bodies to use design competitions, usually (though not always) organized by the Danish Design Council on their behalf. These may be open competitions with designs submitted by all-comers, or invitation-only competitions where a number of design consultants are invited to submit proposals. Copenhagen Transport Authority chose a new logo from over 2000 competition entries and more recently selected a new bus shelter in the same way: the prototype was put up by a bus stop in the main square in 1990, to be tested in normal use by the public. Scanform, one of the furniture firms in Study B, has chosen new designs from competition entries on several occasions. Other examples are Royal Copenhagen (a new dinner service), the Copenhagen telephone company (a new phone box), the Post Office (new uniforms) and Unicon (a cement-mixer lorry). Sometimes retailers sponsor competitions as a way of stimulating new designs and encouraging manufacturers to make them. Hansen now makes a table that was designed for a competition sponsored in Denmark by a retailer in the United States, and in 1990 retailers sponsored a competition for gardening products. An organization for the disabled sponsored a competition for suitable sports equipment for people with various disabilities (see plate 8), paid for by the sales of a specially minted coin (Bernsen, 1990; Flugge, 1990).

Although in the early 1990s the design industry has suffered badly from the effects of economic recession, especially in the UK retail sector, the Design Innovation Group is conducting further research on this new service industry. In Study C we examined the commercial impact on British manufacturers of employing a design consultant for a specific design or product development project. We are currently engaged in a new study of the relationships between design consultants and manufacturers in the UK and other countries, including Scandinavia.

Lessons and Conclusions

In summary, this chapter has described and proposed an explanation for the way in which design has become institutionalized, in separate consultancy firms as well as in-house in manufacturing industry, and in the latter case either as a separate design and development department or attached to another functional department: marketing, production or R&D. In contrast, R&D is typically found as an in-house activity in all but the smallest or most traditional manufacturing firms, although Japanese industry has blurred some of the boundaries between R&D and other functions of the company.

The chapter has also analysed the different human resources devoted to design, the frequency of design being done as a part-time activity, the status of designers in firms and the qualifications of people employed as R,D&D staff. There are significant differences between sectors of British industry and between British and overseas firms.

Several lessons arise from these differences:

1 Although there was little evidence that having qualified designers or technologists on the company board contributed to better commercial performance, it is important that a specific individual or group in the firm is made responsible for design and product development. In small firms this should normally be at board level, but in larger firms an individual or group at senior management level with access to the board is sufficient.

2 There are wide differences in the number of research, design and development staff employed by different firms in the same industry. While there is some evidence that employing a high proportion of R,D&D staff can help commercial and design performance, it is more important that the design skills available in the firm, including those of managers, marketing and other staff whose main job is not design ('silent designers'), are fully utilized, that the design function of such staff is explicitly recognized, and that where appropriate they receive suitable training in making design decisions.

3 The employment of in-house industrial and product designers was most common in 'design-conscious' firms which had a reputation for good design. But equally good commercial results could be obtained by using consultant industrial, product and graphic designers. The successful use

of design consultants depends on whether they are properly managed by individuals at senior level with an understanding of design, and on whether the consultant's work is integrated with that of in-house engineers and other staff. The firms which made most effective use of product design consultants retained them on a long-term basis, rather like in-house staff who could maintain an independent view of design. More important, however, than whether the industrial or product designers were employed in house, were consultants, or both, was that the firm's management regarded design as an investment justifying the best professionals it could afford.

5
Organizing Design and Innovation

Succeeding in getting the right product to the right market involves not only good product design and an awareness of market requirements, but the ability to manage product development. Over the past decade numerous studies have indicated that R,D&D has often produced inappropriate products too late, thus missing market opportunities, because technically capable people are not coordinating their efforts with each other.

The importance of coordinating design effort has featured in several official government-sponsored reports. In the Corfield Report (NEDC, 1979) it was noted that in numerous cases design work was isolated, resulting in the need for costly and time-consuming adaptations after market launch to ensure that the product met market and production requirements. The Finniston Report (Committee of Inquiry into the Engineering Profession, 1980) also advocated that 'the work of engineers and managers in research, design, development and production is integrated and linked to the market strategy' but that 'this integration is often missing'. A NEDC report on design by Pilditch (1987b) recommended a 'multi-disciplined process for product development' with 'engineers, industrial designers, marketing, manufacturing, R&D and finance all working together throughout the life of a product development programme'.

There are numerous ways in which companies organize the design and development of new products. These can depend on a wide variety of factors, like the size of the firm, general management structures, the types of product or service produced, the level of technology used, through to idiosyncratic factors such as peculiarities of the firm's history, how well different members of staff get on with each other, or the unique abilities of one or two senior individuals. This chapter looks at recent studies of managing design and

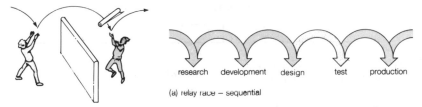

(a) relay race – sequential

Figure 5.1 'Relay race'. In the traditional linear or sequential approach to product development each department makes its contribution before passing the project 'over the wall' to the next department
Source: Course P791 *Managing Design*, The Open University

development and adds to these the results of our own research. From this work a 'map' of product design and development organization has been developed and this is used to identify and clarify associations between types of organization and other characteristics of firms, such as financial and design performance.

One in-depth case study, that of the management of British Rail's Advanced Passenger Train, High Speed Train and InterCity 225 projects, will be used to illustrate the major conclusions of this chapter.

Types of Product Development Organization

In their study of engineering design, Francis and Winstanley (1987) developed a three-fold typology which neatly summarizes the problems faced by traditional methods of managing technical projects. Lorenz (1987) also developed a similar typology for the same purpose, using sporting analogies to describe the management of product development. These are 'Relay race' which describes the traditional sequential pattern; 'Volleyball game' for iterative loops; and 'Rugby team' for group approaches to product development.

Sequential: the 'Relay race'

This is characteristic of many medium and large companies, which are divided into distinct functional departments with their own expertise and career hierarchy. To develop a new product 'the project goes sequentially from phase to phase: concept development; feasibility testing; product design and tooling; pilot production and full

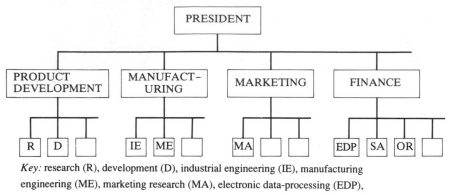

Key: research (R), development (D), industrial engineering (IE), manufacturing engineering (ME), marketing research (MA), electronic data-processing (EDP), system analysis (SA), and operations research (OR).

Figure 5.2 A typical functional management structure. The development of a new product will require the expertise of people in departments separated according to function. The sequential approach is when a design project is handed from one self-contained department to another.

production. The various functions are compartmentalized from each other with different specialists carrying the baton at different stages of the race' (Lorenz, 1987) (see figure 5.2).

Francis and Winstanley feel that such functional structures cope badly with modern pressures for rapid product development, particularly when tight budgets and high product quality are required. Their survey of engineering companies showed that the division between functional departments prevented communication and integration between different areas, particularly between design and production. The terms 'wall' or 'barrier' were used by some people interviewed in these firms. For example, such barriers to effective communication may result in impractical or expensive designs being 'thrown over the wall' to production departments for them to sort out.

Iterative: the 'Volleyball game'

One consequence of a functional structure is that a project may not succeed in being passed sequentially between departments, but is returned to the preceding department for corrections. Francis and Winstanley call this a 'volleyball' process because projects get passed between two departments several times before progressing on to the next stage (for example, several rounds of tests and modifications may be needed). They feel this type of project structure can inspire

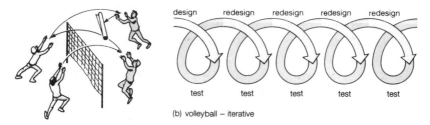

Figure 5.3 'Volleyball game'. In many companies product development proceeds via a series of iterative loops during which the product may be tested and modified several times before passing to the next department
Source: Course P791 *Managing Design*, The Open University

destructive internal rivalries. Production may pass back a design as 'impractical', but do little to aid the designers to improve it. In such an atmosphere, designs may end up being passed around simply so that no individual can be blamed for any faults. All this can be very time-consuming, particularly if communication between departments is poor.

Functional organization, mature industries and small firms

Agreement with Francis and Winstanley's view of product development in functional management structures comes from Holt (1987): 'If specific measures are not taken, a pure functional solution will give a slow sequential processing of projects, moving from department to department.' Yet Holt considers functional management structures to be appropriate in certain circumstances. One example is in traditional industries where technical changes occur in an incremental manner and at a slow pace. In such a situation a high level of coordination between departments might seem unnecessary. However, even in mature and traditional industries the rate of technological change and the speed of product development are increasing. The rail case study later in this chapter will illustrate this point.

Holt's second example of where functional organization is appropriate is 'the small company which often is very innovative due to an informal organization and a strong leadership'. This presumes that a small company has grown to the extent that it has established specialist functional departments, but these do not act as a 'wall' between staff, or that the firm is still small enough for all projects to be coordinated by one individual.

A major danger with such situations is that these small-firm methods of integration need to change as the firm grows. For example, an electronics company we visited in Study C developed out of the music-recording interests of its founder. He had a wide network of contacts in the recording industry and a superb technical knowledge of the technology involved. He initiated ideas for products and updates, knew exactly what the market wanted, and kept a watchful eye on product development, pulling in people and getting departments involved where necessary. The company grew over fifteen years from a hobby into the leader in its field, employing 250 people. But then the founder sold out. Nobody knew the technology and the market in anything like the detail he did; nor was there an organizational structure for product development through which anyone had been trained to replace him. After a period of crisis the firm was taken over by a company in the same business which did possess the expertise to organize product development.

This example shows that, although small firms may be innovative due to their more informal structure and strong leadership, changes have to be made to cope with growth. In our Study A of the plastics industry, the transition to formalized management structures occurred when a firm reached about 100 employees, and the firms identified as 'design-conscious' were noted as being the ones that had successfully made this transition (Walsh and Roy, 1983). Once a firm grows above such a threshold, the small-firm ways of coordinating new product development are likely to become impractical and will inhibit growth.

The results from Study B support such a conclusion. Information was gathered on the way in which the product development process was managed through its various stages. One method was the informal coordination by a specified individual, which, it is argued above, is only appropriate to small firms.

The results from Study B showed a strong correlation between company size and the use of a specific individual to coordinate product development. By this it is not meant that a project manager was appointed to coordinate a particular project, but that one person usually sorted out coordination for all projects. Usually this would be the technical director. Table 5.1 shows that the average size of firm where a specified individual personally coordinated three or more stages of product development was forty-seven employees. There was then a large jump to an average size of 310 employees where personal coordination was used for one or two stages of product

Table 5.1 Size of firms by use of specified individual to coordinate product development (Study B)

No. of stages of product development personally coordinated	Average size of firm (employees)	Size of largest firm (employees)	Sample size
3–4	47	80	4
2	310	650	5
1	313	650	5
0	596	3,500	20

n = 34 British and foreign firms in office furniture, heating, electronic business equipment and computing industries

development, and a further jump to nearly 600 employees for the average size of firms that did not use personal coordination at all.

Overall, the results of our studies and the conclusions of other writers in this field suggest that functional management structures may be appropriate for small firms and for firms in mature industries, but that problems are likely even in these situations.

Multidisciplinary: the 'Rugby team'

Lorenz (1987) and Francis and Winstanley (1988) contrast functional 'relay' and 'volleyball' methods of managing product development with the use of multidepartmental teams, which they call the 'rugby team' approach (a term also used by Uttal, 1987) – see figure 5.4. This basically refers to organizational structures that attempt to break down functional barriers so that 'designers and production staff are all on the same side working towards the same goal with good communications between them' (Francis and Winstanley, 1987). Drawing on Japanese experience, Lorenz typifies this approach as involving a 'hand-picked multi-disciplinary team, with its members working together from start to finish of the development process', which 'goes the distance as a unit passing the ball back and forth. The team usually has a high degree of autonomy, and often included representatives from key suppliers.' Iterative processes may be involved, but as part of a well-integrated team approach.

These writers are keen advocates of team approaches, seeing sequential and iterative methods of product development as time-

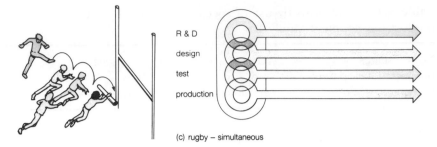

R & D

design

test

production

(c) rugby – simultaneous

Figure 5.4 'Rugby team'. In this approach product development is undertaken by a multidisciplinary project team working simultaneously and in regular communication with each other
Source: Course P791 *Managing Design*, The Open University

wasting and, in many cases, engendering bad communications and internal rivalries. However, Lorenz noted that in Japan, 'it may sometimes be possible to engender a "rugby" spirit without adopting a formal project team structure' and that in many large and successful Japanese electronics companies, project teams were not the norm.

This raises some crucial points. First, as was noted above, in certain industries which only have incremental developments, a functional organization copes perfectly well. It is a good way to pass on specialist expertise, to train people and to provide a clear career structure. Second, although team approaches are good for new developments, a functional approach is often better for routine work, which typically makes up 90 per cent or more of a company's activities. This tension, between the structure that is best for innovative as opposed to routine work, has led to a number of approaches that attempt to blend the best of both worlds.

Some firms get round this problem by having a separate, multi-disciplinary R&D department which works on new and updated products and then passes them on for development, testing and production-planning in the normal functional 'relay race' way. This is one example of what Holt (1987) refers to as an 'innovation-oriented structure', where innovative work is not done by coordinating people and resources scattered around a firm's departments, but where innovative structures are built into the organization of a firm.

There are a number of ways in which this can be done besides forming a separate research and development department. Holt also mentions the use of a separate management unit to develop innovative ideas, a central coordinating group to focus and direct decentralized innovation proposals, a hierarchy of such groups at corporate, divisional and plant level, and 'venture departments' set up to break into a new market.

Blending Functional and Team Approaches

Study B provided some very revealing information on the methods used to undertake the design and development of new products and the consequences of these methods. Companies were asked to describe the way that they 'typically' design and develop a new product, who is involved and how work is coordinated. Six basic approaches were identified:

- Sequential approach between functional departments
- Use of a specified individual
- Development committees
- Project teams
- Informal departmental groupings
- Methods involving the board of directors

Most of the companies in Study B had a functional structure – either entirely according to functional departments, or a divisional structure based upon product groups, each with their own functional departments. Particularly in the more 'traditional' and 'low-tech' companies, the sequential approach was normal. This fits in with Holt's observations considered above. As was noted earlier, in smaller companies, coordination between departments was often the responsibility of just one individual.

None of the companies surveyed had a separate research department as such, but about a quarter referred to 'research staff' who were involved in developing ideas to a certain stage before being fully implemented. These research staff were within functional departments, although in nearly half of the firms surveyed they would be involved in some sort of project team. This type of project team organization, where the members of the team remain within functional departments but are responsible operationally to project managers, is referred to as a 'matrix' organization. Pugh (1986b), in his business design activity model, develops a very detailed structure to integrate new product development teams into a functionally organized business, using the matrix approach. (See also Twiss (1980) for a discussion of matrix organization.)

Table 5.2 Use of project team (or 'task force') for new product development (Study B)

	Office furniture %	Domestic heating equipment %	Electronic business and computing equipment %	'Successful' foreign firms %	All firms %
Yes	24	29	80	72	46
Sometimes	35	0	20	14	26
No	41	71	0	14	28
Total	100	100	100	100	100

n = 46

Project teams (or 'task forces') were used at some time by all the electronic business equipment companies and regularly by most (83 per cent) of them. Under a third of domestic heating companies used project teams and, although only a quarter of office furniture companies used project teams regularly, another third used them sometimes. Seventy-two per cent of the 'successful' foreign firms used project teams (see table 5.2).

Quite what was meant by 'project team' appeared to vary between firms. This is important when thinking in terms of Holt's innovation-oriented structures. If a company's standard practice in developing a new product is to assemble a multidisciplinary team from several departments to see through design and development, this very much constitutes an innovation-oriented structure. A very different concept of a project team is one in which an *ad hoc* mix of departmental personnel sees through a project when it requires more development effort than usual.

Study B was able to explore this in more detail when the interviewee was asked to describe the 'typical' stages of designing and developing a new product and who would be involved in this process. From this it was possible to make a distinction between the use of more structured project teams as opposed to *ad hoc* mixes of departmental personnel. One striking result from this analysis is the correlation between the use of project teams and the financial success of the firms concerned. Fifty-five per cent of the firms using

1 Hille International's moulded polypropylene chair is a classic piece of innovative design. Designed by Robin Day in the early 1960s, the chair won a Design Council Award in 1964 and for many years was included on the Design Council's Index of well-designed British products. In its various versions it has sold over 10 million units and has been widely imitated by other manufacturers. *Photographs*: Robin Roy

2 The Austin/Morris Mini car, designed by Alec Issigonis and introduced in 1959 has set a standard for the design of small cars that has not been superseded. The Mini incorporated several innovations, including front-wheel drive, transverse engine and gearbox, small wheels and rubber-sprung suspension. Although it sold very well, for several years the Mini failed to yield much profit for its manufacturers.
Photograph: Richard Hearne, The Open University

3 Raleigh's 'Chopper' bicycle was an innovative design when launched in 1970 and sold more than any other single-specification bike made by the firm. However, the design was criticized on safety grounds and for attracting children away from the pleasures of 'real' cycling.
Source: Raleigh Industries Ltd

4 The fuel-effect fire, designed to provide the image of the traditional fire-place, is unlikely to win any design awards. However, such products are very popular in the market and are produced by most British manufacturers of domestic heating equipment.
Photograph: Stephen Potter

5 Serious fun – LEGO®

LEGO is a toy *system* in which all the pieces are compatible with each other. The firm has stuck to its basic product idea without chasing fads, but has creatively developed a vast array of variations on that basic idea, and this, combined with a clever marketing strategy, is what lies behind its success. Technical improvements in materials, basic brick design (for better 'grip') and processing have also been important, with an estimated £100 million invested in new plant and equipment in recent years

Source: LEGO (UK) Ltd   LEGO® is a registered trademark

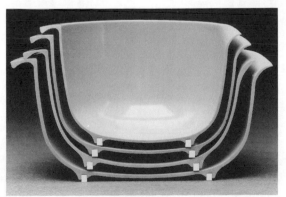

6 The Margrethe bowl, designed by Bernadotte and Bjørn and made by the Danish firm, Rosti, has been in production since the 1950s. The bowl is made from melamine and is to be found in most households in Denmark. The visual appeal is combined with practical function. The lip on one side forms a handle and on the other makes an open spout for pouring. A rubber ring on the underside prevents the bowl from sliding on the worktop.

Source: Danish Design Centre

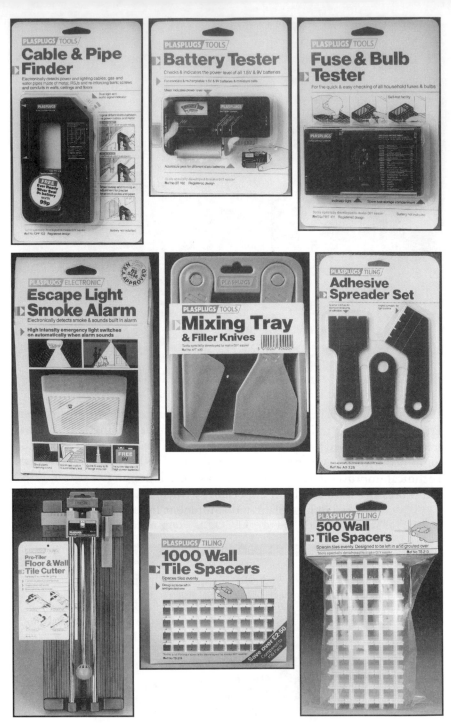

7 Some of the large range of do-it-yourself products manufactured by the British firm, Plasplugs. The company's rapid expansion has been based on its policy of retaining a consultant designer on a long-term basis, thus enabling the firm continually to add to and improve its range. Packaging design is also recognized as being important, and the best graphic design consultants are engaged for this purpose. *Source*: Plasplugs Ltd

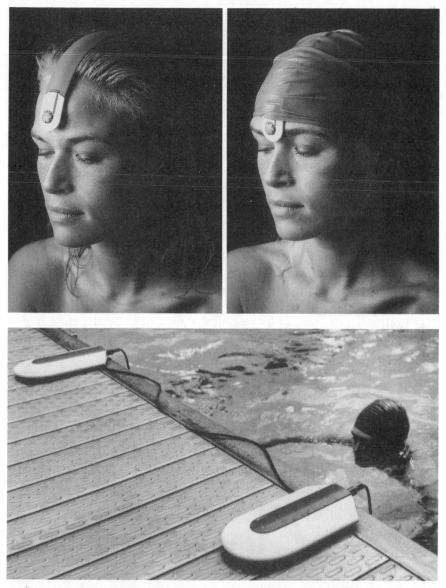

8 Prize-winner in a Danish design competition to provide sports equipment for people with various disabilities. This electronic system is designed to help blind people use swimming pools in safety. The receiver worn on the blind person's head sends signals from the transmitter on the poolside through the skull and so does not interfere with his or her hearing.

Source: Danish Design Centre

9 One of the prototype Advanced Passenger Trains on a trial run. The 155-mph APT incorporated several radical innovations in train design, including a tilting body, high-speed bogies, hydrokinetic brakes and articulated coaches. Development of the APT was hampered as much by organizational problems as by technical difficulties. By the time it was operating reliably the market had changed and the APT was cancelled.
Source: British Rail

10 The InterCity 125 (High Speed Train). This largely evolutionary design, whose only major innovation was a high-speed bogie, was success-fully developed within the functional structure of British Rail's Chief Mechanical and Electrical Engineer's department. The engineers in the Traction and Rolling Stock division were determined to prove that they could develop a 125-mph diesel train to rival the APT. *Source*: InterCity

11 The InterCity 225. The 'Class 91' locomotive for this 140-mph train, developed by GEC-Alsthom Transportation Projects to British Rail's specification, is largely evolutionary in design. The Mark IV coaches used on this train, developed by Metro-Cammell to British Rail's specification, are also relatively conventional, being non-articulated and made from steel.

Source: InterCity

12 The strength of the British electronics company Amstrad has been in identifying customer wants and in designing products to meet those requirements at a highly competitive price. One of Amstrad's most successful ranges has been its complete word-processing systems which include personal computer, software and printer in one easy-to-use package, at an affordable price. *Source*: Amstrad plc

13 The Sinclair C5 electrically assisted tricycle, which was launched in January 1985 as 'a revolution in personal transport', sold only a fraction of the 100,000 units its developers had anticipated. Although production was discontinued in August 1985 after about 5000 C5s had been sold, the vehicle continues to be used by a few enthusiasts, like this Newhaven commuter. The C5 illustrates the difficulty of identifying the potential demand for a radical new design. Nevertheless, more thorough market research and testing at the early stages might have revealed that no mass market existed for a low-performance electric vehicle that offers few advantages over a bicycle and initially cost as much as a moped. *Source*: Camera Press, London

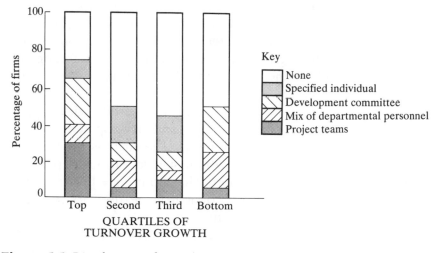

Figure 5.5 Distribution of coordination methods for product design and development (Study B)
Source: Potter (1990)

project teams were in the top quarter of firms with the highest turnover growth (see figure 5.5).

These results are similar to those found in the survey of 369 companies by Service et al. (1989). This showed 'a positive correlation between teams and dedicated new-product departments and better business performers. Conversely there is a negative relationship between product performance (i.e. successful product development) and where companies have either a new-product manager or where the technical department is responsible for new-product and development.'

In our Study B, informal groupings of departmental personnel are, interestingly, associated with both the best and worst financial performances! However, informal groupings are more difficult to categorize than project teams. Whereas the existence of a project team implies close and continuous cooperation, this may not be the case when more informal, *ad hoc* groupings are mentioned. Informal or *ad hoc* groupings could occur for positive or negative reasons. Positively, they could (as Lorenz observed) reflect an 'organic' structure with close informal links between departments. Negatively, they may arise when a project is found to be behind schedule or getting nowhere and people are pulled together to 'sort out a mess'. Also, the grouping may only be for one or two stages of a product's development. Typically, in Study B, this might involve Marketing and

Design getting together to sort out a basic concept and brief for a new product which is then developed and produced sequentially. Another grouping may occur later, involving Production, Finance and Sales, to see through production planning and marketing. This was more typically found among the domestic heating companies than in the other sectors examined.

Forty-seven per cent of the firms in Study B used a 'development committee' to oversee product design and development. Broadly, this is a management team including people such as the technical, financial and sales directors, to whom staff in various departments working on a new product report. This alone may be used to co-ordinate functional departments, or it may be used to coordinate managerial input to a project team.

In fact Evans (1985) felt that much of Japanese manufacturing industry 'adopts a very systematic linear flow of work from the initial concept, market research and planning to various stages of sketches, presentation models and production prototypes'. This sounds very much like the traditional functional sequential process. But Evans continues: 'With near-constant formal meetings to assess progress, many iterative loops and final exhaustive testing of the preproduction units, not much is left to chance'. This enables firms to splice together better marketing, design, engineering and production, with an 'emphasis internally on cooperation rather than competition' (Evans, 1985). This helps to explain Lorenz's seeming surprise at the lack of formal project teams within much of Japanese industry. The coordination may be more organic and informal or involve cooperation and direction of purpose without the dismantling of functional departmental structures.

Service et al. (1989) noted in their study that 'frequent meetings (at least weekly) have a positive relationship with the percentage of turnover accounted for by new products. Again, this agrees with the literature in the area which calls for integration between different departments: frequent contact no doubt facilitates integration and encourages a more multidisciplinary approach.'

Holt (1987) considered that 'proper documentation can be a useful integration device': for example, producing a project schedule, including time-scale, responsibilities, costings, etc., will require inputs from various departments and will show how these have to be integrated. However, this is best used as part of other integration methods, such as the meeting of a development committee to assess project progress. In Study B, we also found such formal review points

Table 5.3 Holt's typology of product development methods

A Ways of organizing routine product development	B Ways of organizing innovation	C Integration methods	D Management style
1 Functional structure	1 Use general development structure	1 Integration unit	1 Organic
2 Product-oriented structure	2 Matrix management	2 Transfer of personnel	2 Formal/ mechanistic
3 Innovation- oriented structure	3 Independent project organization	3 Committee	
		4 Documentation	

Source: Adapted from Holt (1987)

being fulfilled by presentations to the board of directors. For projects that do not need a great deal of day-to-day coordination, such periodic management reviews are often appropriate.

Analysing Functional and Team Approaches

Overall, our research shows that it is not just a matter of team project management versus 'relay race' or 'volleyball' sequential management. There is a whole spectrum of degrees of cooperation, and these may vary at different stages of product development. Lorenz's and Francis and Winstanley's basic division into 'sequential' and 'project team' approaches may be easy to comprehend, but in practice (as Study B has shown) most firms fall between these extremes.

Holt in fact breaks his analysis into a far more complex categorization of four levels. At the first level he examines models of general product development; second, he looks at ways of innovating; third, at methods to integrate the work of people from various parts of a company; and fourth, at management styles. Table 5.3 is a summary of Holt's analysis.

This four-fold distinction is very useful. First, for an individual product, ways of innovating may not be the same as for routine product development. Second, integration methods stand alone from product development structures, as does management style.

For example, a functionally organized company may use a project team for a development job which is more complex than normal. This is made up by temporarily transferring some people from marketing and production into R&D, which is agreed personally by the managing director. This represents one possible path through Holt's four levels, involving a) functional structure; b) independent project organization; c) transfer of personnel and d) organic management style.

This sort of theoretical approach helps to explain some of the apparent contradictions that arise when trying to relate the simple functional/project group typology to actual practice. However, Holt's analysis does provide a very complex typology with dozens of possible permutations. This is particularly difficult if, as in the analysis of Study B, relationships between financial performance, design performance and product development organization are to be examined.

Project organization mapping

A diagrammatic classification was therefore developed which falls somewhere between these two extremes. It takes as its basis the axis between functional sequential and group/team organizations, while allowing for a broad categorization of the major integration methods. This is represented diagrammatically in figure 5.6.

This technique can cope with the fact that many firms use a blend of project management methods. The boxes represent 'ideal types', that is, the perfect version of that management method. If a firm used only project teams for all stages of product development, it would be plotted inside the project team box. If a firm used a blend of organizational and management methods, they would be mapped at a point representing this blend. For example, if a firm used an even mix of sequential and informal groupings, it would appear half-way between these two on the map. If this grouping was then organized by a development committee, its mapped position would swing up to midway between these three boxes.

The major advantage of such a map is that it does not require firms to be classified into one type or another. The methodology reflects the reality it is analysing by allowing for blends of organization and management methods.

Mapping firms from Study B according to industrial sector reveals distinct patterns (figure 5.7). The domestic heating firms cluster close

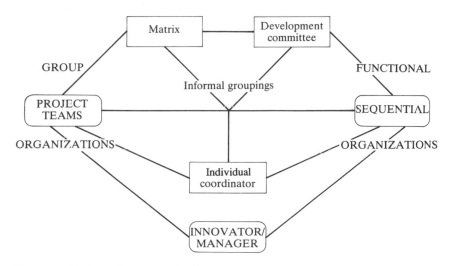

Figure 5.6 A project organization map
Source: Potter (1990)

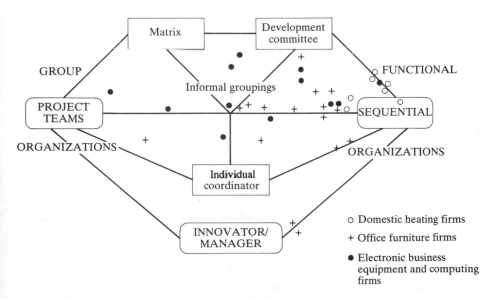

o Domestic heating firms

+ Office furniture firms

● Electronic business
equipment and computing
firms

Figure 5.7 The position of firms in Study B on the project organization map according to industry sector

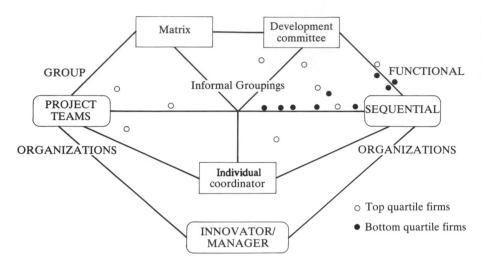

Figure 5.8 Project organization map of the firms in Study B according to top and bottom quartiles of turnover growth

to the sequential type, with what coordination there is being undertaken by a development committee rather than by an individual manager or formal project teams.

Office furniture firms veered more towards personal methods of coordination, particularly in the smaller companies where the influence of the 'innovator/manager' was strong. Most firms in this sector used some form of group working with some project teams, although sequential methods were still used for certain stages of design and development.

Electronic business equipment firms displayed a scattering along the project team – informal group – sequential axis, with coordination tending to be by committee rather than individuals.

Relating the position of firms on the map according to turnover growth reveals an interesting pattern (figure 5.8). Given the general pattern of firms as shown in figures 5.7 and 5.8, where very few are found towards the left of the diagram, it is significant that the top quartile firms are to be found in an arc across the top of the map. The bottom quartile firms are far more clustered towards the functional–sequential 'ideal type'.

Of the three top quartile firms where product development was basically sequentially organized, one was a small firm (twenty-five employees), where coordination would be a relatively straightforward job. The other two firms were larger and used development committees to coordinate the sequential process. This does suggest that methods to coordinate development other than project teams or other ways to group staff can succeed.

Service et al. (1989) gathered information on the involvement of different personnel in new product development, although this was not combined as such with management/organizational structures. Their study showed good performance at new product development to be related to:

a) where the managing director is involved throughout the process (which is related to a strong commitment at board level);
b) where both engineering design and aesthetic design are represented throughout the process;
c) where distributors and suppliers are involved throughout the process.

Good design and project organization

Information was also gathered in Study B on the design quality of the companies' products. Firms were categorized according to 'design-consciousness'. As described in chapter 1, this was done by an analysis of whether their products had won design awards, had received other forms of recognition for good design, or had a reputation in the industry as design leaders. As figure 5.9 shows, design-conscious companies were found mainly in the area of informal groupings organized by development committees rather than individuals.

Overall, there is a general pattern that the companies associated with better design and higher turnover growth have product design and development organizations that facilitate group working. Formally constituted groups or those with a formal coordinating body (such as a development committee) are more successful than those coordinated by a specified individual. A purely sequential approach to product development is associated both with poor design and companies with a poor financial performance. This finding statistically supports the views of the various authors cited earlier, that team working leads to better-designed and more commercially successful products.

Although these are the broad trends, it is also quite clear that there is no simple organizational formula that guarantees the rapid production of well-designed, financially successful products. Both the successful British and foreign firms in the study used project teams

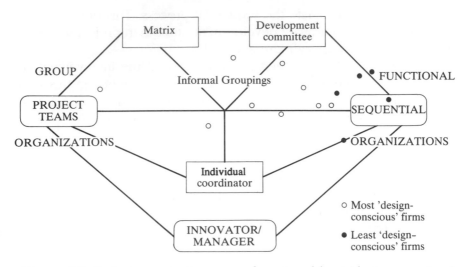

Figure 5.9 Project organization map of most and least 'design-conscious' firms in Study B
Source: Potter (1990)

and other strong methods of coordinating product development more than the less successful firms in the sample. However, there were exceptions and clear sectoral differences which suggest that the market addressed and the complexity of the technology used have much to do with which coordination method is optimal. Rutterford (1989) noted that 'it is much easier to prescribe the use of multi-disciplinary teams than to implement them successfully' and that the 'official reports contained few details about establishing integrative measures and the problems of implementation were not explored'.

Our Study B certainly indicates that different types of coordination may be appropriate in different circumstances, depending on the size of the company, industrial sector, style of management, etc. In order to explore such issues, a specific case study follows which provides a good illustration of many of the issues raised in this chapter.

Organizing Research, Design and Development: a Tale of Three Trains

In the 1960s, a number of countries were developing fast passenger trains capable of 130–170 mph. Most of these combined fast train designs with new, straight track (Japan's Shinkansen, France's Train à Grande Vitesse (TGV), the Neubaustrecken and Directissima lines in Germany and Italy as well as the rebuilding of the North-East Corridor line in the United States). New track made the technical development of fast trains easier, but in Britain no economic case existed for building new lines. Work began in 1968 on the 155-mph (250-km/hr) Advanced Passenger Train (APT) – a very technically sophisticated train which could operate on ordinary, curved lines. This required a host of innovations: high-performance brakes, ultra-lightweight construction and a tilting body to maintain passenger comfort while the train curved at high speed.

At this time, the railways could easily be viewed as being within one of the categories where Holt considered functional structures to be entirely appropriate for product development: a mature industry where changes occur incrementally and at a slow pace. Indeed, in the 1960s and 1970s this was very much the case within British Rail. The department responsible for the engineering design and development was the Chief Mechanical and Electrical Engineer's Department (CM&EE for short). This was then divided and sub-divided according to function (see figure 5.10).

This functionally organized structure had built up historically and had much to do with the 'evolutionary' engineering approach that is characteristic of the rail industry worldwide. Any new development has to fit in with a large existing system of track, signalling and operational methods, only a small part of which can be changed at a time. Consequently, any improvements have to be compatible with the existing infrastructure and vehicles. In most cases, existing designs came to be taken as the starting-point for any new job. Each time a particular design feature was used, it was updated, improved a bit, or another variation tried to see if it worked any better. Such evolutionary engineering generally means that design improvements are slow, but easily managed; experience is readily shared and it certainly represents a low-risk approach to change.

In the early 1960s a separate Research and Development Division had been established. This could be seen as an example of Holt's 'innovation-oriented structure', for it was to 'act as a strategic organization undertaking basic research on project ideas to be implemented by the appropriate engineering department and workshops (or an outside contractor) once their viability had been proven' (Potter and Roy, 1986). The Research and Development Division (BR Research) was purposefully separate and organized differently (on a multidisciplinary project team basis) in order to undertake work unsuited to traditional, functionally organized departments.

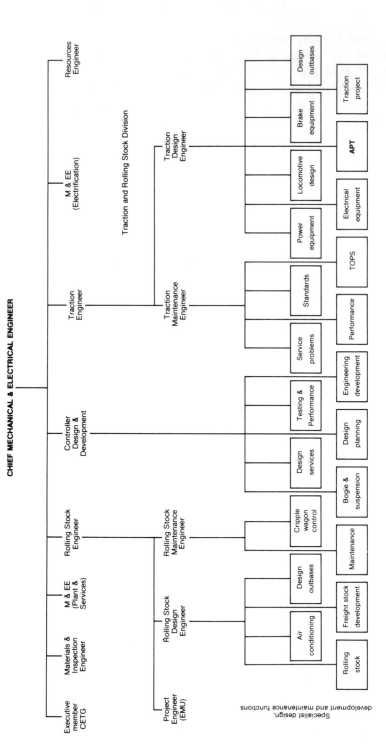

CHIEF MECHANICAL & ELECTRICAL ENGINEER

Executive member CETG   Materials & Inspection Engineer   M & EE (Plant & Services)   Rolling Stock Engineer   Controller Design & Development   Traction Engineer   M & EE (Electrification)   Resources Engineer

Traction and Rolling Stock Division

Project Engineer (EMU)

Rolling Stock Design Engineer

Rolling Stock Maintenance Engineer

Traction Maintenance Engineer

Traction Design Engineer

Rolling stock   Air conditioning   Freight stock development   Design outbases   Maintenance   Cripple wagon control   Bogie & suspension   Design services   Design planning   Testing & Performance   Engineering development   Service problems   Performance   Standards   TOPS   Power equipment   Electrical equipment   Locomotive design   **APT**   Brake equipment   Traction project   Design outbases

Specialist design, development and maintenance functions

APT Project Group (140 staff)

Figure 5.10 The functional organization of British Rail's Chief Mechanical and Electrical Engineer's department in the mid-1970s. Note the location of the APT Project Group as a relatively isolated team within the Traction and Rolling Stock division

Source: British Rail, Potter and Roy (1986)

The Advanced Passenger Train (APT)

The technical basis of the Advanced Passenger Train emerged from basic work at BR Research who then took the development of the APT as far as the construction of an experimental train. Having used a dedicated project team to prove the viability of the APT concept, BR Research passed the project over to the functionally organized Chief Mechanical and Electrical Engineer's (CM&EE) Department for further development and the construction of three prototypes. Because of the complex nature of the APT, the entire project team was transferred into CM&EE. There were problems with this solution; the project team engineers duplicated posts and skills within CM&EE. This made worse an existing problem of internal rivalries, as a number of key engineers viewed the whole approach of the APT as a 'high-tech irrelevance'. Although the APT project team contained very skilled engineers, they were not experienced in dealing with such internal politics. Rutterford (1989), in her survey of firms introducing multidisciplinary teams for R,D&D, noted similar problems: 'Loss of authority, control and status can be threatening and cause functional managers to resist attempts to introduce multi-disciplinary teams.'

The practical effect of this antagonism was that the project team became very isolated. It received little support from people with valuable engineering and managerial experience in CM&EE and work on the development of the train and debugging the three prototypes became more and more protracted. The effects of this isolation and antagonism filtered through to other parts of the railway. In the British Rail workshops, the train came to be viewed as a low-priority 'experimental' job, and this sort of attitude not only slowed up development work, but had a major influence on quality control. There were considerable differences in the quality of work between workshops where the manager was enthusiastic about the APT and those where the manager was not. Many of the problems of reliability with the APT prototypes were a direct legacy of poor quality control. The APT got stuck in a classic 'volleyball' situation, involving iterative loops of modification, tests and further modifications. All of these were prone to delay, but slowly the APT team began to win the enthusiasm of others within CM&EE and British Rail. It was at this point that a new managerial factor came into play that virtually halted any real progress.

Trials of the APT began in May 1979 (see plate 9), and in December of that year one of the prototypes set the British Rail speed record of 161 mph (although the fastest they ran in passenger service was 138 mph).

Holt (1987) notes that many larger companies divide themselves functionally according to the products they make. Each division has specialist development, manufacturing and marketing sections. Such a corporate structure has major advantages for product development. It 'gives a clear responsibility for results, good communications, strong motivation and good possibility for developing managers . . . it also may have relatively informal management systems and thereby get benefits such as speed, flexibility and creativity'.

This was the sort of structure that British Rail created in the 1980s, focused around five major product sectors: InterCity passenger services; regional passenger services; Network Southeast (London commuter lines); Freight; and Parcels. For traction and rolling stock purposes, three basic sectors were identified – InterCity, Freight and Suburban. From 1976 to 1980 CM&EE was restructured around these three sectors. The APT project team was dispersed among the new functional categories (figure 5.11) and was formally wound up in 1980.

From being under a tightly knit project team, development work on the APT came to be simply one of many projects under the Inter-City engineer. The whole project lost focus. In addition, the past awkwardness of the APT project team being based in an otherwise functionally organized department led to further problems. Members of the APT project team duplicated the skills already in the department and they were working on a project that was despised by some people who were likely to become their new bosses. Those who could got out to obtain posts elsewhere which did not involve such uncomfortable circumstances. This rapidly drained the APT project of its most capable and skilled people. Every single APT section head left.

Just when the project required the strongest focus and greatest skill and resources, those resources were being dissipated or lost. The new organizational structure came into being in 1980. For the APT it had disrupted development work since 1977 and continued to disrupt it while the new organization settled down. Embarrassed by the train's absence from passenger services, a limited service was attempted on the London to Glasgow route in December 1981 using one of the APT prototypes. The train only completed one run without a hitch. Although severe weather conditions probably had more

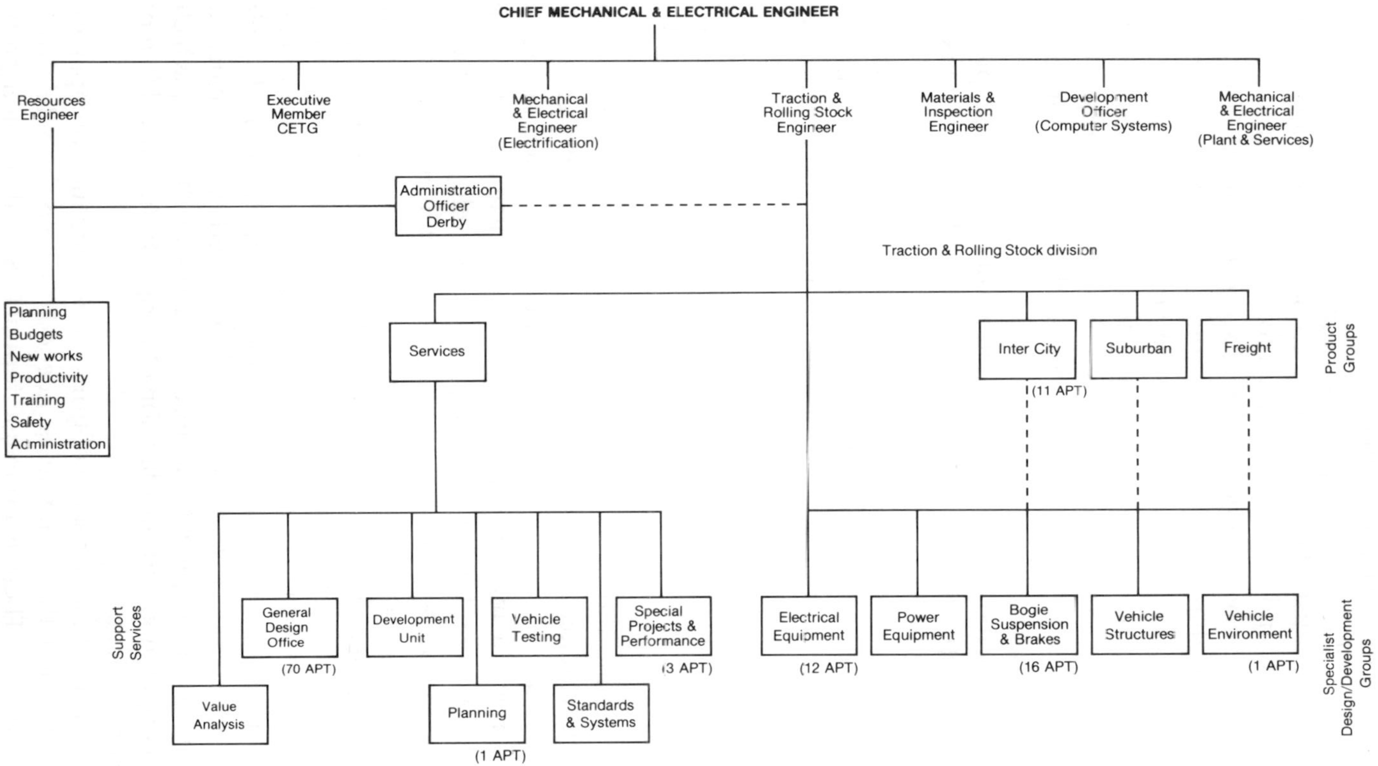

CHIEF MECHANICAL & ELECTRICAL ENGINEER

Resources Engineer

Executive Member CETG

Mechanical & Electrical Engineer (Electrification)

Traction & Rolling Stock Engineer

Materials & Inspection Engineer

Development Officer (Computer Systems)

Mechanical & Electrical Engineer (Plant & Services)

Administration Officer Derby

Support Services

Planning
Budgets
New works
Productivity
Training
Safety
Administration

Services

Value Analysis

General Design Office
(70 APT)

Development Unit

Planning
(1 APT)

Vehicle Testing

Standards & Systems

Special Projects & Performance
(3 APT)

Traction & Rolling Stock division

Product Groups

Inter City
(11 APT)

Suburban

Freight

Specialist Design/Development Groups

Electrical Equipment
(12 APT)

Power Equipment

Bogie Suspension & Brakes
(16 APT)

Vehicle Structures

Vehicle Environment
(1 APT)

Figure 5.11 The CM&EE department of British Rail following the reorganization that came into effect in July 1980. The APT Project Group was dispersed into nine different sections in the new structure, as indicated on the chart

Source: British Rail, Potter and Roy (1986)

to do with this than technical faults, it was clear that the APTs were nowhere near reliable enough for passenger service.

In 1982 the British Railways Board employed the management consultants Ford and Dain Research Ltd to establish what had gone wrong. They were very concerned that work on the APT had become isolated within CM&EE and that some engineers were undertaking work in areas in which they were very inexperienced. That the APT was a project slotted into a functionally organized department was of particular concern. They felt that a focused project team had to be re-created, but must be compatible with the functional structure of CM&EE.

This involved the use of a matrix organization. A new project manager was appointed, whose role was to coordinate the work of people in different sections of CM&EE and other British Rail departments. They were not removed from their sections to work exclusively on APT, but the project manager was given the authority and backing to ensure that his work got done. By not creating an isolated team, it was possible to change the skills and people in the team easily, and this also made the avoidance of internal rivalries easier. Broadly, the aim of this type of project management structure was to combine the continuity and experience of a functional department with the direction and cohesion of a project team.

This overcame the main drawbacks of the original APT project team structure. A major problem with the APT's original project organization was that, because people had been exclusively appointed to the APT project team, the skills in that team remained static. The sorts of skill needed for the different phases of development change all the time. At the beginning, the bulk of the work is in engineering design, but very different skills and experience were necessary for testing and debugging. What happened with the APT project team is that the skills that were its strength in the early stages of the project became less relevant later on. Most of the APT project team had little management experience outside the project itself, so although their engineering experience was extensive, they lacked many abilities to cope with the development and testing phases of the APT, which required cooperation and coordination of people from many different parts of British Rail.

Rutterford (1989), in her study of firms introducing multidisciplinary teams, concluded that 'training is needed to help [people] work collaboratively . . . There is no magic formula.' She also noted problems where, as in the case of the old APT project group, there was a lack of backing for project group leaders. The matrix project team was drawn from within sections of CM&EE as their skills were needed. This meant that it was possible to change skills in the team to match the differing needs of work as it progressed. Training was also more effective as there was a mix of experience within the project team. Equally, from a staff point of view, this matrix structure provided a settled situation, with none of the disturbances associated with the break-up of a team once the project ended. This structure allows people to be moved on from one project to the next. Finally, although internal rivalries will always exist within any large organization, such a flexible project team structure makes avoidance of conflict that much easier.

The effect of this reorganization upon the APT's development was substantial. By early 1984 the prototypes were running reliably and in 1984–5 they saw regular passenger service as relief trains. But too much time had been spent reaching this stage. By the time the new project manager and team had got the bugs out of the APT, the design and market specifications were a decade out of date! Embarrassed by the whole saga, British Rail scrapped the APT prototypes, although one was retained for a while as a research test bed.

The High Speed Train (HST)

What saved British Rail's InterCity services was that, in addition to the technologically radical APT, an incremental development was also authorized. This was the 125-mph diesel High Speed Train (HST) or InterCity 125 as it is more widely known (see plate 10). Nearly 100 of these trains became the backbone of four out of five main InterCity routes and when introduced in 1976 were second in speed only to Japan's Shinkansen trains. The HST design has been licence-built in Australia and its coaches became the basis of the International Coach (plate 19), which has been exported to many countries and is licence-built in Mexico and China. Designed in the early 1970s, twenty years later the HST is still the fastest diesel train in the world.

Besides the use of the innovative high-speed bogie, every other design feature on the HST was nothing more than an incremental 'evolutionary' improvement on existing 100-mph train designs. The 'Mk 3' coaches for the HST were being developed anyway and entered service a year before the HST itself. Hence any serious problems had already been identified and corrected. The power cars housed an upgraded version of an existing diesel engine, but the power cars' aerodynamic streamlining was new, and made a very important contribution to the HST's modern image.

The HST did face a number of technical problems, largely concerning the engines. These had a persistent problem of internal coolant leaks, plus several other mechanical failures. High levels of maintenance became necessary, pushing up operating costs. This maintained the HSTs in service but in 1983, following a series of HST failures, British Rail was forced to reduce its HST fleet so as to have more power cars available in reserve. Improved maintenance methods eventually addressed this reliability problem and by 1989 the mileage between power car overhauls more than doubled to over 450,000.

The HST has undoubtedly been a success, but the debugging of the train's technical problems actually took over ten years.

The InterCity 225

In 1984 the abandoned APT was replaced by the 'InterCity 225' project (see plate 11). A strong management structure was established and an incremental approach adopted in order to get this train into service as quickly as possible. A new passenger service specification was drawn up. Research fed into this specification suggested that 140 mph (225 km/hr – hence the train's name) should be the top operational speed. Commercially it was not worth going faster as the time savings involved would generate insufficient additional income to pay for the costs of higher speeds. A cut of 15 mph compared with the APT may not seem much, but it allowed the use of a much more conventional design, somewhat akin to the technology of the TGV. Also, for the first line on which it would operate – the newly electrified route from London to Leeds and Edinburgh – the track was relatively straight and so tilt would not be necessary. Tilting coaches thus became an option for possible later development. The only really innovative feature was in the 'Class 91' locomotive for this train. In order to reduce track damage, the weight not cushioned by the suspension system had to be minimized. This meant that driving motors and gear-boxes could not be directly mounted on the axle. The train's builders, GEC, developed a new transmission system to do this.

The design, development and construction of the Class 91 locomotive took only two years and it entered passenger service thirteen months later in March 1989. The first Mk 4 coaches entered service in October 1989.

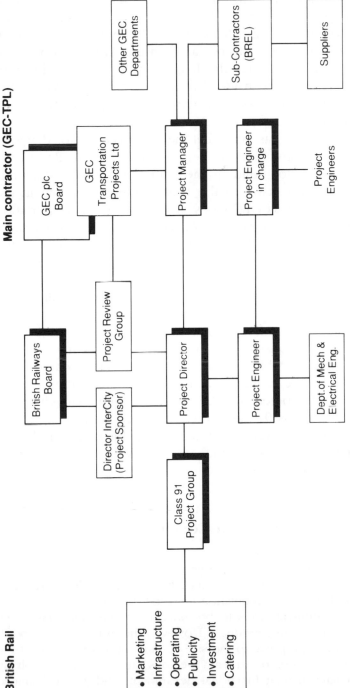

Figure 5.12 The matrix management structure for British Rail's 'Class 91' locomotive showing the links between BR and the main outside contractor

Source: Course T362 *Design and Innovation*, The Open University. Adapted from information supplied by British Rail and GEC Transportation Projects Ltd

One important lesson of the APT saga was that the method used to coordinate project design and development must relate to the organization within which it will take place. The type of project team that saw through the technical research on the APT concept in BR Research was not suitable for the longer, more complex development process requiring considerable managerial skills within the CM&EE department. The reorganization of that department and the disbanding of the APT project team were the final blow.

A significant change has been that the responsibility for development as well as construction has been given by British Rail to the main outside contractor building the train. To a large extent this shifted much of the risk on to the main contractor, which in the case of the Class 91 was GEC (now GEC–Alsthom) Transportation Projects. However, British Rail established a very effective management system to coordinate their internal resources with those of the main contractor. This is shown diagrammatically in figure 5.12 with respect to the Class 91 locomotive on the InterCity 225 train. This structure involves a project director with strategic responsibilities and a project engineer who manages a matrix team.

As well as the InterCity 225 being a more manageable project, the design of the train is considerably more flexible than either the APT or HST. Short-term flexibility is provided in that the coaches and locomotive can be used separately, and in the longer term, the design has considerable potential to be upgraded. With relatively minor modifications, the Class 91 has sufficient power to run at 160 mph and a double-power car version would be capable of 186 mph (300 km/hr). With new trains having a lifetime of at least thirty years, such flexibility is important.

Lessons and Conclusions

1 Companies which create interdepartmental teams for product design and development are among the most financially successful of those examined and have products with a reputation for good design.
2 Sequential development tends to be too clumsy and time-consuming, particularly for innovative products. However, the exact form of coordination must be appropriate to the size, nature and organization of the company involved. Less formal team methods can succeed by involving staff who remain in their functional departments and are coordinated either by a project manager or by a management 'development committee'.

3 A minority of companies that were financially successful, and a substantial number that were noted for good design, none the less had a predominantly sequential organization for product design and development.
4 Overall, this supports the notion that it is crucial to identify the most appropriate structure for organizing product design and development. Factors that influence this are firm size, the nature of the market in which it is competing (for example, fast moving), the technology used and the speed of response required. The latter is of increasing importance in all market sectors.
5 The fast trains case study provides a more detailed set of conclusions regarding the appropriateness of organizational structures for product development. These include:

- Radical technological innovation depends upon strong R&D capabilities and is likely to involve a long period of development, testing and debugging.
- Radical technological innovation, while offering the prospect of major benefits, is inherently risky. If possible, the risks of innovating can be reduced by incorporating the minimum amount of innovation at first and then phasing in further innovations into updated versions of the product. This has been the intention with the InterCity 225, which is designed to be upgraded in service.
- Technological innovation requires commitment and may require organizational change. A company must not only ask, 'Have we the people skilled to make this?' but also, 'Have we the organization to make this and are we all behind it?' British Rail was divided over the APT project, and the way it was implemented did little to heal those divisions. It was not divided over the InterCity 225 project and had an appropriate project organization, both to manage internal resources and to work with the outside contractors.

6 Major innovations usually require the coordination of a project team approach. Linear approaches are appropriate for incremental 'evolutionary' developments, but are too clumsy and time-wasting for the development of more complex or radical projects. Although the type of team may vary, two crucial factors for success appear to be the use of a dedicated project manager and the support at senior management level of a 'product champion'.
7 It is nearly always necessary to change the composition of the team through the various stages of research, design, building, testing and implementation of a new product.
8 Even if a firm has devised a potentially successful product, the involvement of people outside the company is important. It may not even be appropriate for that firm alone to develop the product. An example of this was the new procurement policy in British Rail, which was seen

as a better way to integrate the experience of the railway industry and British Rail. A project team for a major new product should involve sub-contractors, consultants, suppliers and product distributors as well as internal people. It may involve delegating major responsibilities to such outsiders, or even (on a clear contractual basis) the responsibility for leading product development.

6

Designing for the Market

It has often been said that if you design the world's greatest mouse-trap, the world will beat a path to your door. This suggests that success comes to designers and inventors of ingenious products. It even implies that these inventors and designers know what will work, what consumers' preferences are and what the market will stand. Sometimes inventors and designers are successful and sometimes their instinct for what will succeed is accurate. But inventors and designers do not necessarily know what customers want, even on the basis of past experience. And the potential customer will not buy the new product without knowing about its existence, or how it compares with alternatives. Nor will the product sell well unless it is fairly readily available and appropriately priced. Ingenious design, by itself, is not sufficient to bring about commercial success. Marketing is important in achieving success, however good or innovative the design may be.

Conventional wisdom often associates marketing with selling, advertising, creating 'needs', product promotion, brand loyalty and image. Indeed, it is often held that marketing is nothing more than selling products whether or not people really want to buy them. From this perspective, the only role for design is in promotional and advertising material.

Marketing, however, is much more than selling, promotion and getting people to buy anything a company makes. It is about gathering information to help anticipate, identify and satisfy customer needs. It is about linking such needs with the company's goals and objectives in product planning. It is about decisions across the company's portfolio of products concerning the introduction of new products, the adaptation of existing products and the deletion of some items. Marketing feeds vital information into R,D&D departments about the sorts of product a company should be developing.

In the design of new and improved products, the interaction of the designer's flair and the marketing staff's knowledge of customer life-styles, demands, needs, wants and hence potential desires is a central and vital ingredient. As Kotler and Rath (1984) said: 'Good design acquires and incorporates the necessary knowledge of what customers want, what can be most effectively produced and what best fits in with the company's other products.'

Understanding what the customer wants is a central function of marketing and a vital input to the achievement of 'good design'. It is not always easy to know what the customer does want. A powerful slogan in marketing circles is 'find a need and then fill it' (Pilditch, 1978). But finding out what constitutes a need or desire is a perennial problem, especially where innovative technology and design are involved. Potential customers do not always know what they want in the abstract.

From our surveys, we found that companies with a record of successful innovation typically gather market intelligence from many sources, such as surveys of in-house staff or existing customers, trials of prototypes, and studies of social trends and patterns of use of existing products. Companies which have developed an effective approach to marketing tend to be good at anticipating future trends in life-styles, consumer preferences and market opportunities. They are often proactive and anticipate, or even create, market demand rather than reacting to changes when they have happened. Different approaches to marketing are discussed in this chapter.

Having decided what the customer does want, it is not always easy to incorporate customer wants into appropriate designs. One of the arguments we make throughout the book, and which emerged from our studies, is that companies which are successful and sustain a competitive position are good not only at design but also at other key business activities, such as marketing and production. Good communication between marketing and design enables the configuration of products which correspond as closely as possible to customer needs and offer value for money (see chapter 2). It also enables relevant information about customer needs to be fed into the design process at an early stage, thus saving time in getting the product into the market and avoiding subsequent costly modifications.

Product Marketing Strategies

Market demands and user needs are unstable and constantly open to change. For example, at the beginning of the 1990s 'environmentally friendly' became a major selling-point for some consumer goods ranging from washing powder to cars and domestic appliances (see chapter 8). Yet only one or two years earlier 'green issues' were not significantly affecting consumer preferences in the mass market. If companies fail to meet new consumer demands or to respond to changes in the market, then they can quickly be overtaken by their competitors. Consequently companies have to be aware of trends and shifts in consumer preferences and be able to design products which fulfil new demands. Firms have to be able to anticipate changes in the market and also try to keep ahead of the competition.

What is the range of product marketing strategies available to companies to assist them in designing for changes in the market? The matrix in figure 6.1 (adapted from Ansoff, 1965) presents three market choices: maintaining the current market position; increasing market presence; or entering a new market. The corresponding design options to help achieve these market goals are either incremental design changes or more radical and innovative new designs.

Examples of product marketing strategies

Some of these different options and the pros and cons of different methods of acquiring market information are shown by the following examples taken from our Study B.

Product development A supplier of electronic business equipment devised a new text-processing system capable of handling text, technical and graphical information. The product was developed in response to changing user needs. One of the managers interviewed gave the following rationale behind this development: he said, 'Our users noted that the system we were selling fell short in certain capabilities, the product was developed to meet their requirements.'

Product update 1) A terminal for an electronic business machine was redesigned to reduce the cost of manufacture and to enhance its marketability with the addition of new facilities. 2) The implementation of new standards affected a range of desks supplied by one of the office furniture companies. The old desks had to be scrapped and a new range which complied with the standards was developed.

		DESIGN	
		NEW DESIGN	UPDATE/ REDESIGN
M A R K E T	Maintain market	Product development	Product update
	Increase market	Product and market development	Variation of product
	Enter new market	Innovation	Market gap

Figure 6.1 Marketing and design mix to give alternative product development strategies
Source: Bruce and Capon (1990)

Product and market development 1) Following the initiative of one of its main competitors, a new range of systems furniture was designed by one of the office furniture firms. It was expected that the new range would meet changing market demands for furniture which could accommodate office automation. 2) The rising cost of oil had been a prime factor encouraging a heating equipment supplier to design a solid fuel boiler. The increase in oil prices had resulted in a fall in demand for oil-fired boilers and the firm needed to diversify.

Variation of product One of the office furniture companies had been operating at both the lower and the top end of the market, with huge price differences between the products it sold in these different market segments. The company felt that it had lost its identity and was failing to be as competitive as firms which had a range of product brands with prices matched to various market segments. The range of products the company made was rationalized and new variants introduced.

Innovation A voice storage device integrated with a workstation was launched by one electronic business equipment supplier. The firm had carried out a study to identify the requirements of users working in totally electronic offices or 'paperless offices of the future'. The voice storage device was one of the products designed for such an office environment.

Market gap A supplier of computer accessories introduced a number of products ranging from a copy holder to a dehumidifier to fill gaps in the market. These products would meet existing market demand and were likely to be profitable.

It is possible for a company to adopt more than one strategy for product planning and design. Once major British bicycle manufacturer participating in Study A had the following approaches:

- updated versions of standard products, such as permutations of components, frame sizes and colour on its range of sports bicycles;
- replacements for existing products, such as redesigned bikes with oval-section frame tubes and alloy components;
- a new market opportunity (or market gap), such as revival of traditional designs of bicycle with roller-lever brakes, hub gears, etc. aimed at the 'nostalgia market';
- a new design concept, such as a fun bike for children with electronic instruments, built-in radio and sound effects synthesizer.

This company drew on its marketing knowledge to assist in the design process in order to meet changing market needs and satisfy different consumer preferences. The firm was attempting to find a need – in this case several needs – and fill them.

It is worth considering in greater depth examples of firms which fall into some of the categories identified in the design/marketing matrix illustrated in figure 6.1. These firms have taken different approaches to marketing and its integration in the product planning and design process.

Risks and rewards of innovation

An example of a company following the dictum of 'find a need and fill it' is that of the British consumer electronics company Amstrad, which diversified in the mid-1980s from its product base of audio and television equipment into the personal computer market. One of Amstrad's first and most successful products in this new area was designed to fill a market gap by providing a complete package of hardware and software for a microcomputer system designed mainly for word processing and other office tasks (see plate 12). The product was specially designed to meet the needs of the target market and was competitively priced. The system was based on existing technology to keep costs down, and was well promoted and distributed via established retail chains.

The success of Amstrad word-processing systems can be attributed to the ability of the innovating firm, and in particular its chief executive, to perceive changes in demand which were creating new openings in the market and then to act on this market knowledge to design a product which met consumers' preferences. Moreover, the firm entered the market at the right time. Competitors quickly followed suit. Amstrad has continually redesigned the product to stave off the competition and to meet new consumer needs as new uses for the product have come to light (Roy et al., 1987).

The above is an example of a company creating a new design to fill a market gap. In this case there was an individual in the firm who had an excellent feel for the market. But what happens in a situation of much greater uncertainty, and where both the product and market are unknown? Can innovators find out in advance whether a potential demand exists and what the customer requirements for the innovation may be? The pitfalls of the individual 'gut feel' approach to innovative design is illustrated by the now well-known example of the Sinclair C5, an electrically assisted tricycle which spectacularly failed to identify or create the market demand expected for the vehicle by its planners and designers (see plate 13).

Whilst the failure of the C5 can be attributed to design deficiencies, such as low riding position, limited range and luggage capacity and a maximum speed of 15 mph fixed by legislation, there were also marketing deficiencies which contributed to its failure. Clive Sinclair relied on his conviction that a market existed, or could be created, for a vehicle like the C5, and based the design specification on his own views of customer needs and preferences.

Some market research was carried out, but only after the basic concept had been decided upon. The market research that was done was mainly intended to help promote the vehicle. Had the firm made some attempt to investigate the market systematically before the design and launch of the C5, it might have discovered that the main demand for an electrically assisted tricycle was limited to a few leisure uses rather than for general family transport (Roy et al., 1987).

In this example there was a general disinclination to study the market and identify user needs before developing the product. The innovators believed they were creating a 'breakthrough in personal transport' and that a market for the innovation would be created. The C5 shows clearly that ingenious design by itself is not always sufficient to create market demand, especially if the product does not offer potential customers sufficient advantages over existing products to induce them to try out and switch over to using the new product.

One of the most successful consumer electronics products of recent years is the personal stereo player. The Sony Walkman was the first personal stereo and this innovation opened up a market that did not previously exist. Again, this is a situation characterized by both technical and market uncertainty. But unlike Clive Sinclair with the C5, Akio Morita, who conceived the Walkman, was correct in spotting a potential new market. In this case the 'gut feel' approach worked. Since its introduction over a decade ago, several million personal stereos have been sold world-wide and there are many variants available from different manufacturers who quickly entered the market. To keep up with the increasing competition, Sony has developed a range of personal stereos aimed at different market segments. It has also differentiated its products from the competition, for example by introducing new designs like the water-resistant 'Sports Walkman' and the 'My First Sony' range aimed at the children's market (see plate 14).

Sony has the ability to create products that anticipate and open up new market demands, and then to develop the original innovations into a product range aimed at different groups of consumers. How does it do this? Sony welcomes ideas for new products from many sources including engineering, production, marketing and sales staff, and from outside the company. The ideas are fed into the Product Planning Centre which is responsible for 'software thinking', that is, anticipating future trends in life-styles, consumer preferences and market opportunities. Promising ideas are developed into concepts which are presented to top management and, if selected, the ideas are then developed further.

What the C5 and Sony Walkman have in common is that both these product innovations are rooted in a 'gut feel' approach and where formal market research was non-existent or minimal. The 'gut feel' approach did not work in the case of the C5 but obviously did for the Sony Walkman. Sony used market research for the incremental changes to the Walkman to keep ahead in the competitive market subsequently created. With radical innovations it is difficult for market research to lead the way. Finding a 'need' is a perennial problem because potential customers do not always know what they want in the abstract. Extensive and systematic market research can at best reduce the risk of failure of radical innovations. This point is taken up again later in the chapter.

Anticipating market change

It is clear that looking ahead and planning products which meet changes in consumer tastes and keep ahead of the competition are vital, not only to discover the basis for a product's superiority and uniqueness, but also for a firm's survival. The demise of well-known British toy producers in the 1970s and 1980s (firms with household names like Airfix and Meccano) gave way to producers from overseas, notably from the Far East. Why did this happen? Airfix was one of the toy producers visited as part of Study A and it was producing construction kits and model vehicles similar to those it had produced for decades. It did not develop toys to meet the changing tastes of children. Airfix targeted its promotional material at adults, at uncles and fathers, to buy model kits for children out of feelings of nostalgia and a desire to use the toys themselves. New market opportunities (for example, capitalizing on the 'Star Wars' space craze which followed the film) were sought too late. Promotion was aimed almost exclusively at boys, and the firm ruled out product variants aimed at girls, or even advertising existing products to them, and thus ruled out the potential doubling of their market. In addition, lack of investment in process innovation meant that an old and inefficient plant was making expensive products which were perceived by potential customers as being too much hard work for too little fun. Airfix fell into the trap of selling what it made, rather than making what it could sell. It doggedly persisted in the belief that because the products were good in the past they would continue to be good in the future. Airfix did not respond to changing consumer tastes and preferences nor to the changing nature of competition. Cheaper imported toys as well as up-market expensive toys appeared to offer better value for money to consumers. The company could not compete and closed down, selling its trade names to overseas firms.

This example shows that a lack of attention to design, innovation and market research can be fatal, given ever-changing markets and shifts in consumer tastes and preferences. Complacency and a failure continually to adapt, redesign and change threaten survival. Lego is a successful toy company whose contrasting approach to strategy was discussed in chapter 3.

The problems faced by many of the companies participating in our studies were not so much the risks of innovation; rather, they were those of market penetration and moving into related product markets, as well as the redesign and adaptation of existing products to sustain and expand their markets. In our Study B, the commercially more successful firms were those with an evolutionary approach to design and product development. It was also true that these companies were usually not innovators in the sense of creating wholly new products. As is shown in chapter 7, they tended to use existing ideas, and competitors' products, as a starting-point to introduce improved products on to the market and to fill gaps in the market or in their product ranges. The companies we encountered in our surveys were all gathering market intelligence of some sort to assist in their design and product development activities. However, there were marked differences in the approach to marketing of the successful and less successful companies in our Studies A and B. The more successful firms tended to gather market intelligence from a wide variety of sources and to feed this information into the planning and design process. They had an understanding of marketing that had a much more vital role to play than just being about the promotion and selling of the finished artefact.

How did the firms in our surveys collect market information? What were the differences between the more successful and less successful firms? We go on to discuss these issues in the next sections.

Sources of Market Intelligence

On a day-to-day basis the marketing department is concerned with the prices and market shares of the firm's products and those of its competitors. On this information are based the company's strategies for selling its existing products more efficiently and information about demand is conveyed to the production department so that short-term increases or decreases in production may be implemented. Marketing is also able to observe longer-term changes in patterns of demand which result from the complex interaction of changes in incomes and cultural patterns and changes in the range of products made available by other firms. This information is fed into the decision-making process about the firm's range of products, how they might be modified and what new products might be possible or necessary.

The main sources of market information used for product planning

Table 6.1 Sources of information for product planning (Study B)

	Office furniture %	Domestic heating equipment %	Electronic business and computing equipment %	'Successful' foreign firms %	All firms %
Companies that relied on feedback from customers via the sales staff	82.3	50.0	64.7	100	74.5
Companies that carried out formal market surveys	11.8	25.0	58.8	88.9	46.1
Companies that monitored sales of existing products	5.9	25.0	5.9	0	9.2
Companies that monitored competitors' products	41.2	25.0	35.3	55.5	39.2

n = 51
Note: Several firms used more than one source of market information.

by firms in Study B are shown in table 6.1. Feedback from customers via sales staff was the most important source of information, used by about three-quarters of firms. Fewer than half the firms relied on formal market surveys or monitored competitors' products, while less than 10 per cent of firms monitored sales of their own products, at least for new product planning purposes.

What is interesting is that the sample of successful foreign firms were the most active in seeking market information. These firms drew on a range of techniques including feedback from customers and sales staff, carrying out market surveys and monitoring competitors' products. One firm had set up a panel of experts to discuss new product ideas and another firm had 'a special monitoring system

Table 6.2 Attitudes to formal market research (Study B)

	Office furniture %	Domestic heating equipment %	Electronic business and computing equipment %	'Successful' foreign firms %	All firms %
Formal Market Research					
Used often	7.7	50.0	42.1	21.4	23.0
Used sometimes	0	0	21.1	21.4	11.5
Used infrequently	15.4	0	0	7.1	8.2
Not worth cost/ don't use it	38.6	50.0	5.2	28.6	26.2
Not necessary/ inappropriate	11.5	0	21.1	7.1	13.1
Use general market research reports	3.9	0	0	7.1	3.3
Unsure about what market research is	23.1	0	5.2	0	11.5
Other	0	0	5.2	7.1	3.3
Total	100	100	100	100	100

n = 51

used to question "special" customers as to what their needs are'. Managers from the foreign firms stated that key factors in their successes were the 'ability to define and predict a market niche' and 'to be in the market with the right product at the right time'. Another comment was that the key factor contributing to success was 'marketing – the industry is no longer technology-driven'.

Attitudes towards market research

The participants in Study B were asked to express their attitudes towards formal market research, and a comparison of views across the sectors is interesting. The attitudes to market research are shown in table 6.2. About half of office furniture firms regarded market research as 'not worth the money', 'not necessary' or 'inappropriate'. The firms in this sector relied on customer feedback and their sales staff as their main source of market intelligence. One supplier had 'informal discussions with dealers, interior designers and end-users to get reactions to existing products'. None of the British companies in Studies A or B mentioned that they had established panels of experts or panels of users to discuss ideas or to help in the development of new products, as did some of the foreign firms. None of the British firms we visited suggested that they had devised any kind of monitoring system to use with certain customers to help identify their needs and assess them. The interaction with users and dealers was informal and the information was not gathered in a systematic or formal way. Indeed, one person interviewed from the office furniture sector was adamant in his view that 'market research is not very useful for guiding new product development.' Another firm used market research to assess its 'price position in the market sector – we look at the prices of competitors' products'. These companies tended to have a view of marketing as being more about selling and promotion rather than collecting market intelligence in a systematic way to help to identify and anticipate changes in user needs and market demand. Such a perspective comes through in such statements as 'Market research is used to promote customer awareness of the firm.'

These views of market research were particularly strongly expressed by companies in the British domestic heating equipment sector. For example, one manager had considered using market research to 'help overcome the problem of brand awareness'. The firms in this sector tended to be rather complacent about the need to do market research. This is illustrated by one manager's comment that 'market research is not needed because the market is known and is static.' Half of the firms in this sector saw market research as being 'too expensive' and 'unlikely to be of use'.

It is also the case that the office furniture and heating equipment companies tended to introduce variants and updates rather than innovative designs. They were rarely at the forefront of changes in the market and reacted to changes in consumer needs and to competitor actions rather than operating in a more challenging and proactive way. A view of market research being akin to promotion and sales can limit firms to a more evolutionary-based design strategy.

In contrast, the electronic business equipment firms generally viewed market research in a more positive light. These firms are

(a)

(b)

14 Since Sony's introduction of the Walkman personal stereo in 1979, a large number of competing designs from other manufacturers have been introduced. Sony has kept its 40 per cent share of the market by developing new designs to meet the needs of specific market segments, such as 'my first Sony', aimed at younger children. The 'my first Sony' range was conceived by Sony's US design team for the American market, but its success has led to its introduction into Europe and Japan.

(a) (b) *Source*: The Conran Foundation (c) *Source*: The Sony Corporation of America

(c)

15 A successful British manufacturer of gas cookers bases each of its designs on many sources of market information, including a variety of quantitative and qualitative market research techniques. Using a limited number of standard chassis, the company produces a wide range of different models designed to meet the requirements and aspirations of different groups of customer. *Source*: New World Domestic Appliances Ltd

parts should be supplied painted and screened where appropriate.

. . .

2:8 Future products to use common parts

We will want to make various other products, which may be used with the LCA 1, and which will use basically the same case parts, or at least as many common parts as possible. These include:–

(a) F.M. Tuner. This will have a digital frequency display, but otherwise similar facilities to our existing T21 tuner. There will, of course, be no heat-sink on the rear and many fewer connectors.

(b) Higher-Powered Amplifier. This will be similar to the LCA 1 except that it will have more switchable facilities, possibly more connectors, a larger heat-sink and a larger mains transformer. The latter will probably have to be a toroidal type.

There is no intention to design these products at this stage, but the constraints they would impose must be taken into account during the LCA 1 design. Both of these units are likely to be produced in lower volumes than the LCA 1 (3,000 plus per annum).

3. SPECIFICATION

3:1 Facilities – Front Panel

Controls Volume, balance, bass and treble – preferably in that order. The spindle centres are all 12.5mm above the PCB top surface (12.5mm mounting height).

Mains Switch Probably a push-button type, but open to suggestion if an alternative (internationally approved) type is available.

Input selector switch Either a rotary switch (12.5mm mounting height), possibly with one or two push-buttons, or a push button bank with four or five buttons. Push-button switches are available with 6.5 or 12.5mm mounting height.

"On" indicator probably an LED of some sort.

3:4 Heat Sink

The heat sinking capability from the output transistors to the surroundings must be good. We have data for the A60 heatsink/chassis and this is about the level of performance required of the LCA 1.

The higher power model referred to in 2:8 will require more heat-sink efficiency so the facility to modify the thermal performance of the chassis is important, unless it is over-designed initially.

3:5 Dimensions

The overall size should not exceed 430mm wide × 80/90mm high × 250mm deep.

3:6 Cost

The total cost to A & R (not including tooling and set-up costs) of all those parts referred to in section 1:1 (except packaging) should not exceed £7.50 in production quantities in the third quarter of 1984.

The Alpha brief

A & R (Cambridge) Limited

CONFIDENTIAL

To: Cambridge Industrial Design

DESIGN BRIEF FOR LCA 1 AMPLIFIER – MECHANICAL DESIGN & STYLING

1. SCOPE

1:1 Areas to be designed by CID

We wish you to design, specify and assist with the specification of, all mechanical parts of the amplifier, including:– all case parts, screws and other fasteners, heat-sink (with thermal performance constraints), mechanical fixing/support of PCB, control knobs and buttons, and, possibly, packaging.

The above is to include, where appropriate, advice on parts suppliers or manufacturers – particularly with bespoke parts. Second sources may also be required for some parts.

We would like advice on any special production techniques which might be required.

1:2 Areas to be designed by A & R

A & R will design the amplifier's PCB(s) complete with all controls and connectors, and also the transformer and all wiring. This, together with those parts covered in 1:1 plus an owner's handbook, should complete the amplifier package to be manufactured.

1:3 Specification

A & R will specify the general design parameters and constraints. Some of these are detailed in sections 2 and 3. Further discussion/advice on various aspects of the specification (e.g. ergonomics of the user interface) are welcomed.

2. GENERAL

2:1 Quality

The perceived quality (externally) should equal or exceed that of comparably priced (£80–£140) Japanese products. The internal appearance should, in keeping with our other products, be of significantly higher quality than Japanese products which usually look rather messy inside.

2:2 Styling

The styling of the LCA 1 must be in keeping with the Company's image. However, it need not match any existing product. Indeed this may well be a disadvantage. The product should appeal to a wide range of ages and nationalities.

2:3 Serviceability

The top and bottom of the PCB must both be accessible without removing the PCB from its case. Removal of electromechanical parts (pots, switches and connectors) should be straightforward.

Access to the top of the PCB should be achievable by the user with a single standard screwdriver, preferably without having to turn the amplifier upside down. This is to allow the user to plug in additional internal modules.

2:4 Production requirements

The cost constraints of this product dictate design for the minimum in-house labour content. This implies minimising the number of parts and maximising the extent of pre-finishing (see below).

2:5 Parts/purchasing requirements

All bespoke parts must be designed such that they are economic to produce in the required volumes (i.e. 10 000 plus units per annum). All parts must be available reliably from suppliers in the required quantities and to the required (consistent) level of quality.

As far as possible all parts should be supplied to A & R in a "finished" condition, requiring minimum additional labour content. For example, metalwork

---

16 Part of an exemplary design brief/specification for the original model of the Arcam Alpha low-cost hi-fi stereo amplifier launched in 1984. Since then several new models have been introduced. *Source*: A&R (Cambridge) Ltd (Arcam) and Course P791 *Managing Design*, The Open University

17 Netlon plastics mesh was made possible by an innovation in extrusion technology that used the revolutionary integral extrusion process. The firm has succeeded by constantly seeking new applications and designing new products – from garden netting to components for renal dialysis filters – using this technology. Photographs by permission of Netlon Ltd with whom the copyright remains

18 Market testing of prototypes

In a hall test potential customers evaluate realistic mock-ups or prototypes of a successful British company's gas cookers against competing products of a similar type and price. Only if a new design emerges with a substantial majority preferring it to rival products is it put into production.
Photograph: Robin Roy

19 Design for economic manufacture

In the 1980s British Rail Engineering Ltd designed a railway coach for the world market using modular construction and a standard kit of parts that could be built to a wide range of specifications on a simple system of movable jigs and tools. BREL's International Coach, and the technology for making it, have been exported to several countries round the world.

Photographs: Robin Roy, Mike Levers, The Open University

20 Speeding up product development

As one of the ways it is attempting to reduce concept-to-market lead times, the Ford Motor Company has invested heavily in computer-aided design and manufacturing (CAD/CAM) equipment, used here in the body shell design of the Ford Granada.
Source: Ford Motor Company

21 The 'Impact' prototype electric car developed by General Motors in response to the air pollution problems caused by internal combustion engines. The Impact is powered using conventional lead acid batteries, but its lightweight glass fibre body, high-pressure tyres and very low drag coefficient allow it an acceleration of 0–60 mph in eight seconds and a range of over 100 miles. Although electric cars may help to reduce air pollution in cities, unless the energy needed to charge the batteries comes from renewable sources, their use merely transfers environmental problems elsewhere. *Source*: General Motors Corporation

22 'Green' product design: using computer-aided graphic design to redesign the typefaces used in the BT Phonebooks. The new typefaces, combined with changes in typographic design and layout, enabled more information to be included on each page, thus producing substantial savings in the amount of paper needed for the 25 million Phonebooks printed each year. The Phonebook won a Green Product Award from the Royal Society of Arts in 1988.
Source: *RSA Journal*, Vol CXXXVII, No 5397, August 1989, p. 538

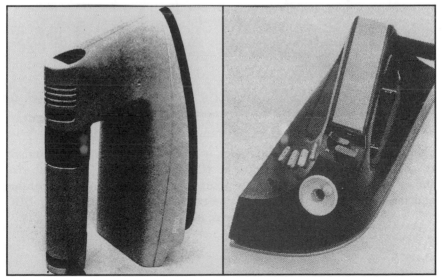

(a)   (b)

23 Domestic irons designed to the same brief by a) male and b) female industrial design students. The male designer was more concerned with the styling of the product, while the female designer focused on user needs, for example in designing a product which was compact and could be used for difficult tasks such as ironing sleeves.
Source: Bruce (1985), by permission of the publishers, Butterworth-Heinemann Ltd

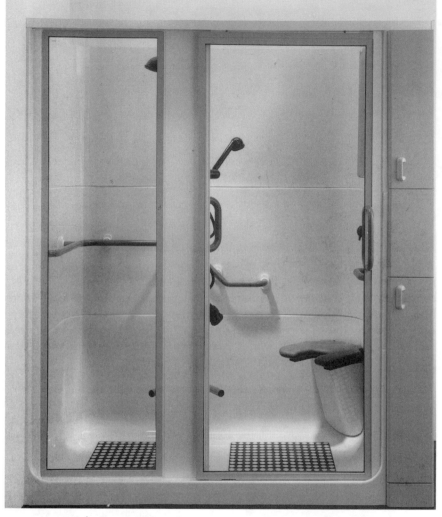

24 Good design for the unmet needs of the elderly

Shower designed by Kenneth Grange in conjunction with Ideal-Standard to be suitable for all users, but especially elderly people. The bath-size shower, which has a non-slip floor, a seat, handrails and high- , medium- and low-level shower-heads, was one of the finalists in the 1990 BBC Design Awards. *Source*: Ideal-Standard Ltd operating in a market characterized by uncertainty and rapid change, and some of the managers we interviewed felt that in such a market situation formal market research could provide information about users to assist in product planning and design. It was recognized that market research could also help to establish competitive 'price and product positioning'. Other firms in this sector, however, said that their products were too innovative to attain any meaningful assessment from a market survey. A statement from the manufacturer of the innovative Microwriter (see chapter 7) expressed this point of view by saying: 'Microwriting is a new concept, how do you assess the market?'

Another manager interviewed as part of Study B suggested that 'Very few people in a market research sample can make the step to evaluate conceptually new designs.' This comment reinforces those made earlier with regard to the C5 and the Walkman and shows the dilemma of those producing radical innovations: can market research ever lead the way?

Despite this difficulty, one of the more successful electronic business equipment suppliers from Study B attributed its success to its approach to marketing. This company used a range of techniques to collect market intelligence. These entailed the close interaction between users and sales staff, analysing the feedback from service technicians who are in direct contact with users, and listening to the reports of the company's overseas agents. Marketing staff visited trade exhibitions to look at and evaluate the competition. These activities helped the firm to identify trends in the market so it could anticipate changes and be ready to respond to these quickly. The company felt that if it did not exploit new market opportunities as these appeared, then others would do so and any advantage of being first in the market would be lost to the competition. The need to get the timing right to make the most of new market opportunities was made earlier and seems to be particularly acute in fast-moving, high-technology product markets.

Multiple approaches to market research

For the majority of the foreign firms, formal market research was used alongside other market research techniques and served to complement other approaches to market intelligence. One manager stated that 'Multi-client reports show trends in the industry and marketing staff use these to support their own proposals.' A manager from a different company argued that 'Consultants increase our confidence in finding a market identity and identifying user needs.' In some instances, market research was used for quite specific purposes, such as 'a detailed examination of competitors' products' and 'to canvass small groups of users for their views on a concept' or 'to buy in expertise from someone who can do it better than you'. There was some scepticism expressed about formal market research, however. This is reflected in the views of one of the managers we spoke to. He regarded 'market research as often biased and used to prove a point rather than to ascertain global and historical trends'.

Companies operating in dynamic markets, like electronic business equipment, used market research to help them to anticipate changes in the market and to respond quickly to change. The more successful firms in our study, the foreign firms, used formal market research alongside other sources of market intelligence, either to bring in additional expertise or to gather data that the firm did not have in house. On the other hand, companies in less dynamic markets and with a more reactive approach regarded formal market research as not worthy of investment of time or money. Such firms relied more extensively on informal contacts with existing customers and distributors and did not see that formal market research could complement or strengthen their more informal approach.

Stimuli for New Product Development

The factors influencing new product development mentioned by the firms in Study B fall into three categories, namely, market stimuli, technological stimuli and company stimuli (see table 6.3). Except in the relatively rare cases of radical product innovations, the overwhelming stimulus and therefore the starting-point for product design and new product development is market demand or opportunity. For example, firms are aiming to exploit gaps in the market, to move into different market sectors or to meet customer orders.

Companies in the relatively stable office furniture market were attempting to meet new customer needs or to keep up with their competitors by introducing variants or product updates. One of the office furniture suppliers referred to the role of the competition in its approach to the introduction of new products. The manager we interviewed said, 'We follow the initiative of our competitors in keeping up with the market trend for furniture designed around computing equipment.'

Table 6.3 Reasons for introducing a new product/product range

	Office furniture %	Domestic heating equipment %	Electronic business and computing equipment %	'Successful' foreign firms %	All firms %
Market stimuli					
Move up-market	0	0	0	9.1	1.9
Expand exports	0	0	0	27.3	5.7
Move into new market sector	4.6	16.7	21.4	18.2	13.2
Gap in market	9.1	16.7	14.3	9.1	11.3
Change in market demand	27.3	33.3	7.1	9.1	18.9
Customer commission	9.1	0	0	0	3.8
Compatibility with other machinery	0	0	7.1	0	1.9
Total	50	67	50	73	57
Technological stimuli					
Technical developments in product	0	16.7	0	0	1.9
Spin-off of other development	4.6	0	0	0	1.9
Development potential of existing product range near limit	4.6	0	0	0	1.9
Improved specification	4.6	0	14.3	0	5.7
Total	14	17	14	0	11

Table 6.3 (cont.)

	Office furniture %	Domestic heating equipment %	Electronic business and computing equipment %	'Successful' foreign firms %	All firms %
Company stimuli					
Gap in company range	9.1	16.7	7.1	0	7.6
Rationalize company range	4.6	0	0	0	1.9
Change in marketing	0	0	7.1	0	1.9
Suggestion from marketing department	0	0	7.1	0	1.9
Cut costs	4.6	0	7.1	0	3.8
Improve identity	4.6	0	0	9.1	3.8
Total	23	17	28	9	21

n = 51

The heating equipment firms in the sample had a similar view. Responding to market gaps and moving into new markets with variants and updates was their strategy. But, in addition, the heating equipment firms emphasized the role of technological change (such as the development of new materials) as being an important reason for introducing new products. This was the only sector to do so.

The electronic business equipment sector was described by the managers we interviewed as dynamic and constantly changing in both technology and market. This turbulence was reflected in the market opportunities available to these suppliers. Many of the people to whom we spoke referred to 'new market opportunities', such as the demand for intelligent workstations with configurations designed for different categories of office staff, but which are compatible and can communicate with each other. The companies we surveyed regarded market stimuli, such as responding to specific customer requirements and improving ergonomic design, and company stimuli, such as filling gaps in their range of products or cutting costs, as far outweighing technological stimuli as the reasons for introducing new products or product ranges. This may seem surprising, given the rapid changes in electronics technology. The reason is that the firms in our survey were not radical innovators, but were more concerned with using existing technology continually to improve their product specifications and reduce costs. The more successful firms we visited in this sector had an approach to new product development which integrated design and development activities closely with those of marketing and production. The companies which were not as successful relied on their designers' and engineers' interpretations of user needs and their desire to improve the company's products.

The successful foreign companies in the sample tended to be looking ahead to anticipate and then meet changing consumer needs, and their approach to product planning reflects this. These firms relied on market stimuli as the main justification and incentive for introducing new products.

Overall, the companies in our Study B were responding to changes in the market, either to meet customer needs or to keep abreast of the competition. This was particularly apparent for manufacturers of office furniture and domestic heating equipment where the technology was fairly stable and hence the 'technological opportunity' was relatively low (see chapter 3). However, the heating firms responded to such changes as the development of new materials, and the market opportunity experienced by the furniture firms was caused by technological changes in another sector, that of electronic office equipment. Companies in these industries were reacting to changes rather than working pro-actively to anticipate and generate new market demands. In the electronic office equipment sector and for foreign firms, constant product development was essential to keep ahead. These companies were more actively seeking new market opportunities for both new and updated products, even in sectors where there was high technological opportunity.

These findings from Study B support those of Study A and also those of other researchers (e.g. Rothwell, 1977; Freeman, 1982) by showing that understanding user needs and keeping close to the market are vital to commercial success. The more successful and design-conscious firms placed a high value on marketing and market research. The identification of a new market opportunity, as a result of market or consumer research or feedback from customers or experts, was usually mentioned as the starting-point for product design. However, most of the firms in our studies are not radically innovative, high-technology based firms. If they were, then there would probably have been more emphasis on technological relative to market stimuli.

Traditional and Creative Marketing

Understanding the market and user needs can be straightforward for orders from existing customers, but much more problematic when attempting to satisfy a large and variable group of customers, or when breaking into new product markets. How can companies gather market information to enable them to design products which meet future customer needs?

Traditionally market research yields quantitative data about social trends, the sales of the product in the market, and so on. But this provides information about the product after its launch and from a designer's point of view can be too general and imprecise. Consequently, market research may not always provide sufficient information for the development, adaptation and modification of products, or the generation of new designs. Qualitative information, such as how the intended product is going to be used, by whom and for what purpose; strengths and weaknesses of competing products; the problems users have with current products; and customers' and users' attitudes to new product concepts, is needed. One of the electronic business equipment companies in Study B summed this up in the statement: 'Market research doesn't tell you what the product needs. To do this, information is required from the user.' In other words, 'motivational' information, the information about 'what makes people tick', is required. The term 'creative marketing' has been used to describe market research techniques which are more qualitative in nature and which provide information about people's use of existing products and their ideas about possible future alternatives (Alexander, 1985).

There are various techniques and methods available for firms to collect market information. These range from formal market surveys to analysis of sales reports or running user panels. As noted earlier, what distinguishes the successful from the less successful firms is the former's efforts to be user-oriented and their willingness to draw on a variety of sources of marketing intelligence. This is borne out by Study B and other research (e.g. Holt, 1987) which showed that the

Table 6.4 Sources of information for product planning and design

I	II
Senior management's 'feel for the market'	Customer feedback/inquiries/ complaints Service reports/warranty claims Trade shows/exhibitions Technical/trade literature Market surveys
Sales/market statistics	Developments in related industries Competitors' products User groups/customer panels
Sales-force feedback	Workshops involving engineers, marketers, customers and users, etc.

Commercially successful firms in Study B employed sources listed under both I and II. Less successful firms tended only to use I.
Source: Walsh, Roy and Bruce (1988)

commercially successful firms tended to gather market intelligence from several sources, as shown in table 6.4.

In contrast, the less successful firms used a much more limited range of sources to gain knowledge of the market to help in design and product development. Typically, the methods for market research in these firms were *ad hoc* and informal. The firms relied on senior management's 'feel for the market'; comments about products gathered through informal discussions with customers; or a kind of 'blind faith' that those designing and developing the product knew what was wanted.

We discovered that the more successful firms had in addition developed an approach to marketing which helped them achieve good design. This creative approach to market research is much more wide-ranging than traditional approaches. It is about probing for complex motivational information to try to get to grips with the problem of understanding what customers and users want, by involving them in the new product development process and tapping into any ideas they may have for product improvements and developments. This way of gathering market intelligence aids and supports the work of the design staff. Marketing and design are regarded as complementary activities which identify and create the sorts of product that the company should and could be making.

Examples of creative marketing

An example of a company which has adopted this wide-ranging creative approach to marketing and design is a British manufacturer of cookers (Roy et al., 1987). At the centre of this company's highly market-oriented approach is a desire to understand what it is about customers' aspirations and underlying motivations, as well as specific product features, that makes people buy one cooker rather than another. What the company is striving to do is to establish a continual dialogue with the customer to attain a better sense of their concerns and preferences. To achieve this, the manufacturer uses a range of quantitative and qualitative methods, including:

- carrying out in-depth interviews with customers in their own homes, in which life-style aspirations and the role of cookers, kitchens and cooking are discussed;
- workshops and discussion groups involving designers, marketers and customers to identify features for new cookers and get feedback about new concepts;
- the use of 'hall tests' (see chapter 7 for more details) and small group surveys in customers' homes where customers evaluate new designs and compare these with competitors' products.

As mentioned earlier in this chapter, the two Japanese electronic business equipment companies we visited also had elaborate methods of gathering marketing information, including a 'special monitoring system' comprising a panel of customers and users who were regularly asked about new products. Philips, the Dutch electronics giant, also engages in major creative marketing exercises. For example, in the 1980s it introduced a Youth Task Force to identify product opportunities for the teenage market. A series of workshops, involving the company's in-house designers plus marketing staff and potential users, created the concepts which led to the highly successful, innovatively styled 'roller radio' range and subsequently to a whole series of audio products, 'Moving Sound', for the youth market (Blaich, 1990). One company described by Bruce (1988) is a major UK electronics supplier diversifying into a new software market. This company was not just concerned with releasing another technical product but wanted to identify business problems and then design the appropriate software package to meet those problems. The company wanted to market solutions for a host of business applications. To achieve this goal, it held a series of workshops with existing customers from different industries to obtain 'market know-how' about customer needs and their plans for the future in order to assist in the development of value-added applications. In another study of the enzyme industry (Rodgus, 1989; Bruce and Rodgus, 1991), it was found that one leading supplier had devised a system of 'dual visits' of marketing and technical specialists going together to visit existing and potential customers. The dual visits not only helped to assess and understand customer needs but also ensured good communication between marketing and technical staff.

Intensity of customer requirements

As well as changing market demands during the product life cycle, the intensity of desire for a product varies for different groups of consumers depending on their specific needs. For example, in the design of production machinery, flexibility may be beneficial for smaller manufacturers but less so for volume producers of standardized goods. On the other hand, improved reliability is likely to be valued highly by both types of firm.

It is possible to identify design features that fulfil a set of user needs and to estimate the intensity of demand for each feature. Techniques ranging from sophisticated market research tools to informal discussions with sales staff can help in separating out the high- and low-intensity requirements. The high-intensity features are those that must be included in the design, and the low-intensity features are optional. These characteristics can then be built into the design specification as a list of design priorities ('demands' and 'wishes'), as discussed in chapter 7. The supplier may decide to meet different user needs by offering a range of products, or by providing a degree of customization. This is illustrated by Roy et al. (1990) who describe a company designing a microcomputer. The supplier may have segmented the market into business users wanting high storage capacity and scientific users who would select a machine on the basis of its processing speed. A compromise design with a reasonably fast processing speed and a moderate storage capacity would fail to meet user needs in either of these markets. So the supplier has to decide whether it can produce two models to address both markets or if it should go for only one, depending on the commercial viability of each of these options.

Although a creative and thorough approach to market intelligence appears to be common sense to more successful companies, this is not necessarily the case for a majority of firms. Many of our observations – like the importance of good communications and an understanding of user needs – appear at first sight to be common sense, but it is surprising how many firms do not adopt apparently 'common-sense' practices. As we have stressed throughout this book, the design process has to be dynamic and based on the best possible information to be effective in meeting changing customer needs and market demands.

Customer Involvement in Design and Innovation

The formation of close contacts between manufacturers, customers and users contributes to the identification of user needs and the discovery of new concerns and requirements in advance of the competition.

The direct involvement of the customer and/or the end-user in the product development process can:

- provide invaluable market know-how to convert an idea into a commercially viable product and give guidance on the best performance/price blend;
- result in a flow of user-initiated improvements to the original design;
- provide an 'opinion leader' to endorse the design in the market-place, so enhancing the success of the product.

One of the main advocates of the 'customer-active' approach to design and innovation is von Hippel (1978). He discovered that out of a total of 160 innovations in the scientific instrument and electronic manufacturing equipment industries, 117 were invented by users (although it is not clear what von Hippel means by 'invented'). In some cases users would have built the first of a new type of machine, but in other cases would only have contributed ideas about new ways of doing things. In a recent study of the factors determining the commercial viability of innovations in the enzyme industry (Rodgus, 1989; Bruce and Rodgus, 1991), it was found that 'maintenance of links with customers' was crucial. Nearly four-fifths of the companies in the survey involved the customer in the design and development process. Idea-generation and problem-solving were the main areas of collaboration. This study also pointed to the vital role customers play in improving the product after it has been launched.

Some of the more successful companies in Studies A and B established close interaction with customers and end-users to obtain market information to help in the design process. The foreign firms had set up panels of users and experts to assist in the design process and made comments like 'Users give hints during regular talks' and 'The impetus for change comes from users'. In the case of one of the companies from the electronic business equipment sector which was in a 'leading edge' position, the main thrust of the marketing effort with regard to hardware and software design was to foster good contacts with users 'to try out ideas on them and to listen to them'. Board members of this supplier had direct contacts with senior executives of their larger account customers, so enabling the firm to test new products and new concepts before market launch. Understanding user needs and feeding such knowledge into the early stages of the design process has been shown in many studies to be a key factor discriminating between successful and less successful firms (see Freeman, 1982; Cooper and Kleinschmidt, 1988).

However, there are some pitfalls with customer involvement in design. Developing a close contact with selected customers raises questions about the representativeness of these users for the whole market. Customers who are demanding and forward-looking are likely to be more effectual than customers who are 'behind the times'.

For example, West German textile firms in the 1950s and 1960s demanded new and superior equipment from textile machinery manufacturers, and the collaboration between them stimulated innovation. Meanwhile, UK textile firms were reluctant to adopt innovative equipment and not only failed to stimulate innovations by UK machinery firms but made them complacent about not innovating, which contributed significantly to the decline of the British textile machinery industry (Rothwell et al., 1983).

There is also an important difference between effective collaboration with users, and dependence on users as a source of market intelligence to the exclusion of other sources. In Study B, British furniture and heating firms were inclined not only to rely on customers who were not very demanding or stimulating compared with overseas buyers of such equipment, but to do so to the exclusion of other sources of market intelligence. They therefore concentrated on up-dating and redesigning products rather than introducing innovative new designs. They were reactive to changes around them rather than pro-active in creating new demand.

Lessons and Conclusions

1 One of the most important lessons of our research is the importance of listening to the customer. There are various ways of doing this, from obtaining informal customer feedback via sales staff to engaging in systematic market research methods. Keeping a continuous 'dialogue' with the market helps the firm to be aware of shifts in customer needs and market demands so as to be able to anticipate likely trends. Creative marketing contributes to the collection of information for the design and development of future products and is likely to reduce the risk of failure.
2 Successful firms are those which are open-minded and draw upon a range of sources of market intelligence, both informal and more systematic, to aid the design process. These companies invest more resources in marketing than the less successful ones.
3 Linking up with 'lead users' – those who 'know tomorrow's needs today' – is one tactic for integrating 'user needs' into the early phase of product planning and design. Collaboration between supplier and customer can be extensive with joint design projects. Such collaboration can be of mutual benefit, with the customer gaining access to the supplier's competences and skills and the supplier acquiring market know-how to develop value-added applications for that market. But it should not be the only source of market intelligence.
4 Effective communication between technical, design and marketing staff can lead to products which reach the market at the right time and do not require extensive adaptations after market launch. The strategy of 'dual visits' of marketing and design or technical staff to customers is an interesting approach encouraging the close collaboration and integration of these activities.
5 Awareness of the competition is another aspect of good marketing. Knowing the competition can help to identify market gaps and to enter markets at the right time with superior or unique products.

7

From Design Brief to Manufactured Product

In this chapter we look at the core of the product development process, namely, the conversion of the brief from management or marketing into a design ready for manufacture. In earlier chapters we stressed the crucial importance of strategic product planning, creative marketing and appropriate organization. But in much design management literature the actual creation of the product tends to be ignored. It is often regarded as a mere technical problem to be solved by the 'backroom boys' – the firm's designers, engineers and production staff. Yet of course without their creative and technical skills there would be no product, even given the most far-sighted plan, imaginative marketing and good organization.

In this chapter, therefore, we will examine the product design and development process in different industries as it moves from brief to manufacture, in order to see if success is associated with any particular activities or practices.

The Product Design and Development Process

Many models of the design and development process have been proposed. As was noted in chapter 1, there are no generally agreed definitions in this field, and so in some models design and development is viewed as being synonymous with the whole product development process. Hart et al. (1989), for example, have shown that companies using multi-disciplinary team approaches tend not to separate design from other parts of the product development process. While this emphasizes the importance of not artificially detaching design and development from product planning, marketing and manufacture, it has led to some confusion.

As was made clear in chapter 1, in this book we tend to view design and development as the core of the new product development or innovation process: the stage in which market needs or opportunities identified in a brief are transformed into detailed instructions for manufacturing a product. A variety of such models shows that, from a managerial perspective, there is a remarkably similar pattern to the design and development process across different industries and types of product (Cross, 1989).

A model that has gained wide acceptance during the last decade is that developed in Germany by Pahl and Beitz (1984), based on ideas about systematic approaches to engineering design. In this model, which gives detail to the central part of the innovation model given earlier in chapter 1 (figure 1.1), the design and development process comprises several broad phases:

Specification The stage during which the brief is elaborated from a set of broad objectives into a more detailed list of market and technical requirements. Producing the specification often involves market and technical feasibility studies.

Conceptual design The stage during which alternative-solution principles and design variants for satisfying the specification are generated and selected for further development. This is generally considered to be the highest level of design, involving the most senior designers working in consultation with management, marketing and production staff. Typically, it will involve the production of sketches, drawings, mock-ups, 'lash-ups' or models to test basic feasibility, etc.

Embodiment design This is the stage in which one or more design concepts are translated into layout drawings and/or prototypes or full scale mock-ups for technical development and testing and for evaluation by management and/or customers for financial and market acceptability.

Detail design At this stage the design chosen from the embodiment stage is developed and optimized in detail at component level. The materials are specified, the design is engineered for ease of manufacture, maintenance, etc., given final technical and market testing and presented as final production prototypes and detailed working drawings and specifications or as computerized instructions for manufacture.

Figure 7.1 illustrates how a design evolves through some of these stages, using the example of an automatic tea-maker. Although many

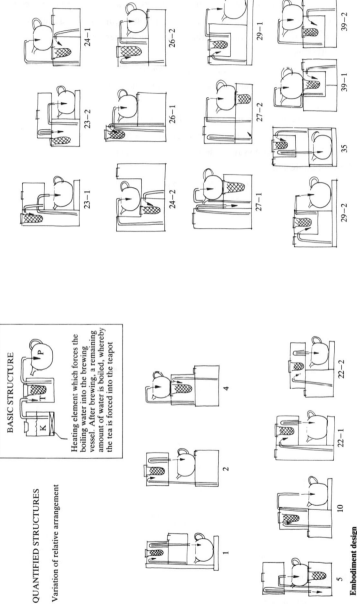

Figure 7.1 Stages in the design of an automatic tea-maker
Source: Tjalve (1979); Hubka, Andreasen and Edet (1988)

Brief

Design a machine for office use to make naturally brewed tea without the need for the user to stop the infusion when the desired strength is reached. The tea should be made available in a container from which it can be served.

Specification

The tea-maker should meet the following criteria:

As easy to use and to clean as an automatic coffee-maker

Retail price in range £40–50

Size not to exceed two or three times volume of the serving container

Reliability to equal that of similar small appliances for office use

Attractive appearance to suit modern office environments

Conceptual design

Alternative solution concepts for the automatic tea-maker

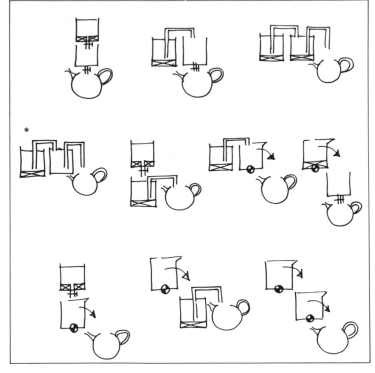

* Chosen concept

Figure 7.1 continued

Detail design

Assembly drawing of final tea-maker design and working drawing of component

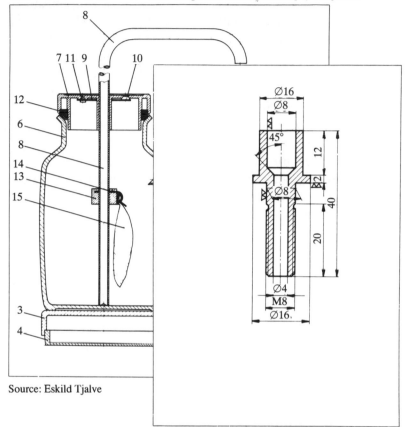

Source: Eskild Tjalve

Figure 7.1 continued

more steps are involved, this example clearly shows the overall 'convergence' from many possible design concepts at the early stages into the detailed drawings of one chosen concept required for manufacture.

The model, as well as showing the main steps through which a product is gradually defined and shaped, is also useful in clarifying the place of creativity in the design and development process. While it is commonly supposed that the creative part of design and development comes at the conceptual stage, in fact creative thinking is required throughout the process. Thus in the tea-maker example, considerable creative effort was needed not just at the concept and embodiment stages, but also at the detail stage – for instance, to design a seal for the lid of the heating vessel.

Of course, like all models, Pahl and Beitz's is a simplification. In reality there is considerable overlap, blurring and feedback between the different phases, and often other activities, such as production planning and component purchasing, take place in parallel. Indeed, in 'concurrent engineering' such parallel working is vital (see below). But despite many differences in the details of what firms in our various studies did during design and development and in how the process was organized, the broad pattern of stages closely matched Pahl and Beitz's model.

As was described in chapter 1, the main steps we found during design and development were: initial specification; concept design; prototype development and testing; detail design and production engineering. Let us look at a specific example.

The example of bicycle design and development

In Study A we visited TI-Raleigh, Britain's largest bicycle manufacturer, before its sale in 1987 to an American consortium, Derby International, as part of TI Group's strategy of focusing on engineering rather than consumer products. At Raleigh the development of a new design began with the preparation of a brief or marketing specification based on information on sales of various models, marketing research, design ideas, etc. The specification, prepared by Marketing in consultation with Concept Design, defined in non-technical terms the general type of bicycle to be developed, together with the requirements of price, design features, target market, appearance and image. It was the task of Concept Design's industrial, engineering and graphic designers to translate this marketing specification into design ideas, and usually several design options were created and presented as drawings, models or mock-ups in wood, plastic or even metal. At the same time the Product Planning department prepared rough costings for tooling, components and prices at various production volumes.

The design options, together with information on commercial viability, were put to a product planning committee (with representatives from Design, Manufacturing, Marketing and Planning) for approval before prototype development of one or more designs could proceed. Development involved extensive technical testing of full-scale prototypes in the company's laboratories to ensure that the design could withstand the rigours of use and meet international standards. In addition, prototypes were usually subjected to market acceptance tests in a product clinic and further evaluation by the product planning committee before approval for production.

Before trial production could begin, the Technical department prepared full engineering drawings of the final chosen design and developed any necessary tooling, while Product Planning began the ordering of components. Full-scale production and launch only took place after successful trial production runs and testing of pre-production prototypes.

This elaborate and thorough procedure for product development at Raleigh – which for a new model could take up to two years – was in contrast to that observed in Study A of several smaller British cycle manufacturers. In such firms new models are usually variants or improvements of existing designs, using new combinations of components, colour schemes, frame materials etc. Typically, design is undertaken by one or more senior managers, who are frequently keen cyclists but often do not have any particular technical or design qualification. Prototypes are rapidly made in the firm's model shop for evaluation by the firm's employees, sales staff and managers, and possibly a few dealers, before being put into production. Since there is usually no great variation in basic design or large-scale production facilities involved, such manufacturers do not consider it necessary to undertake the extensive testing done by Raleigh or to engage in the elaborate system of product and production planning. As a result new models can be planned, designed and launched within a few weeks or months to exploit the latest market trends.

The design and development process at Raleigh in the early to mid-1980s was typical of a highly systematic and thorough, but rather traditionally organized, 'sequential' approach (see chapter 5). It was effective in producing novel designs as well as updates and variants of existing models, but relatively slow in responding to new market and design trends. This failure to keep up with the market, coupled with problems in introducing a computerized manufacturing system, were two reasons for the financial difficulties that preceded the sale of the company in 1987. In contrast, the approach in Raleigh's much smaller competitors was typical of an *ad hoc* informal approach to design carried out by a few individuals. This allowed rapid responses to fashion trends in the market, but was only really capable of producing variations on existing designs using components bought in from suppliers.

Since the takeover, Raleigh still dominates the British cycle market. However, the company has closed its R&D department and become more market-oriented. By relying increasingly on bought-in components and confining design changes mainly to variations of components, accessories and styling, Raleigh has reduced concept to market lead times, enabling the company to produce new and updated models more rapidly in response to market changes and to compete on quality and price with growing foreign competition (Challis and Crump, 1990).

The problem of being able to do the thorough job of design and development to produce innovative designs that can be economically manufactured to high quality, but sufficiently fast to exploit changing market demands and opportunities, lies behind all the recent thinking on multidisciplinary team approaches and 'concurrent engineering' already discussed in chapter 5 and taken up again later in this chapter. But first it is necessary to examine some of the main stages of product development in more detail.

From Brief to Specification

As the examples given above show, the design and development process proper usually starts with the issue of a brief.

The Corfield Report (NEDO, 1979) and Oakley (1984) argue that a clear brief and a comprehensive specification are vital to successful product development. Thus the draft British Standard on *Product Design Management* (BSI, 1988), issued as BS7000 in 1989, notes:

> The importance of the design brief cannot be over-emphasized. An inadequate design brief is a dangerous document: it may mean that management does not know what it wants, but it certainly means that the designer is misinformed about what is required. . . . It is regrettable that many designers are obliged to work to briefs that are inadequate – or are even non-existent.

And Pugh (1986a) says, 'The product design specification forms the bedrock upon which any competitive design should be based. Whilst not of itself generating good sound competitive design, without it the chances of achieving this are slim indeed.'

As is shown later, the results of our studies confirm that the brief and the specification derived from it are indeed among the key ingredients of successful design management. But first, let us consider the nature of this stage of product development.

The brief from management or a customer provides the design team with a statement of the general objectives and requirements of the product to be developed. As we have seen from chapter 6, the brief should be based on a proper understanding of customer requirements or market opportunities. But usually the brief is not detailed enough to provide a proper basis for design and development: it is necessary to produce a product design specification (PDS). The specification lists in detail the parameters that define what the product must do, preferably without saying how the required performance should be achieved. For example, the specification for a measuring instrument might state the accuracy to which it must operate, without stating the method by which the instrument is to make the measurements.

In practice, of course, briefs and specifications are rarely produced without some idea of design solutions. Indeed, the specification may only be produced after the basic solution concept has been created and its feasibility tested. In technologically complex areas of design, a feasibility study is often needed before completing the specification. But a design team should not be given a specification that unnecessarily constrains the range of possible solutions. For example, the specification might state that a particular material, say aluminium alloy, should be used, when what is really required is a certain strength or weight which might be better satisfied at lower cost by an engineering plastic. Designers justifiably complain when the brief or specification is so specific that it virtually makes all the main design decisions, leaving them with just the details.

Marketing and technical specifications

This difficulty is overcome in many industries by making a distinction between the marketing or business specification and the technical specification.

The marketing specification is essentially a detailed, written version of the brief which describes the target market, price and requirements of the product ideally wanted by management and the customer, often in relatively non-technical terms. The technical specification translates the marketing and business requirements into more precise technical parameters, compromising as necessary from the ideal in order to be feasible.

For example, a major British manufacturer of lift trucks generates the brief for the development of a new design from a very thorough study of customer needs, market opportunities and technical trends. Before a new product idea is approved for design and development it is given an appraisal by marketing and engineering staff to produce detailed marketing and technical specifications. The marketing specification gives an overview of the market plus the design parameters – capacity, weight, speed, turning circle, etc. – required by customers in the ideal truck. The design and production engineers have to translate these ideals into a feasible technical specification. Any compromises needed are discussed with marketing to ensure that no crucial customer requirements are lost or changed for reasons of technical feasibility (Roy, et al., 1987).

Some items in the marketing specification (such as power output and total weight) may be given quantitatively and are easily incorporated into the technical specification. Other marketing requirements may be given only qualitatively as statements (for example, 'reliable'; 'attractive modern appearance'). The design team will often have to gather further information or make judgements – in consultation with management, production and marketing representatives – in order to define such statements precisely enough for them to be usable as part of the technical specification. The technical specification is thus typically longer and more detailed than the marketing specification which in turn is more detailed than the initial brief. For example, the business specification for the locomotive for British Rail's new InterCity 225 train (see chapter 5) ran to thirty pages, while the technical specification was 200 pages!

The aim of the specification, whether two or 200 pages long, is to produce a set of parameters from which to create feasible design concepts and a set of criteria against which to evaluate alternative solutions. Thus 'reliable' may be defined more precisely in terms of average hours of operation between failures. This might involve further contact with customers to clarify their requirements or reference to the specification of similar products. Or, if that is not practical, the design team may have to produce sketch designs, mock-ups or prototypes to assess customer, user or management reaction to alternative solution ideas before finalizing the technical specification. In this way even parameters like 'attractive appearance' may be pinned down more precisely, for example to mean that a mock-up is judged by a panel of customers, dealers and users to be more attractive than rival products.

Some requirements in a specification must be met to produce an acceptable design. For example, a particular material may have to be used to satisfy an international standard, or there may be a maximum dimension to fit a space in which the product is to be installed. Other requirements will be of varying importance and the design team will have to make trade-offs – for example, between reliability and cost; weight and durability; appearance and ergonomics – when drawing up the technical specification and creating the design.

It is therefore extremely helpful if the requirements in the specification are prioritized according to their importance, for example into 'demands' and 'wishes' or using a system of points. Designers are rightly annoyed when they have struggled to meet technically a requirement given in the marketing specification, perhaps at the expense of the product's performance, only to discover later that the requirement was 'optional'.

Specification check-lists

In many industries writing good specifications is a matter of experience. It is clearly much easier to do for a variant of an existing design than for an innovative product.

But whatever the degree of innovation involved and the experience of the product development team, it is very easy to leave out major points, particularly those concerned with less obvious aspects, such as packaging and servicing, which may be crucial to the customer. So one of the most useful aids to producing specifications is a check-list of points to be covered.

Many such check-lists have been produced. For example, for the engineering industry there is a British Standard publication, *Guide to the Preparation of Specifications* (1967), and other useful lists may be found in Pahl and Beitz (1984) and Pugh (1986). But none of these is universally applicable because so much depends on the particular type of industry and product involved. The British Standard *Guide to Managing Product Design* (1989) recommends that the following elements are essential to a proper brief or specification:

Performance requirements: including what the product must do and the range of conditions under which it must perform; size, weight, location, safety, reliability and standards; appearance and visual quality; ease of use and maintainability.

Cost requirements: including development costs, tooling and manufacturing cost, maintenance and warranty costs.

Time-scale requirements: including product launch or delivery date, planned production volume and sales life and product life.

Many of these key elements, especially those relating to cost and time constraints, are often omitted from briefs and specifications. This may lead to serious problems as the result of misunderstandings between designers and management and errors, such as delays in launching a product or cost over-runs, that result in loss of sales to competitors.

Briefs and specifications in practice

We have seen that the ideal brief and product specification is a comprehensive list of all the requirements that affect the design, manufacture and marketing of a product. But what happens in practice? In our Studies A and B there were striking differences in the amount of effort different firms put into developing briefs and specifications and in the detail they provided.

At one extreme, a manufacturer of gas appliances briefed its design team simply by telling them that two new gas fires were needed to replace existing models. The designers attempted to get management to clarify what was wanted and to obtain customer responses to their design ideas, but without success. Not surprisingly, the resultant designs failed on the market. At the other extreme, a manufacturer of hi-fi equipment provided its own designers and an outside consultant with a five-page written brief/specification covering quality, styling and finish; cost constraints; production and purchasing requirements, servicing; relationship to existing and planned future products; required facilities and internal details. Plate 16 gives part of this exemplary brief. The clear specification, plus the skill of the designers in meeting it, produced a successful new product (Roy and Walker, 1988).

Among the British and foreign furniture, heating and electronics firms visited in Study B, most (84 per cent) drew up briefs and specifications at the beginning of product development, and in three-quarters of the firms this was a formal document. There were, however, significant intersector and international differences. Whilst all the UK electronics firms and all the leading foreign firms always

Table 7.1 Specifications for new and updated products (Study B)

	Office furniture (%)	Domestic heating equipment (%)	Electronic business and computing equipment (%)	'Successful' foreign firms (%)	All firms (%)
Before work commences on a new product or a major update of an existing product is a specification drawn up?					
Always	75	50	100	100	81
Sometimes	12	12	0	0	6
Never	13	38	0	0	13
If a specification is drawn up, what form does it take?					
Formal document	47	100	100	67	78
Verbal message	29	0	0	33	16
Other (e.g. sketch or diagram)	24	0	0	0	6
Who draws up the specification for a new product?					
Chief executive/ director/senior manager	90	40	62	22	53
Group of people	5	40	28	78	38
Other (e.g. designer)	5	20	10	0	9
Total	100	100	100	100	100

n = 51

drew up formal written specifications, many UK heating and some UK furniture firms said they did not even provide an informal brief to designers (see table 7.1).

Often the lack of a brief or specification was because the same individual (usually the managing director or another director or manager) was responsible for initial design concepts as well as the specification: 'There is no brief – ideas are based on the technical director's understanding of the market' was a typical comment. In the furniture sector especially, 'new' products were often modifications of existing designs, so only a verbal brief was considered necessary. Or the firms were small and a very informal briefing was used.

Informal methods of briefing can work if the project concerns a minor modification to an existing product or if very few individuals who know each other well are involved in product development. But in the majority of situations such an approach is unlikely to be adequate. Work by Oakley (1984) has shown that inadequate specifications often lead to delays in product development and designs that are costly to manufacture and ill-matched to customer needs.

In Study B we statistically analysed business performance of the firms against their design management practices. We found that the factor that most significantly distinguished the commercially successful firms from the others was the care they took in drawing up a comprehensive marketing and technical specification at the start of any major product development project. While less successful companies tended to provide a specification that merely gave the required function and price of the product, the rapidly expanding, profitable firms were significantly more likely to include at least the following additional information:

● evidence of market demand;
● details of target market and customer requirements;
● relevant national or international standards;

and where relevant:

● guidelines on appearance, style and image;
● guidelines on ergonomics and safety.

Probably the most striking differences were between the typical UK and the successful foreign firms, both in responsibility for the brief and in its form and content. Although not all the successful foreign firms used formal briefs, developing them was usually a group responsibility (see table 7.1). This is an aspect of the importance of team work in product development which has already been discussed in chapter 5. In contrast, in many of the typical UK firms the specification was drawn up by the chief executive or other senior individual with advice from colleagues. One consequence was that the successful foreign firms generally produced specifications that contained more comprehensive sets of product requirements. Figure 7.2 shows that 'selling price' was the only element of the specification

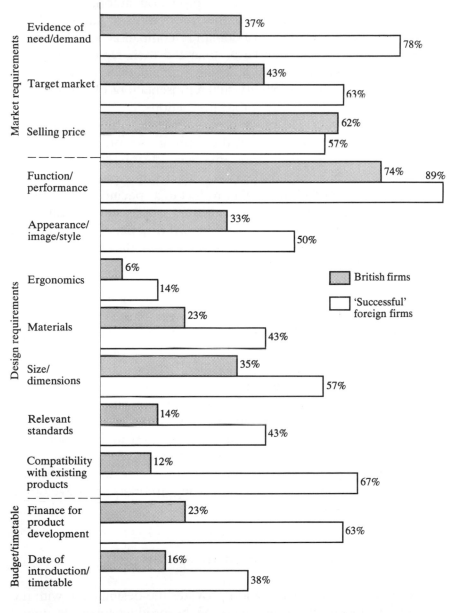

Proportion of firms who said they included this element in the brief/initial specification

Market requirements

Evidence of need/demand 37% / 78%

Target market 43% / 63%

Selling price 62% / 57%

Function/ performance 74% / 89%

Design requirements

Appearance/ image/style 33% / 50%

Ergonomics 6% / 14%

Materials 23% / 43%

Size/ dimensions 35% / 57%

Relevant standards 14% / 43%

Compatibility with existing products 12% / 67%

Budget/timetable

Finance for product development 23% / 63%

Date of introduction/ timetable 16% / 38%

British firms

'Successful' foreign firms

Figure 7.2 Factors included in the brief or initial specification by a sample of forty-two typical British and nine successful foreign firms in the office furniture, domestic heating, electronic business equipment and computing industries (Study B)
Source: Roy (1990)

included by more UK firms than their overseas competitors, reflecting a greater emphasis on price competition among typical UK manufacturers. Significantly, a higher proportion of successful foreign firms included 'evidence of demand', 'compatibility with existing products' and 'relevant standards' than did their typical UK rivals. The foreign firms were also significantly more likely to provide briefs that included sketches, or other visual representations of design ideas, combined with written and verbal instructions.

Despite what was said in chapter 6 about the value of customer involvement in design, except in the furniture sector, there was surprisingly little evidence of firms involving customers and users in drawing up specifications. In the case of the UK firms any involvement was usually confined to making a product to a specification provided by an individual customer, while all three successful Scandinavian furniture manufacturers we visited involved a panel of users and other external expertise (such as ergonomists) in drawing up a specification for the general market.

The vagueness of the briefs and specifications provided by many typical UK firms, while apparently giving lots of freedom to designers, often inhibited creativity and wasted time, as in the gas fire example given earlier. This was because design time and effort had to be spent on defining the problem, often by producing unsuitable designs which had to be modified, rather than on solving it. Nevertheless, the existence of a detailed brief or specification cannot guarantee a successful design and development process. Designers sometimes ignore or modify the brief given to them, if they feel it unnecessarily constrains their creativity or goes against their professional judgement. This again points to the need for a collaborative team approach to product development in which designers are involved with other professionals in drawing up briefs and developing specifications.

From Concept to Prototype

In theory the brief or specification provides the design team with the market and technical requirements of the product to be de-signed without saying how they are to be realized. The design and development task is to transform the specification first into a general solution concept and finally into detailed instructions for manufacture.

Sources of design ideas

In chapter 6 we saw that ideas for new or updated products might stem from various sources – customer orders, senior management, market surveys, sales-force feedback, competitors' products, in-house research and development, outside consultants, etc. – but that successful firms would draw on as wide a variety as possible of sources of marketing intelligence for product planning. At the conceptual design stage such initial ideas provide the starting-point for an exploration of possible product concepts that are likely to meet the requirements of the specification.

The key contribution of designers is widely regarded as being that of creating new concepts, forms and configurations, often in advance of market demand. But it is important to appreciate that these ideas and solutions do not arise 'out of the blue'. They are almost always stimulated by something in the context or experience of the designers concerned. Darke (1979) writes about the 'primary generator' in design – the image, constraint, etc. that gives a designer a starting-point to create a solution to problem. For example, she describes how an architect got the idea for a housing layout from a pattern he had seen on a doormat. Holt (1987) argues that creative design ideas arise from a 'fusion' between the designer's perception of a problem and possible means of solving it, both of which depend on the information available to the designer. Thus the brief and specification provide the boundary to a 'solution space' within which there are many different design possibilities, only some of which will occur to a particular designer or design team.

We have seen that it is important to define the solution space as clearly as possible using the product design specification, but it is equally important to employ the best possible designers and to allow them scope to search widely for ideas within that space.

Several sources provide designers with ideas and solution concepts. Among the most important are:

- Existing products made by the firm and its competitors in the same or related industries;
- Experience of existing and new technologies, materials, components and manufacturing processes and knowledge of new ones;
- Current ideas from the design community, from exhibitions, magazines, etc.

In addition, design solutions may arise wholly or partly from:

- Creative thinking and problem-solving by individuals or groups using both informal meetings, workshops and discussions and formal idea generation techniques such as brainstorming and analogical thinking;
- Technical or theoretical analysis of a problem, increasingly involving the use of computer aids to design;
- Systematic searches of patents and the technical and trade literature;
- Ideas and suggestions from customers, users, dealers, suppliers, marketing staff and managers;
- Designers' personal experience of using existing products;
- 'Cut and try' experimentation and testing.

Conceptual design in practice

For most firms in our studies it was clear that design more often involves modifying or improving existing products than creating novel ones. In all the sectors we examined, the influence of competitors' products was therefore strong. Only 8 per cent of the typical UK and the successful foreign firms in Study B claimed either that they were uninfluenced by competitors or were the design leaders in their field. The remainder used competitors' products in one or more ways as the starting-point for their own designs: nearly half (48 per cent) used them as a source of ideas; a similar proportion (52 per cent) would adapt or try to improve on the competition; and a few (6 per cent) admitted to imitating competitors' products. For example, in the office furniture sector the comments on the influence of competitors ranged from 'They don't [influence us] – we are the design leader' (from the highly design-conscious US-owned company Herman Miller) to 'Our chairman notices a product in our sector of the market that appears to be selling well and says "How do we knock it off" – don't quote me!' However, more typical approaches are indicated by comments such as 'We look at other people's ideas, not only office, but domestic and shop furniture too' and 'The company takes new concepts introduced by competitors and looks at how it can translate them. The concept of systems furniture led to our range of flexible furniture.'

As is shown in figure 7.3, the world-leading foreign firms in all sectors modified or even imitated competitors' designs – or at least used competing products as a source of ideas – more than their typical British rivals. The fact that the foreign firms were specifically chosen for their commercial and design performance suggests that

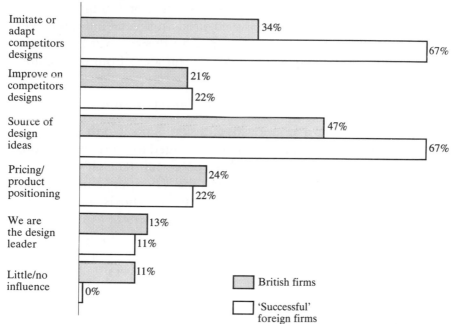

Proportion of firms mentioning this influence on their products

Imitate or adapt competitors designs — 34% / 67%

Improve on competitors designs — 21% / 22%

Source of design ideas — 47% / 67%

Pricing/ product positioning — 24% / 22%

We are the design leader — 13% / 11%

Little/no influence — 11% / 0%

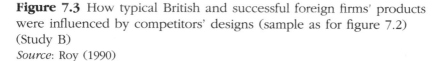

British firms

'Successful' foreign firms

Figure 7.3 How typical British and successful foreign firms' products were influenced by competitors' designs (sample as for figure 7.2) (Study B)
Source: Roy (1990)

this can be a successful approach. Indeed, Japanese companies, including Sharp and Ricoh which we visited, are renowned for the detail in which they study, cost and reverse-engineer their competitors' products before developing their own (Pilditch, 1987).

Of course British firms study the competition too, but in some that we visited the designers said they preferred to 'start from scratch' to retain their professional integrity. There was often a tension in such firms between the desire of designers to be creative and original, of marketing staff to satisfy often rather conservative customer demands, and of management to avoid undue risk. Other empirical studies of the design process (Samuels, 1989) have shown that, while designers do indeed aspire to create original designs, they appreciate that innovation represents a high risk of failure both for themselves and for their companies and that improving other's innovations may be a more realistic design approach.

There was evidence from our statistical analysis that an evolutionary design approach is more likely to be commercially successful. Firms that modified competitors' products were significantly associated with aggregate financial success measured on several indicators. Perhaps surprisingly, firms that had won most design awards were also significantly more likely to have got design ideas from competitors.

Innovative and evolutionary design

This does not mean that innovative design is not worth attempting. Several of the UK firms in our studies managed to produce individual innovative designs that were highly successful. Raleigh's most successful single-specification bicycle was the 'Chopper', a novel design with 'high-riser' handlebars and thick-tyred wheels aimed at the children's market, which sold over three-quarters of a million units in the UK alone and led to a whole range of 'fun' bicycles (see plate 3). Hille International's pioneering moulded polypropylene chair, designed by Robin Day in the 1960s, has sold over 10 million units in various versions and has been widely imitated (see Plate 1). But the problems which have affected these two firms show that producing individual innovations is not enough. Netlon, one of the most successful British firms from Study A, went beyond individual innovations and exploited the technology of extruded plastic mesh it developed in a wide variety of applications (see plate 17).

Moreover, our studies produced several cases of innovative products that were technically excellent and well designed, but which had failed to find or keep a profitable market. The cycle industry produced several examples, including an automatic bicycle gear and the Swedish 'Itera' bicycle with frame, forks, wheels and handlebars made of reinforced plastics (Roy and Cross, 1983). We also found several examples in the electronics sector, including the Maltron computer keyboard which was sculpted ergonomically to fit the hands, and the Microwriter system.

The Microwriter, the world's first fully portable word processor, launched in 1980, employed a unique five-finger keyboard to generate the full range of letters and symbols. However, by 1986 production of the Microwriter had ceased after only some 13,000 units had been sold worldwide. Among the reasons for this were that potential users believed the novel five-key typing method was more difficult to learn than it actually was, the cost of the system was relatively high, and by 1985 low-cost conventional computer word-processing systems had appeared. Nevertheless, market research indicated that the Micro-writing system still had considerable support and potential, and in 1989 the company launched a new product, a hand-held electronic personal organizer called 'Agenda' with a dual conventional/five-key keyboard.

These novel products failed because they had insufficient advantages over existing designs to overcome the resistance to innovation posed by well-established technologies and skills. In other cases the innovation was overtaken by rival firms that produced improved designs. For example, Redring Electric's innovative 'Autoboil' plastic jug kettle, launched in 1979/80, created a new market and achieved sales in excess of a quarter of a million units in 1981, including substantial exports. But in 1982 seven rival designs, some made of improved plastics and with additional design features, were launched by competitors on the UK market, backed by major marketing campaigns. Redring's share of the jug kettle market rapidly declined in the face of the competition (Roy et al., 1987).

The conclusion that may be drawn from these and other examples is that innovative design is inherently risky and failures are inevitable. Even if an innovation succeeds, only the best-managed firms will be able to gain the rewards of being first on the market and staying ahead of competitors by continuously improving their products and extending their range.

Evolutionary design, while less risky, also requires creative thinking. As one designer said, 'Creativity lies in integrating available components in a new way.' So even though the products in our studies were mainly evolutionary in design, over three-quarters of the designers we interviewed said they created alternative proposals in the early stages of a project and employed a variety of approaches to stimulate creativity. These included brainstorming, sketching, making models, holding meetings of the design team 'to thrash out ideas' and 'lateral thinking by bringing together designers and people from other departments'. However, the alternative designs would normally be variations on a theme rather than fundamentally different concepts.

A few firms in our studies used more adventurous approaches at the concept design stage. One successful British gas appliance manufacturer – whose various methods of creative marketing were outlined in chapter 6 – held regular workshops in which customers, dealers, designers, marketers and outside experts met to produce new design concepts. Some of the successful foreign firms set different designers or design teams on to the same project to propose

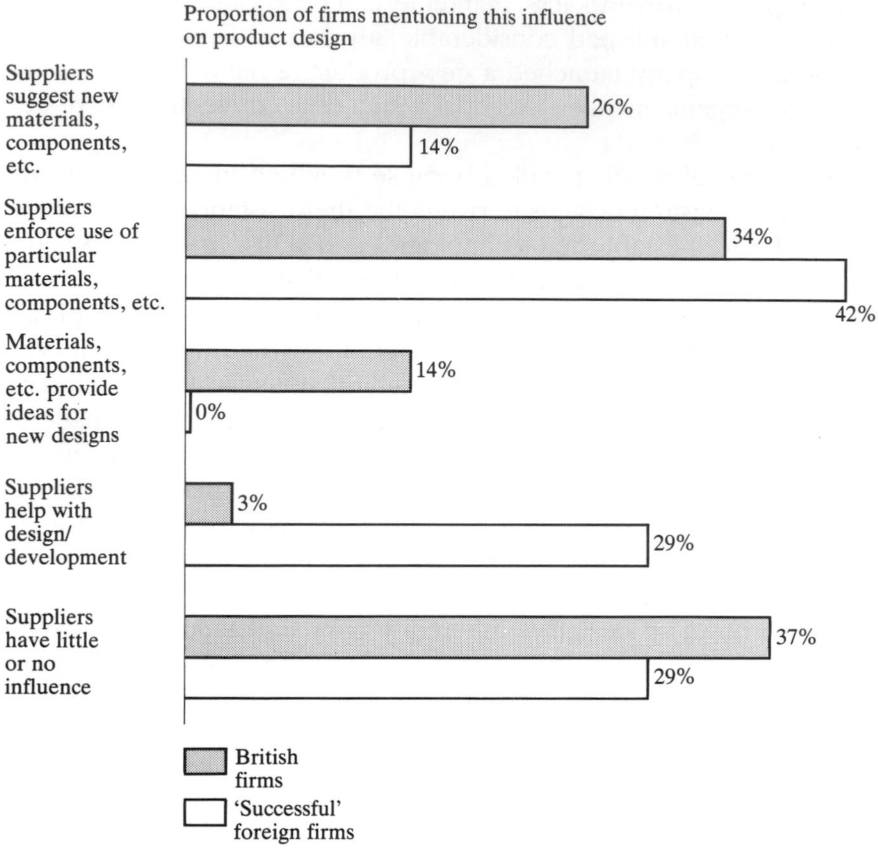

Proportion of firms mentioning this influence
on product design

Suppliers
suggest new
materials,
components,
etc.
— 26%
— 14%

Suppliers
enforce use of
particular
materials,
components, etc.
— 34%
— 42%

Materials,
components,
etc. provide
ideas for
new designs
— 14%
— 0%

Suppliers
help with
design/
development
— 3%
— 29%

Suppliers
have little
or no
influence
— 37%
— 29%

British firms

'Successful' foreign firms

Figure 7.4 How outside suppliers of components and materials
influenced product design in typical British and successful foreign
firms (sample as for figure 7.2) (Study B)

alternative solutions. In the Japanese electronics firms these competing design teams were usually in-house. As was noted in chapter 4,
the Danish furniture firms would hold competitions in which outside
designers and consultants were invited to submit proposals, the
winners being awarded the contract.

By constraining designers to use particular components or materials or by suggesting particular items, suppliers were another
important external influence on design (see figure 7.4). Over half
(65 per cent) of all firms in Study B acknowledged the influence of
suppliers, but the impact in electronics was particularly strong where
the introduction of a new microelectronic component could stimulate

the development of whole new product ranges or where particular components formed the basis of the design.

Nearly a third of the successful foreign firms used suppliers to help with design and development, compared to only 3 per cent of their typical UK competitors. However, the typical UK firms were as willing as the successful foreign ones to devote at least some of their output to making products to specifications provided by large purchasers or dealers.

Many of the typical British firms were thus more insular in their approach to design than was really necessary, while the foreign firms were willing to expose their designs to external influences and assistance. This confirms other research (see Roy et al., 1990) which shows that one of the factors that distinguishes successful firms from the less so is a willingness to use external expertise to help with design and development.

All this suggests that for the majority of firms who cannot aspire to be the design/technology leader, modification or even imitation of competitors' products and joint development with suppliers or customers can be an effective method of creating well-designed, commercially successful products. In other words, for most firms, being an 'offensive' or innovator is not necessarily the path to success. But to be a successful 'fast follower' or 'improver' also requires designers with creative ability to make the improvements that give products a competitive edge.

From Prototype to Production

It is rare for a product design, unless it involves a minor modification, to remain on paper or computer-aided design (CAD) screen, as sketches, drawings or calculations until it is ready for manufacture. At some stage its designers will usually wish to model the product in three-dimensional prototype form. Often these will be mock-ups rather than a full representation of the final design – for example, a computer terminal with a wooden instead of a moulded plastics casing containing wired circuitry rather than printed circuit boards.

Prototypes and mock-ups are used for a variety of purposes. The use of laboratory models and mock-ups to test basic technical feasibility has already been mentioned. The traditional and most common use of prototyping is for technical development and testing once the design concept has been established, to ensure that the product will meet standards of performance, safety, durability, etc., and to sort out design details. An example of this process for the development and testing of bicycles at Raleigh has already been described.

In some firms, however, mock-ups and prototypes are used at the concept stage. Some designers like to work in three dimensions as early as possible to get the 'feel' of the product and to have something more tangible than drawings to evaluate and discuss with other staff. In our surveys this was more prevalent in the design-conscious firms. The Danish toy manufacturer Lego, one of the successful design-conscious firms in Study A (see chapter 3), provides an example. When new product ideas are being developed, one of the first activities is to make mock-ups for discussion with the managing director, production and marketing staff. Staff are employed solely to spot errors in the models. Such errors may be dimensional – new Lego components have to fit with all existing components – or might relate to the most efficient method of manufacture. Likewise, in a British design-conscious firm which makes plastics consumer products, the chief designer said that it was very important to have something to look at, hold and try out when a new design was being discussed. In this firm a new product evolves via up to six mock-ups, each representing modifications proposed by the managing director, marketing and production staff, the design group and indeed any member of staff with an interest in the design. The modifications result from in-house user trials of new products to test function and ease and convenience of use, together with considerations of production efficiency and ideas about 'what looks right'. Use of prototypes and mock-ups at an early stage can therefore be helpful in allowing different categories of staff to contribute to the design process to produce something which works well and can be made economically. The drawback is the increased time and cost involved in working in three dimensions rather than two, and to be practicable it is important that the firm has good workshop facilities for rapidly producing and modifying prototypes, mock-ups and models.

Market testing of prototypes

Another less common, but also very desirable, use of mock-ups and prototypes is for customer acceptance testing and user feedback before manufacture and launch. It has been argued that proper consumer testing of prototypes provides a middle way between the risky 'technology/design-push' and the unadventurous 'market-pull' approaches to product development. For example, Kotler and Rath (1984) say that: 'designs need not be market-sourced but at least they should be market tested. Consumers should be asked to react to any proposed design because often consumers have ways of seeing that are not apparent to designers and marketers.'

Consumer testing of prototypes thus provides one answer to the marketing dilemmas posed in chapter 6. Obtaining customer reactions to prototypes or mock-ups can also help avert expensive errors – ranging from identifying products that would have failed on the market had they been launched, such as British Leyland's 1977 proposed replacement for its Mini car, to locating design changes wanted by users before the product is in production.

There are many methods of market-testing prototype designs: from gathering informal comments from employees or at trade shows to full-scale evaluation techniques such as 'product clinics' used in the motor industry and 'hall tests' used to test consumer durables. An excellent review of these methods may be found in Holt (1987).

Market testing in practice

In our Study B the most common method of evaluating the likely acceptability of a product before launch, used by over half (57 per cent) of all firms, was to get comments on prototypes and pre-production models by customers. 'Customers' were often distributors and specifiers rather than end-users, for example British Gas for heating appliances or architects for office furniture. Some firms had arrangements with a group of 'friendly' customers in order to get feedback on prototypes. Other low-cost methods of assessing product acceptability included getting comments from sales staff, used by a fifth (19 per cent) of firms, and seeking reactions to new products or prototypes at trade shows and exhibitions, used by a similar number (17 per cent). One British furniture firm had discovered that dealers and sales staff could evaluate one-tenth scale models of new designs set in scale office environments, so it could get feedback on design ideas before going to the expense of making full-scale prototypes.

Formal marketing methods for getting customer feedback, such as product clinics and hall tests, were used by less than a third of firms (29 per cent across all sectors), with no intersector or international differences. This is partly due to the cost and complexity of applying formal methods, which restrict them to larger firms, and partly due to the negative attitudes towards market research in many firms, as discussed in chapter 6. However, as we also noted in chapter 6, there were notable exceptions, such as the successful British gas cooker manufacturer that systematically applied a variety of techniques to get market reactions to new designs and prototypes. Only if a new cooker design 'trampled on the competition' in a series of hall tests with potential customers was it put into production (see plate 18).

Nevertheless, successful foreign firms were significantly more likely than typical British ones to get feedback on prototypes, not just from customers and users but especially from sales staff (figure 7.5). The Japanese firms in particular had elaborate arrangements with panels of end-users to evaluate prototypes (which was part of a 'special monitoring system', mentioned in chapter 6, to get feedback from selected customers at all stages of product planning, development and use). Study A highlighted the very successful practice of two foreign toy manufacturers, Lego and Fisher Price, of subjecting all their prototypes to extensive trials by users – in this case children – and rejecting all designs that did not meet with the users' approval. Fisher Price runs a nursery for staff and local children, while Lego employs the services of school children. In both cases the children play with prototypes of new toys and if they reject the prototype the project ends. Fisher Price prototypes which meet with the children's approval are also shown to a sample of parents and then given extensive safety tests before approval for manufacture.

Except in heating equipment, most firms (78 per cent) made internal use of their own products and prototypes in order to get user feedback, and some would not release a product until it had performed satisfactorily 'in house' for several months. Sometimes this led to useful ideas for improvements, for example, a furniture manufacturer coated its chair bases with polyurethane after complaints from staff about scuffed shoes. But this had dangers, for example when technical staff (usually male) evaluated word-processing equipment, they were unable to anticipate the problems and requirements of (usually female) secretaries in keyboard and software design. This is one aspect of a more general problem, namely, that in order to obtain reliable market feedback on product designs it is necessary to use proper test procedures with representative customers and users.

Thus, while a few firms, notably Scandinavian ones, took care to subject prototypes to proper user or ergonomic trials before final design and production, some relied merely on the intuition of senior management and marketing staff to assess product acceptability.

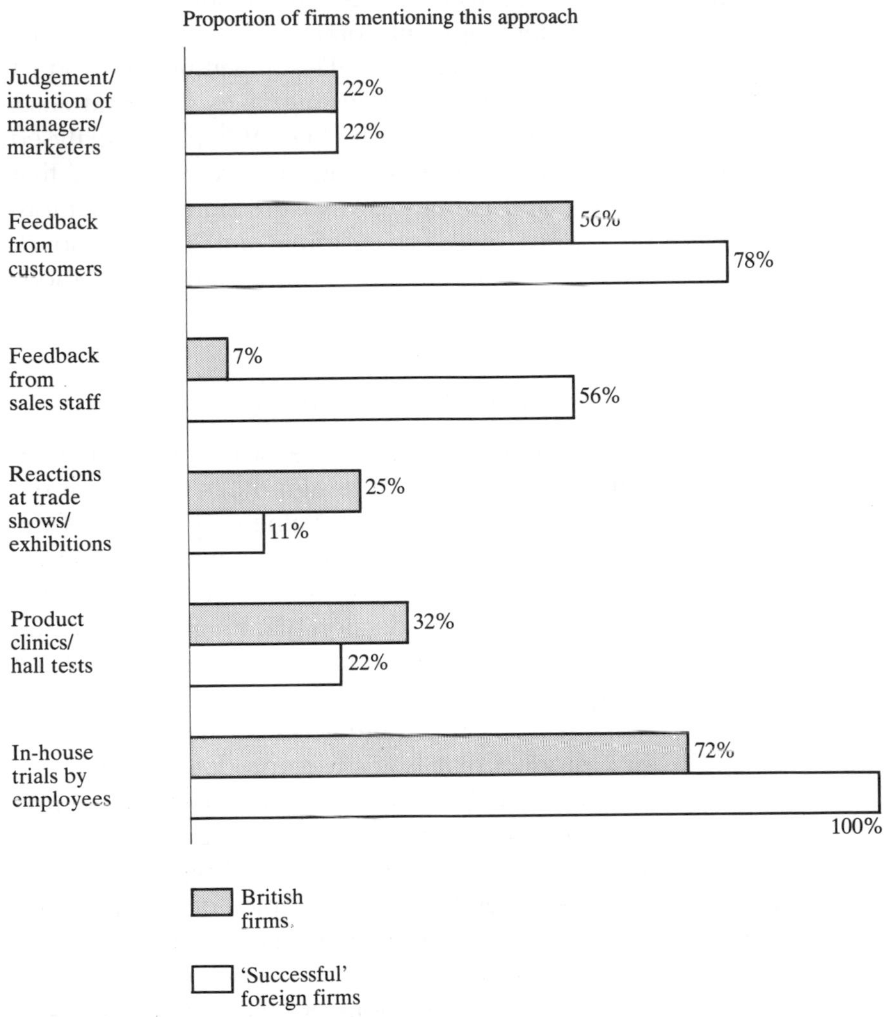

Proportion of firms mentioning this approach

Figure 7.5 How typical British and successful foreign firms assessed the likely acceptability of a product before market launch (sample as for figure 7.2) (Study B)

Typical comments from such firms were: 'We keep our fingers crossed'; 'I put myself into the position of a potential customer. If I like it I expect others will too'; 'Commercial instinct – we make things that give us pleasure'; and 'Prototypes are almost as expensive as the real product, so we usually launch products and see how they go.'

We were surprised to discover, given the usual Japanese commitment to extremely thorough market testing, that one of the Japanese multinationals surveyed undertook no user trials but relied on the judgement of a product development committee to assess product acceptability. This was in order to avoid delays in getting the product on to the market. But although market testing takes time and costs money, the evidence is that it is worthwhile. When we analysed business performance against market testing practice, we found that firms with high turnover and profit growth were significantly more likely to subject prototypes to direct customer and user feedback than those that relied just on intuition or simple, indirect methods like asking sales staff for their comments.

Design for manufacture

Much has been written about the importance of taking production facilities and constraints into account in design. Rolls Royce, for example, estimates that design decisions determine 80 per cent of the final production cost of many of the components it makes (Whitney, 1988), while the Ford Motor Company estimates that design decisions are ten times as effective as production planning decisions and one hundred times as effective as production changes in reducing costs and improving quality.

Failure to consider production requirements at the design stage thus often results in a product that is costly to produce and may be of poor quality because of difficulty of manufacture. Substantial savings can be made at the design stage, for instance by designing a product range using common modular components, by redesigning a product with fewer parts to be assembled, or by choice of materials and components to allow automatic manufacture. Delaying action until the production planning or manufacturing stages will usually be too late, resulting only in minor cost reductions or quality improvements.

For example, the design brief for Arcam's low-cost amplifier shown in plate 16 specified that the total cost of all assembled mechanical parts should not exceed £7.50 in production quantities. This target was achieved by designing the amplifier casing around extruded aluminium end-pieces to permit rapid assembly without the need for drilling or tapping (Roy and Walker, 1988).

Often a product, like Arcam's amplifier, is designed to be economically manufactured using a company's existing facilities, but production-efficient designs may also be stimulated by changes in manufacturing. For example, when Kenwood had to replace the tools used for injection moulding of plastic components for one of its food mixers, the company decided to redesign the mixer to improve its appearance and also reduce the cost of production. By replacing complex metal and plastic assemblies, fixed together with screws, by one-piece moulded plastic components, materials, scrap, labour and inspection costs were reduced and appearance and quality were improved (Dagger et al., 1985). In this case the product was redesigned when the tooling was being changed, but increasingly product and manufacturing systems design have to be considered together, as in the example of British Rail's International Coach shown in plate 19.

Several approaches may be used to ensure that manufacturing requirements are incorporated into design decisions. Organizational methods aim to ensure that staff with knowledge of production facilities and constraints are involved in product development (see Dean and Susman, 1989). These range from subjecting designs to regular review by someone with production expertise, and exchange of staff between design and production departments, to the product development committees and multidisciplinary product development teams discussed in chapter 5. Educational methods aim to ensure that designers have knowledge of production processes. These range from the practice in some Japanese companies that designers must first work on the shop floor and in production engineering before entering the design office, to the practice common in Germany of providing designers with training courses in manufacturing technology and methods. Technological methods, in particular the introduction of systems for computer-aided design and manufacture, can provide designers with manufacturing information at an early stage and thus help them incorporate production requirements into their designs.

Designing for manufacture in practice

Despite the view that designing for production is neglected in British industry, research by Oakley and Pawar (1984) indicates that this is not really true, with two-thirds of the firms they studied saying that production staff were involved throughout the design process. This finding was confirmed in our Study B. Over two-thirds (69 per cent) of the UK firms surveyed claimed they always designed for ease of production, and only 2 per cent said they never did so. However, it is clear that they were not all successful in achieving this, as about two-thirds (65 per cent) also said they always or sometimes had to modify their designs at the production stage. There were no significant intersector or international differences in the above respects. However, the usual method of designing for production differed between sectors.

In office furniture this was typically achieved by designers being aware of the skills and production facilities in the firm and taking these into account. In heating, with much larger fixed investments involved, production considerations were paramount and were usually specified in the brief or formally considered by a development committee at the concept stage, and very largely dictated what design changes were possible. In electronic business equipment, production staff were usually involved in the design and development team or regularly consulted during the development process. Table 7.2 lists some of the methods that the firms in Study B used to design for ease of manufacture.

Production facilities also affect design both as a constraint and as a stimulus. In Study B two-thirds (65 per cent) of firms viewed production and design as opposing factors between which a compromise had to be struck, giving rise to comments such as 'We always consider what the factory is capable of making, but would not compromise design because it could not be manufactured easily'; and 'Ergonomics and human factors are our major concerns. If we were doing the product for manufacture, it would never have been designed like this.' On the other hand, over half (55 per cent) of the Study B firms, almost all UK furniture makers, said that changes in production had generated ideas for new or improved products. For example, new high-pressure lamination equipment allowed one firm to produce furniture looking like wood at reasonable cost; a new multiborer enabled another firm to replace dovetail joints by dowelling and to improve quality by permitting more precise alignment of panels; while new computer-numerically controlled machine tools enabled a third to make metal components that snapped together, eliminating welding in its sheet metal furniture.

In summary, the evidence from our own and other work suggests that the majority of firms are at least aware of the need to take production considerations into account during the design process, but that not all firms actually manage to achieve this in practice. A wide range of approaches is used in the attempt to design for production, but the most effective seems to be the team approach in which production staff are involved throughout the process or, in firms too small to justify this, regular review by a product development committee containing someone with production expertise.

Table 7.2 Ways of designing for ease of manufacture: illustrative quotes from Study B

Awareness by designers of production facilities/skills	'Familiarity with machinery and skills in the factory' (*furniture*) 'Making design staff aware of the problems inherent in production. Having the production director involved in design' (*electronics*)
Involvement of production staff in product development team	'Production always have the opportunity to discuss changes with the design team and are involved at an early stage in design/development' (*furniture*) 'Continual discussion between designers and production engineers, who are both in the technical department' (*furniture*) 'Involvement of those responsible for design, quality, materials and manufacture in product development. Everyone can have an input and be involved' (*electronics*)
Committee of senior managers to oversee product development	'Production is considered carefully at the brief stage. The development committee includes our production director. This is the foremost consideration in design' (*heating*) 'Designs are vetted for ease of manufacture, in terms of assembly, time for manufacture, ease of testing, etc. – all these factors add to cost of production' (*electronics*)
Part of brief/concept	'We try to take this into account at the stage of the design brief – production staff are only brought in at the prototype stage' (*furniture*) 'Production engineering are involved at the concept stage. Whether a design can be made is crucial from the beginning' (*heating*) 'This is always thought out at the concept stage – at what cost can we build it?' (*heating*)
Part of prototype evaluation	'Production staff are involved in prototype evaluation' (*furniture*)
Rely on component suppliers	'Most crucial design for manufacture decisions are made by component suppliers' (*electronics*)

Post-launch Design Changes

It is a mistake to assume that the design process is finished once a new product is launched on to the market. As was noted in chapter 1, there is considerable evidence (e.g. Rothwell and Gardiner, 1983; Georgiou et al., 1986) that updating and improving a product after its first introduction can be as important as the initial innovation process. It has been suggested that British industry is insufficiently concerned with this aspect of the design and innovation. For example, Sir Terence Beckett, former CBI Director General, has said:

> British companies have often been first in the market-place, but have failed to produce the mark two and subsequent develop-ments to stay ahead. . . . Innovation is not just about new ideas, welcome as those may be. It is also about minor improvements to products, range extensions, slight differences which can make considerable differences, and also unexpected spin-offs. (Quoted in Rothwell and Gardiner, 1985)

Certainly British companies well known for their competitive success, such as J.C. Bamford and Rolls Royce, are also renowned for the attention they devote to continuous development of their products – to improve quality and performance, add features and reduce costs. Thus JCB's highly successful backhoe excavator range, which in 1987 had 21 per cent of the total world market, is subject to continuous design improvement, with the occasional major update. Other successful companies, from British Aerospace to Netlon and Lego, are noted for their skill in continuously extending their product range to exploit the design and technology they have developed. A good example is British Aerospace's innovative Harrier 'jump jet', which has been subjected to both continuous incremental improvements and major redesigns and is produced in a whole family of versions for different applications (Roy et al., 1990).

Improvements based on customer and user feedback are especially important. For example, in response to feedback from hi-fi reviewers, users and dealers, Arcam brought out an improved version of their low-cost amplifier with a new transformer to reduce hum and coloured fashionable all-black (instead of the original grey and black). Sales of the incrementally improved version were nearly double those of the original design (Roy and Walker, 1988). Many similar examples of the commercial benefits to be gained by redesigning existing products are emerging from our Study C (see Potter et al., 1991).

Product improvement in practice

Firms were asked in Study B about the frequency with which they introduced new products and major updates of existing products. Nearly half (43 per cent) of all firms launched new products and a third (36 per cent) made major updates on average every two years. Almost all firms made frequent minor improvements to their existing products. Perhaps surprisingly, a third (35 per cent) of office furniture firms introduced new products at least every year – despite a view in the industry that 'the office furniture market does not change' – compared with 18 per cent of electronics firms, who were very aware of having to compete in a very rapidly changing market. This was due to the relative ease with which furniture could be redesigned to respond to fashion changes compared to electronic business equipment where new components and technologies had to be incorporated into redesigns. Because of the constraints on design changes imposed by capital-intensive production facilities, none of the heating firms made annual new product introductions, only 14 per cent made annual updates and nearly one-third (29 per cent) did not even make minor improvements to existing models.

However, across all sectors almost two-thirds of firms recognized the need for product improvement, as they deliberately designed products that could readily be modified in response to market or technical changes. Table 7.3 gives some examples of how firms designed products to be adaptable.

What is surprising is that fact that the typical British firms in the study tended to introduce new products more frequently than their successful foreign competitors, who tended instead to make frequent major updates to their products. Although the differences are not great, they suggest a possible international difference in the relative priority given to new product development and product improvement, which is consistent with the tendency noted earlier for the foreign firms to put much of their effort into evolutionary rather than innovative design.

Product improvement, therefore, seems to be as essential a part of a successful design programme as new product development. However, an improvement programme cannot guarantee the continued success of a product. Technology or markets may change and leave the product behind; competitors may design something better or be better at marketing; or the product may never have had much chance of success in the first place. In such cases the only option is to undertake a major redesign or to design something completely new.

Table 7.3 Designing for flexibility: how firms in Study B designed products to be readily modified in response to market/technical change

---

Office furniture
- A 'Meccano kit' approach. The system has 1000 items, only 5 per cent will be becoming outdated at any time
- The product is an adaptable kit that changes to suit customer needs
- We try to take existing products further, for example five ranges developed from one
- Colour changes can allow for flexibility at low production cost

---

Domestic heating
- As much interchangeability between components as possible
- Where possible we make use of standardized components

Electronic business equipment
- Modular approach allows for expansion through the addition of extra boards and optional features
- Hardware and software are modular and can be adapted to the requirements of a range of users
- Flexibility is built into products, for example circuit boards can take more advanced components when these become available
- Using a more expensive microprocessor that can be programmed to drive terminals, run videotex or provide other applications

---

Speeding Up Product Development

One of the factors that has emerged since we began our studies is the growing importance of the speed of product development. Rapidly changing technology and markets and shorter product life cycles have meant that getting products on to the market ahead of the competition has become one of the main preoccupations of managers and design staff. The ability of a firm to respond sufficiently fast to the changing market, technical and business environment is becoming an increasingly important measure of competitiveness. This affects firms in all major manufacturing countries. For example, a major study of the reasons for the declining competitiveness of American manufacturing carried out at the Massachusetts Institute of Technology (Berger et al., 1989) argues that:

> US firms are increasingly perceived to be doing poorly in comparison with their foreign competitors in such key aspects as

the cost and quality of their products as well as the speed with which new products are brought to the market. . . . US industry shows systematic weaknesses that are hampering the ability of many firms to adapt to a changing international business environment.

Kim Clark, Professor of Business Administration at Harvard Business School, has put the argument for speed more dramatically:

Time is of the essence. Today companies make history or are consigned to it, quickly. In many industries, six months can be packed with moves and countermoves. Products are born, sold and phased out. . . . Customers will not wait . . . Companies that shorten development times often prompt associated improvements in product quality and lower development costs. (Quoted in Roy et al., 1990)

Clark's views derive at least partly from his studies of lead times in the American, European and Japanese car industries. These showed that the time between design concept and market introduction averaged about 3.5 years in Japanese car manufacturers and 5 years in their US and European rivals (Clark and Fujimoto, 1989).

Fast response includes the ability to monitor and anticipate trends in markets, fashions, technologies, etc. and then to plan, design, develop and introduce products in time to match the competition. Speed of product development has always been important in new technology sectors such as electronics and in fashion industries such as clothing and footwear. But shorter concept-to-market or order-to-delivery lead times are becoming important in most other sectors too. The role of lead times in the car industry has been mentioned, as well as examples of firms such as Raleigh and projects like the Advanced Passenger Train that ran into problems at least partly because of protracted development times.

However, these examples also highlight the potential conflict between the requirements of speed and thoroughness in product development. Various approaches are being used by companies to speed product development without compromising on the care and effort they put into the process. The introduction of CAD systems has significantly reduced the time required for drafting and is beginning to have an important impact on the time needed for other areas of product development such as modelling and testing. To some extent, however, CAD systems are being used to explore more design alternatives than was possible with manual methods, and so some of the gains are in better or a greater variety of designs rather than in shorter lead times.

The full benefits are only achieved with the introduction of computer-aided design and manufacturing (CAD/CAM) systems, which enable design information to be fed directly to computer-controlled manufacturing equipment (see plate 20). Such systems are beginning to give many firms – when have overcome the inevitable initial learning problems – the ability to offer customers a wider variety of high-quality products with greater speed. Firms in traditional as well as newer industries are benefiting: the example of the introduction of CAD/CAM into a few leading firms in the knitwear industry was given in chapter 1.

However, many firms are attempting to speed product development, as well as improve product quality and reduce costs, through organizational and managerial as well as technical changes. This change from 'sequential' to so-called 'simultaneous' or 'concurrent' engineering is being adopted by major firms such as Ford, Rover, Rolls Royce, Hewlett Packard and Xerox as well as by many smaller ones. Concurrent engineering is really another term for the multidisciplinary 'rugby team' approach discussed in chapter 5, and means that all the different functions in the product development process – planning, design, manufacturing engineering, purchasing, etc. – are carried out as far as possible in parallel and with maximum communication between the different groups involved (Duffy and Kelly, 1989). In some firms this may involve very major changes and investments – the German car manufacturer BMW, for example, has built a new research and development centre the architecture of which is designed to facilitate close collaboration between all the various groups involved in product development. However, as was noted in chapter 5, the precise organizational means for obtaining the benefits of teamwork in product development can vary from firm to firm depending on its size and the complexity of the product involved.

Lessons and Conclusions

1 Despite many differences in the details of what firms did during product development, the overall process was very similar for successful and less successful firms and for different sectors. Business performance did not

therefore depend on the various steps that a firm went through during product development, but on how thoroughly and systematically the process was carried out: for example, whether a prototype design is subjected to detailed technical, user and market testing before launch, or whether this is done by *ad hoc* methods or guesswork.

2 A balance has to be struck between the degree of thoroughness with which product development is undertaken and the time required to bring a product to market. Firms that have a thorough and systematic design and development process can nevertheless fail if this is too slow. Successful firms have therefore adopted ways of speeding up product development – including concurrent engineering and the use of CAD/CAM systems – without compromising on the care with which the process is carried out.

3 One of the most striking features of the successful firms was the amount of effort they put into the briefing stage of product development and in drawing up a comprehensive written marketing and technical specification at the beginning of any project. Whereas less successful firms might rely on a verbal brief or a specification which only defined the basic function and target selling price of a product, successful firms generally provided a detailed written brief including requirements for performance, marketing, use, servicing, etc., as well as constraints on costs, manufacturing, timetable, launch date, etc.. Except in smaller firms where one or two individuals were responsible for product development, drawing up this detailed briefing document was a group responsibility in which all relevant people/departments were consulted.

4 Many commercially successful firms, especially the leading foreign competitors we studied, did not attempt to be the first to market with a novel technology or design. Instead, they either used competitors' products as a source of conceptual ideas or improved upon, modified or even imitated competitors' designs. These successful 'fast follower' and 'improver' firms got their competitive edge by attention to design details, product enhancement and systems integration rather than by being highly innovative. In contrast some British managers and in-house designers felt they had to 'start from scratch' or produce original designs in order to retain their professional integrity, even if this conflicted with advice from marketing colleagues.

5 Successful firms tended to have the facilities rapidly to make models, mock-ups and prototypes of new designs for technical and ergonomic testing, in-house evaluation and customer feedback. Only designs which, after necessary modification, satisfied those trials were put into production. Less successful firms tended to rely on the 'experience' or 'intuition' of managers and marketing staff to assess the acceptability of a product before launch on to the market.

6 Most firms attempted to take production constraints into account when designing a product. However, the different methods of achieving this

varied in effectiveness. The most successful firms tended to take production (and other) considerations into account by employing a 'systems' approach in which the various design requirements were considered throughout by a multidisciplinary team or where decisions were regularly reviewed by a development committee (see chapter 5).

7 The successful foreign firms in our sample tended to introduce new products less frequently than their typical British competitors, but instead updated their products more frequently and added to the range. This is in line with the strategy of post-innovation improvement and was often made easier by a deliberate policy of designing using standard components or modules to permit rapid modification and/or additions to a range.

8

Issues in Design and Innovation

So far in this book we have mainly considered design and innovation at the level of the individual firm. In common with other literature in the field of design management and innovation studies, we have tended to take the view that good design and effective innovation by such firms would not only improve their competitiveness and business performance but would also yield wider economic and social benefits. In this chapter, therefore, we look beyond the firm and show that this view is inevitably a simplistic one and raises many questions. We will not attempt to answer these difficult questions, as to do so would be well beyond the scope of this book. However, we raise them to show that deciding what constitutes 'good' design or 'successful' innovation is not just a question of an individual firm's profitability or competitiveness, but concerns issues of economic and industrial policy as well as cultural and social values.

Company Performance, Competitiveness and Economic Growth

In chapters 1 and 2, when discussing company performance, business success, international competitiveness and economic growth, we tended to use these terms almost interchangeably. It is necessary, however, to examine the relationships between the performance of the firm and the growth of the economy a little more fully.

The performance of an individual firm – especially, as we have shown, its capability for good design and effective innovation as part of a generally well-managed business – is an important factor in international competitiveness and economic performance. But the relationship between firm performance, competitiveness and growth is complex, and it does not automatically follow that improved performance at the firm level will lead to increased market share or growth in output for the firm, an improved trade balance for the relevant sector, or increased GNP for the economy. If other firms in the same sector have similar approaches to marketing and design or adopt the the same technological or organizational innovations, the result will be rather like that observed by Alice in *Through the Looking Glass* – running harder to keep in the same place. The same might be said of the competitiveness and growth of national economies.

Of course, it is unlikely that all firms in all sectors will improve their performance in similar ways, by similar amounts at similar times with a zero net result and, if a firm or an economy is not to fall behind, it is vital at least to keep up with competing firms and nations. In chapter 1 we noted that technical, organizational and other innovations in the design, production and distribution process, coupled with increased efforts in marketing, could stimulate the continued growth even of highly traditional industries, such as knitwear. But without a major increase in overall demand, because of, for example, significant population growth, or market and social changes, or the take-off of entirely new industrial sectors (or all three), an increase in the relevant economic indicators cannot be certain. This is precisely why, as we argued in chapter 1, emphasis has been given to policies aimed at stimulating radical technical innovations, radical new designs, and the many other components of a new technology system (Freeman et al., 1982) or new techno-economic paradigm (Freeman and Perez, 1988). And, as has been stressed so often in the recent literature on technology policy and economics of technological change (e.g. Dosi et al., 1988), these policies necessarily include support for the scientific, social, financial and industrial infrastructure.

So far we have referred to growth in the firm and the national economy as though the latter were simply an aggregate of the former, and the factors stimulating one stimulated the other. However, it cannot be assumed that the whole economic system is equal to the sum of its parts – what Klein (1977) calls the 'fallacy of composition'. Thus actions designed to increase the capability of individual firms to design better or to innovate more effectively, though very important in most circumstances and essential in the short term, will not always lead to improved competitiveness or growth for the firm, and improving the performance of the individual firms in the national economy is not necessarily the recipe for improving the performance of the national economy itself. As important in the longer term are the competitiveness, growth and performance of certain firms and certain sectors, possibly even at the expense of other firms and sectors. Recent work on innovation suggests that newer sectors are faster-growing than mature sectors and so technology contributes to economic growth through structural change (Coombs et al., 1987; Dosi et al., 1988). Over time the contribution of different sectors to the economy shifts, with the faster-growing, innovative ones becoming relatively more important, until they begin to have a net positive effect on economic growth. Governments have attempted to reflect this by targeting incentives and support at 'winning' sectors, which they regard as having most potential for future growth, although declining sectors have also been supported for political rather than economic reasons.

Incremental and radical change

At various times in history, improving the performance of industries, firms and technologies that had been the basis of past economic successes – such as steam technology in the era of electricity, heavy engineering in the era of precision engineering, materials and energy-intensive industries in the era of microelectronics – if done at the expense of the new technologies and sectors, were all short-sighted (if understandable) policies. They ultimately resulted in the firms and national economies concerned losing out to their more far-sighted competitors who were focusing their efforts on new fields by encouraging the establishment of new firms, diversification by established ones and the development of new technologies and industries in general. It is a difficult task to get the right balance between investment in future technologies for future growth and extracting the maximum benefit from established technologies, for example through market-oriented design improvements and product differentiation. Ideally it should be possible to do both, but limited resources require choices to be made. Firms with established investment in existing machinery and plant and committed to established product ranges and research trajectories, are not necessarily best placed to take optimum decisions in the interest of the national economy.

For example, investing in the design of, say, better steam engines or valve-based audio equipment, prolonged the life cycle of products based on those technologies and extended for a short time the profitability of the firms making them. The A4 Pacific steam railway engine, for instance, was developed in Britain in the late 1930s in response to the threat from imported German diesel locomotives, and set the speed record for steam traction of 126 mph. But steam was reaching the limits of its technological trajectory, while progress in diesel and electric railway technology was forging ahead. After years of successfully seeing off potential rivals, the once dominant steam railway technology suddenly collapsed in the 1950s; less than eight years elapsed between the construction of the last steam locomotive and the total phasing-out of steam on British Rail (Potter, 1989).

For the individual firm or industry an incremental strategy is attractive, as our studies have clearly shown. Improvement of designs based on existing technologies usually carries a lower commercial risk than the development of innovative technologies and design concepts. In any case, some firms do not see any alternative: they do not have the necessary expertise or finance to diversify into the new technology. Or they may be inhibited from innovating by professional, organizational or social barriers. But there are almost always diminishing returns on such effort – especially, as was noted in chapter 3, in industries where the opportunities for technological change are high. Thus in the above examples, when in other countries firms were putting resources into electric or internal combustion engines or solid-state audio equipment instead, there came a point when prolonging the life cycle of the old paradigm would not have contributed much to the the overall performance of the economy, even though it may have staved off the decline of individual firms. And in the longer term, if resources were not put into newer areas, it might have contributed to the absolute decline of the economy.

Design Policy and Technology Strategy

Individual firms may not therefore make decisions that are in the best interests of the national economy or even be willing or able to take the risks and make the investments needed to ensure the long-term development of existing industries and stimulate the growth of new ones. This is one of the functions of government policy towards design and innovation.

In chapter 2 we outlined some of the policies and programmes that British governments have pursued in support of design and technology. We also showed that, in numerous reports from the National Economic Development Office and other bodies, there has been official recognition at least since the late 1970s of the importance of design, innovation, quality and other non-price factors in improving Britain's competitiveness and economic performance (Blackaby, 1989; NEDC, 1989). So why is it that the growth of UK manufacturing – if not the whole economy – during the 1980s still lagged behind that of most of the major industrial economies, and the trade balance in manufactured goods has steadily worsened since it first went into deficit in 1983 (OECD, 1989)?

Price and non-price competition

These are big questions and without exploring both economic policy generally and the deep-seated historical factors affecting British manufacturing (discussed for example by Wiener 1982), we can only suggest partial answers. Certainly one major factor seems to be the fact that competitiveness is still defined in most government, industry and financial circles as being mainly to do with price. Exchange rates, wages, productivity and inflation are still the main focus of economic discussion and political concern. Investment in research and development, design, education and training – all the factors that contribute to non-price competition – are still generally considered of secondary importance, relatively poorly resourced in comparison with many other industrial countries and subject to budgetary cuts in times of economic hardship. Although the obsession with inflation, interest rates, etc. is justified in the sense that international competition is indeed a matter of both price and non-price factors, the balance of advantage for countries like the UK (and the United States which shares similar problems) has shifted towards non-price competition in many markets. The newly industrialized countries and highly efficient manufacturing nations like Japan can often beat UK and US manufacturers on price as well as offering high quality. With the integration into the world economy of Eastern Europe and the former Soviet Union – who are likely, at least initially, to compete on price – we can expect an increase in the pressures on Western Europe and the United States to compete on design, innovation and quality rather than on price.

During economic recessions or booms, the various price and non-price factors are likely to change in relative importance, while trade performance of rapidly changing high-tech industries and of mature industries will be influenced in different ways. The introduction of completely new products gives the innovator a temporary monopoly during which time price competition is relatively unimportant. It may lead in some cases to the take-off of new firms and even new sectors of industry, with significant effects on national output and growth. But the appearance of 'swarms' of secondary innovators, or the period of take-off of new technology systems with their clusters of interrelated and upstream and downstream innovations, brings price back into the picture as cost-reducing process innovations as well as new versions of the product appear.

The relative significance of price factors thus changes over the life of products and sectors. High-technology products, firms and sectors, where design embodies major innovative changes, are often the ones where market demand is growing most rapidly and are therefore those with the most scope for contributing to economic growth. In these sectors, price competition is likely to be least important. This is why the importance of price to national economic competitiveness has been challenged and innovation and other non-price factors emphasized in recent theories of international trade, discussed in chapter 2. But the sheer size and pervasiveness of the more mature sectors, such as clothing, white goods, agricultural machinery and heating equipment, where quality is a matter of incremental and design innovations rather than high-technology state-of-the-art advances, make them important in terms of present employment and short- to medium-term policies and strategies. They are important as today's bread-and-butter industries, even if they are likely to represent a declining contribution to the economy in the future.

In industry, technology and design policy, it is clearly essential to have a perspective for future economic growth and thus to propose an array of measures that will foster such future growth. Hence the current emphasis on strategic technological developments with the potential for future macroeconomic impact, such as information technology and biotechnology. However, it is also important not to forget that new technologies with major potential as the basis for future economic growth actually have their economic impact in the working-out of the technology, its adaptation to other sectors and its application to the process innovations and the many incremental product innovations that appear after the initial 'take-off'. Thus the industrial sectors which are now mature, or maturing, where incremental and design innovations are paramount, represent the realization and established operation of past new technology systems. In planning for the future, the present must not be neglected, which is why our research has emphasized design as an equally important counterpart to new technology.

Investment in research, design and development

In both new and mature industries an increasing number of products – from clothes to computers – are designed for global, or at least international, markets (Clipson et al., 1986). For example, the Sony Walkman and its many variants are sold in most countries. Benetton, the Italian knitwear firm, has identified different markets for its garments in different parts of the world. Competition between firms and economies is also increasingly international and the more successful ones are often only those that can meet the standards of design, quality and innovation set by the best in the world. Thus, although Britain was the first country in the world to establish an official body (the Design Council) responsible for promoting design, and Britain's design education system and design consultancy industry are famous throughout the world, British manufacturing has lagged behind many other countries in its use of this design expertise. Britain also still suffers from the historically low status and investment accorded in many industries to engineering and technology. In an increasingly international market, there is little point in half-hearted measures to correct these problems if these do not match and keep up with what is being done by rival firms and economies, at least in those industries and markets where there is the prospect of effective competition. The discrepancies between what world-leading foreign companies are doing to maintain their price and non-price competitiveness compared to more typical British firms have been highlighted throughout this book.

Such discrepancies are highlighted in the UK's investment in research, design and development (Roy et al., 1990). While Britain's total expenditure on R&D at 2.3 per cent of GNP in 1985 was above average for the major industrial countries, when non-defence R&D is measured the position is much less favourable, especially in comparison with Japan and Germany. In 1987 three-quarters of Britain's R&D was concentrated in three sectors: aerospace, electronic engineering and chemicals. UK government-funded R&D expenditure is even more concentrated. In 1987 nearly 90 per cent of total government R&D support went to aerospace and electronics, in which about half of R&D work is defence-oriented. It is perhaps not surprising that aerospace and chemicals are two of the few remaining sectors in which Britain has had a trade surplus, worth nearly £17 billion in 1988. By contrast, the UK electronics industry is less successful in international competition, despite high R&D expenditure, because of the high concentration on declining defence markets, whereas the growing new markets are in information technology and consumer electronics (NEDO, 1988).

So, although there are a few sectors in which UK industry is matching world competition in R&D, the rest of manufacturing industry has been relatively starved of funds, as well as of qualified scientists, engineers and designers, to develop world-competitive products and processes. In any case innovative performance, or the effectiveness of any country's firms in international trade, is not just a question of the scale of investment in R&D or design. They are also related to the way in which those resources are managed at the level of the firm and the economy. A country like Japan, with limited resources, made rapid progress after the Second World War by combinations of imported technology and local adaptation, design and development. On the other hand, abundant resources in other countries may be squandered by inappropriate objectives or ineffective methods (Freeman, 1987).

So far as design work is concerned, we have already noted that the human and financial resources devoted to design and development in typical British firms are often not sufficient to match world-competitive levels. UK government design policy in the 1980s, although widely admired and undoubtedly in advance of that in most other countries, is probably on far too small a scale to bring British manufacturing to the levels of design investment common in Japanese and German industry. The most significant part of the policy was the Funded Consultancy Scheme/Support for Design programme (outlined in chapter 2) which between 1982 and 1987 provided government subsidies to enable small and medium-sized firms to employ a professional design consultant to help in the development of new or updated products, components, packaging and graphics. This scheme continued as the Design Initiative within the DTI's Enterprise Initiative, again intended for small and medium-sized enterprises. A parallel DTI/Design Council programme, which publicized the commercial benefits of good design without providing financial support, was aimed at UK industry generally, including larger firms.

Our Study C has examined the commercial impact of 221 product development and other design projects, involving inputs of professional engineering, product, industrial and graphic design expertise, within the FCS/SFD programme. It shows that over 90 per cent of the implemented projects have yielded good financial returns for the firms involved, there has been some positive impact on international trade and there have also been important indirect benefits such as improved management attitudes to design and increased use of professional designers by the firms. Full details and results of this study are given in Potter et al. (1991) and the Design Council has prepared a summary of the main findings (Design Council, 1991). However, as the DTI's own evaluation of the programme admitted, despite the positive results for most of the firms involved, FCS and SFD only reached a very small proportion of the firms in British manufacturing that could benefit (quite apart from larger firms which were ineligible). In addition, the programme fell short of its aim of ensuring that 'design becomes an integral part of corporate strategy and incorporated at all stages of product development' (Shirley and Henn, 1988). Indeed, it may be argued that such programmes of public design promotion and support are needed more in Britain than in countries with an established 'design culture', such as Denmark or Italy, because of the apparent unwillingness of UK manufacturing industry to make full use of the undoubted talent of British designers. It is clearly insufficient just to educate and train designers and technologists. There is also a need to educate managers in how to make best use of design expertise and to manage design projects. Indeed, most of the failed projects in Study C owed their failure to poor design management (see Roy and Potter, 1990). Very few business and management schools offer courses in this area, despite pioneering work at the London Business School, the development of a design management curriculum by the Council for National Academic Awards, a course on 'Managing Design' from the Open University's Business School and promotional efforts by bodies such as the Department of Trade and Industry in the UK and the Design Management Institute in the United States.

Limits of government policy

The effectiveness of government policies and programmes on R&D, design and technology depends on the scale of support and on how well they are carried out. But such programmes also have their limitations. In the civil sphere at least, government programmes provide the infrastructural support and a framework within which industry makes its own decisions. Given the short-term, profit-oriented objectives of many British (and American) companies, there is no guarantee that such programmes will succeed, especially if they attempt to generate strategic technological and industrial changes.

A good example of the difficulties is provided by the case of a radical British innovation, the 'Transputer', a microprocessor chip capable of parallel processing which could form the basis of a new generation of much faster, cheaper and more powerful computers. This technology was developed by Inmos, a company set up in 1978 with public investment from the National Enterprise Board under the then Labour government as part of the strategy to revitalize British industry. Under the subsequent Conservative administration, ideologically opposed to public enterprise, Inmos was sold to Thorn–EMI (McLean and Rowland, 1985). However, Thorn–EMI ultimately proved unwilling to sustain the losses and make the long-term investment needed to exploit the Transputer, and in 1989 sold Inmos to a French–Italian company, SGS Thompson. Although this was probably a perfectly sensible commercial decision by Thorn–EMI, it resulted in the loss of a potentially important technology for the UK.

Despite such examples, there is probably more evidence of resistance to intervention and long-term industrial planning by the Conservative government than by British industry. For example, strategic programmes such as the Alvey programme on advanced information technology, which were generally welcomed by industry (Guy, 1989), have been replaced by less ambitious support, while schemes such as the Enterprise Initiative with more limited commercial objectives have been introduced. Since 1988, apart from greater support for small firms involved in R&D and innovation and more collaborative research, Conservative government policy has been to support projects that private enterprise is unwilling to fund. Yet, as many observers of international industry and technical change have argued (e.g. Dodgson, 1989), for long-term competitive success and economic growth a design and innovation strategy is needed that involves government and the whole of industry as well as the financial system. This approach is of course best exemplified by Japan where, as other countries begin to catch up in the ability to manufacture well-designed, high-quality products at affordable prices, major corporations with support by government and banks are exploring a variety of new technologies and concepts. Such developments include moves by some Japanese corporations from making individual products to providing complete systems and services, and attempts to produce a variety of devices and systems that incorporate artificial intelligence (Rzevski, 1990).

Designing for a Better Quality of Life

At various historical periods, certain countries have appeared to lead the rest of the world in innovativeness, international competitiveness and economic growth. These are the countries that were, at the time, seen as the model with which to 'catch up'. Britain during the Industrial Revolution, Germany after 1870, the United States at the turn of the century and during the post-Second World War boom, and Japan after about 1960 were all noted for their industrial performance and competitive success in international markets, particularly in new and technically sophisticated products for which demand was rapidly growing. More recently the newly industrialized countries such as Korea have experienced very high rates of economic growth as a result of a particular combination of factors described, for example, by Kaplinsky (1982).

Japan is currently still seen as a model for economic growth by many other countries, especially in South East Asia. Many people in the West, including the authors of this book (for instance in the previous section of this chapter), have concluded that there are important lessons to be learned from Japanese industrial policy and practice.

In this concluding section, however, we wish to emphasize that competitiveness and economic success are not without human, social and environmental costs. In each of the countries mentioned above, rapid economic growth took place, but at the cost of pollution, work hazards, sharp differentials in wealth, acute poverty and hardship for many, and unequal access to food, housing, health care and other welfare services. Even after a quarter-century of startling industrial and economic growth, Japan has been described as a 'rich nation but a poor people'. The quality of life for the Japanese population is often considered to be lower than that of less economically successful countries, reflecting features of Japanese society such as comparatively poor housing, crowded cities, pollution, long working hours, the low status of women, and so on.

Macroeconomic performance is usually measured in terms of output, national income or growth in either, relative to competing national economies. However, as was noted in chapter 2, aggregate figures used as proxies for economic performance are not accurate indicators of the quality of life, the quality of the human and natural environment, the share of the national wealth spent on such items as health and education, or the way in which the national income is divided among social classes, geographical regions, ethnic groups and so on. We argued that countries with, for example, high rates of literacy, low rates of infant mortality, low levels of pollution or relatively small income differentials might be viewed as being at least as 'successful' as countries with higher absolute levels of economic output or higher rates of growth, but where substantial sections of the population suffered from bad housing, inadequate health provision, pollution and so on, and where relatively small numbers of people earned high salaries and were responsible for a large share of consumer spending. We would argue, therefore, that in assessing the contribution of design, technology or other activities to a country's 'success', it is important to take into account their social and environmental contribution to the quality of life, as well as the effect on business or economic performance.

Design for the environment

After the Second World War, when policies aimed at promoting technology began to be adopted by the governments of most advanced countries, they were justified with reference to economic growth. As mentioned earlier, in the 1980s, governments have become much more aware of design and the desirability of promoting good design as well as technological innovation, again using arguments related to economic performance.

In the early 1970s, the economic growth objective of government economic and technology policies began to be challenged, and it is worth considering these arguments, given the way in which design is now being promoted in a similar way to the promotion of technology over a longer period. The grounds for challenging the growth objective were that the pollution associated with exponential growth threatened the future of human society itself, and that the exhaustion of materials and energy would, in any case, make such growth unsustainable. The computer-based models of a group of American systems dynamicists, published in *The Limits to Growth* (Meadows et al., 1972), showing scenarios in which world supplies of materials, food and fuel would run out or pollution levels would rise out of control, were quickly challenged, among others, by a British group of computer modellers and policy analysts and published for example in Cole et al., 1973. The debate which followed became a major issue of the early 1970s and took place very much in the public and political, as well as in the academic, domain. The main argument of those who questioned the doom-laden scenarios of *The Limits to Growth* was that the issue was not so much a question of how much economic growth took place, as what sort of growth, and in whose interests. They made the point that technological innovation – and we would add design choices – in use of materials and energy, use of lower-grade ores, recycling and the efficient use of capital stock, combined with social and institutional changes, could avert the catastrophes predicted by Meadows and his collaborators. To do so, appropriate technology policies would have to be developed, integrated with economic and social policies, and successfully implemented in rapid response to environmental problems.

Environmental objectives were indeed adopted in technology policies and resulted in some reallocation of resources (Freeman, 1982). Although many further attempts were made to develop more sophisticated computerized 'world modelling' techniques (reviewed by Cole, 1987), for predicting future resource depletion and other environmental problems, there was nevertheless quite a long period in the 1980s when, in practice, environmental concern lost prominence in both public opinion and government policy. But the late 1980s and early 1990s have seen a resurgence of international scientific and political concern about a variety of environmental problems such as global warming, acid rain, and depletion of rain-forests and the ozone layer, plus major shifts in public and political opinion about environmental issues. In Britain the environmentalist Green Party won a surprising 15 per cent of the vote in the June 1989 European Parliamentary Elections, although the Greens' support has since fallen. A 1988 Gallup poll found that three-quarters of a sample of the British population felt that care for the environment was more important than the government's top priority, the control of inflation. A major opinion survey conducted in 1989 for the Department of the Environment produced similar results (ENDS, 1989).

This environmental awareness has been accompanied by a new emphasis – a demand for 'environmentally friendly' products from 'green consumers' who wish to express their environmental concerns through purchasing decisions (Burke, 1989). A survey of 2450 members of the Consumers' Association, for example, found that

81 per cent would pay extra for products that are less harmful to the environment (Consumers' Association, 1989). The Department of Environment survey mentioned above showed that a majority of their sample of British consumers were already using, or were considering using, CFC-free aerosols, recycled paper products, unleaded petrol and phosphate-free detergents, as well as being prepared to take actions such as recycling paper and glass, avoiding garden chemicals and even reducing car use and electricity consumption.

The new interest in environmentally friendly products took place at a time when a great increase in awareness of design, on the part of consumers, retailers, manufacturers, advertisers and government, has also occurred. One result has been to stimulate both design and innovation on the part of manufacturers and retailers. Not only has development of 'greener' products – like cars which run on lead-free petrol and are fitted with catalytic converters or domestic appliances which use less energy – become a new factor in competition in some sectors of the market, but the use of green images by advertising and graphic designers is playing an increasing role in the promotion of manufactured products. In this new area of non-price competition there is some evidence that British manufacturers were failing to anticipate and were slow in responding to the demand for environmentally friendly products, and that as a result most of these were being imported, especially from Germany and Holland. The response of UK manufacturers to the emerging green product market is the subject of a new study by the Design Innovation Group.

Pearce (1990) has, however, noted a decline in consumer demand for green products since the late 1980s. This resulted at least partly from poor control over manufacturers' claims regarding the 'environmental friendliness' of their products and lack of agreement on a proper scheme of environmental assessment and labelling, such as the 'Blue Angel' scheme for labelling goods introduced in Germany in 1978. Inaccurate or misleading claims by some manufacturers gave rise to public confusion and even cynicism about green products and fuelled the environmental activists' view that 'green consumerism is a target for exploitation' and that 'consumerism was the problem not the solution to the world's ecological ills' (Irvine, 1989). The position of most environmentalists was that the need was to consume less rather than to consume different sorts of products and, in particular, there was no such thing as an 'environmentally friendly' car. For example, it has been pointed out that, while several major car manufacturers – including General Motors and Peugeot – have announced plans to develop and market electric cars in order to reduce air pollution, this has sometimes been done without fully assessing the environmental consequences of generating the electricity needed to charge the batteries (see plate 21 and Hughes, 1991).

It has become clear that there are no simple answers. To give another example, the new BT Phonebooks have used clever typographic design to reduce the amount of paper needed for each (see plate 22). While this is a worthwhile attempt at green design, still greater savings could have been made if Britain had supported its Prestel videotex system to provide electronic access to telephone numbers, as in the French Télétel system. Certainly, market forces or green consumerism alone cannot be relied upon to protect the environment or the consumer. To tackle environmental problems effectively, changes to product design, and to industrial processes and use of materials, will have to be accompanied by government regulatory, promotional and fiscal policies to control pollution, stimulate innovation and encourage changes in the behaviour of both individuals and organizations.

Design for human and social needs

As well as having environmental consequences, technical and design decisions – as was noted in chapter 1 – have a major part to play in the process of meeting human and social needs. Different people have different objectives, needs and wants and hence criteria for judging the quality of a product and its design. At present many products (even those supposedly 'designed for the market' as discussed in chapter 6) are designed more for the needs of the designer, manufacturer and purchaser than the end-user. For example, office furniture and equipment are often designed by men who are not always fully aware of the requirements of the users, who are mainly women. A newspaper colour supplement recently carried an article reporting an experiment in which the male designers of buses and trains each spent a day as users of public transport, and hence of their own designs, loaded down as women often are with babies, toddlers, pushchairs and heavy bags of shopping. In every case it was a revelation, if not a deeply shocking experience.

There are many reasons why the needs of a particular group, such as women, are ignored or poorly considered in design, but one reason is lack of involvement in the product development process. Although women have traditionally worked in the fields of textile and fashion design, only one UK firm in Study B employed a female industrial designer (Bruce, 1985) and only 10 per cent of all research, design and development staff in these British firms were women. The proportion of female R,D&D staff in the foreign firms was even lower at 4 per cent. Likewise, Study C found that two-thirds of the 221 small and medium-sized manufacturers we surveyed employed no women in research, design or development (Bruce and Lewis, 1990). So the application of 'tacit knowledge' about women users' needs happens only rarely in product design, while explicit market research may be oriented towards the purchasers of, say, office equipment rather than the users. Even for products where the purchasers are typically the users, such as domestic appliances, the needs of the users may end up as being secondary to other design, manufacturing or marketing considerations. Bruce (1985) argues that women could bring valuable skills and knowledge to the design process and gives as examples ways in which cars could be redesigned according to criteria of women users and how a domestic iron designed by male and female industrial design students differed widely in the relative emphasis placed on factors such as styling and ease of use (see plate 23).

Designing new products or redesigning existing ones could be done in such a way that the needs of different individuals can be met in as full and imaginative a manner as possible, and environmental damage eliminated or at least minimized. Some examples might include: well-insulated houses that are easy and efficient to run; a transport system which has the economic and environmental advantages of public transport and the flexibility of private transport; remote-control handling equipment which utilizes the skills of highly trained workers (rather than automating their jobs out of existence) without exposing them to the dirt, danger, heat or other unpleasantness of their existing work; a vast array of safety equipment and devices; products developed to meet the needs of the disabled, the elderly (see plate 24) or users in different geographical or climatic conditions; products made in, or using, appropriate materials for minimum environmental impact; products modified to make more economic use of materials; and products by the best designer for the mass market, not just for the rich (see discussion on Scandinavian design in chapter 3). Similarly, production processes could be designed or redesigned so that they are human-enhancing not human-diminishing, and again, have minimum adverse impact on the environment (Cooley, 1987).

Conclusions

To sum up, economic 'performance' or growth is an indicator of the state of a national economy which ignores many important social characteristics of the country concerned and the lives of its individual citizens as well as most environmental problems. It is nevertheless still the most commonly used indicator, especially for comparative purposes, as reasonably up-to-date information is available for most countries, and it gives some indication of the potential for investment in improvements to the quality of life and the environment as well as in the overall productive wealth of a nation. Most of the arguments which emphasize the importance of either design or technical innovation are concerned primarily with their potential to stimulate economic growth. However, if governments seek to support design activities – by grants to firms employing professional designers, by ensuring an adequate supply through the education system of suitably qualified designers, engineers and design-conscious managers, and by means of fiscal incentives, award schemes, purchasing policy and other actions – their activities could reasonably be justified with reference to the contribution design and technology can make to the quality of life and the environment, as well as to competitiveness and national economic growth.

In the 1970s, the wave of regulatory policies designed to control the unwanted consequences of technological change were often opposed by industry on the grounds that regulations would make innovation and product development more difficult and expensive. In many cases, it turned out instead that new technical and market opportunities were created (Coombs et al., 1987). More recently, as demands for 'environmentally friendly' products have shown, a greater awareness of the environment, scarcity of resources and unmet human needs can create market opportunities that are not necessarily incompatible with competitive business practices. However, commercial exploitation of these opportunities can be counterproductive in broader terms unless accompanied by government policies and actions which attempt to reconcile economic, business, environmental and social needs.

It is clear that the 1980s – the era of Thatcherism, Reaganomics, monetarism, 'yuppies', the 'new right', Eastern Europe's embrace of the market, the identification of state intervention as a cause rather than a cure for social problems, and the emphasis on 'me first, now' – has seen a shift in official attitudes if not public opinion. Technological innovation, design, improved competitiveness and economic growth are not ends in themselves. They are the means to achieve better standards of living, reduced unemployment and greater environmental conservation, and thereby to improve the quality of life, without jeopardizing the future. If the emphasis in the 1980s was to stress competitiveness and growth rather than the quality of life and environment in this equation, we hope that the balance will be redressed in the 1990s.

References

Aldersley-Williams, H., 1989: Design is more than matt black chic, *New Scientist*, 12 August, 58.

Alexander, M., 1985: Creative marketing and innovative consumer product design – some case studies, *Design Studies*, 6 (1), 41–50.

Allardt, E., 1973: A welfare model for selecting indicators of national development, *Policy Sciences*, 4 (1), 63.

Allen, T. J., 1969: The differential performance of information channels in the transfer of technology. In W. H. Gruber and D. G. Marquis (eds), *Factors in the Transfer of Technology*, Boston: MIT Press.

Allen, T. J., 1977: *Managing The Flow of Technology*, Boston: MIT Press.

Annerstedt, J., 1986: Art and industry. Part of course 'Explaining Technological Change', Inter-University Centre of Post Graduate Studies, Dubrovnik, April (mimeo).

Ansoff, H. I., 1965: *Corporate Strategy*, New York: McGraw-Hill.

Archer, B., 1976: A new approach to Britain's industrial future: design. Lecture given to the Royal Society of Arts, London, 15 March.

Baba, Y., 1985: Japanese colour TV firms: decision-making from the 1950s to the 1980s. Unpublished D.Phil thesis, Brighton: University of Sussex.

Baden-Fuller, C. and Stopford, J., 1990: Flexible strategies: the key to success in knitwear, *Long Range Planning*, Fall.

Beer, J. J., 1959: *The Emergence of the German Dye Industry*, Urbana, Ill.: Illinois University Press.

Bell, D., 1974: *The Coming of Post Industrial Society*, London: Heinemann.

Belussi, F., 1989: Benetton: a case study of corporate strategy for innovation in traditional sectors. In M. Dodgson (ed.), *Technology Strategy and the Firm*, London: Longman, 116–33.

Berger, S., Dertouzos, M. L., Lester, R. K., Solow, R. M. and Thurow, L. C., 1989: Toward a new industrial America, *Scientific American*, 260 (6), 21–9.

Bernsen, J. (Director, Danish Design Council), 1990: Personal communication.

Besford, J., 1987: Designing a quality product, *Journal of Marketing Management*, 3 (2), 133.

Blackaby, F. (ed.), 1979: *De-industrialization*, London: Heinemann.

Blaich, R.,1990: The global, regional and national product dilemma. Paper presented at *The Financial Times Conference*, Product Strategies for the Nineties, London, 15–16 October.

Bruce, M., 1985: A missing link: women and industrial design, *Design Studies*, 6 (3), 150–6.

Bruce, M., 1986: Designing for quality (Open University Course PT619 *Quality Techniques* Unit 1), Milton Keynes: Open University.

Bruce, M., 1988: New product development strategies of suppliers of emerging technologies, *Journal of Marketing Management*, 3, 313–28.

Bruce, M. and Capon, C., 1990: The role of design in strategic marketing. In A. Pendlebury and T. Watkins (eds), Recent developments in marketing, *Conference Proceedings*, Marketing Education Group, 1, 97–113.

Bruce, M. and Lewis, J., 1989: Divided by design? Gender and the labour process in the design industry. Paper presented at the 7th Annual UMIST/ Aston Conference on the Organization and Control of the Labour Process, UMIST, 29–31 March.

Bruce, M. and Lewis, J., 1990: Women designers – is there a gender trap?, *Design Studies*, 11 (2), 115–20.

Bruce, M. and Rodgus, G., 1991: Innovation strategies in the enzyme industry, *R and D Management* 21 (2), 319–25.

Bruce, M. and Roy, R., 1990: Design: its role in innovation and competition. In J. McCalman, C. Beard, D. Brownlie, and N. Gunson (eds), Proceedings of the 4th British Academy of Management Conference, 9–11 September, Glasgow Business School.

Bruce, M. and Whitehead, M., 1988: Putting design in the picture: the role of product design in consumer purchase behaviour, *Journal of the Market Research Society*, 30 (2), 147–62.

BSI, 1987: *Guide to the Preparation of Specifications PD 6112*, London: British Standards Institution.

BSI, 1988: *Draft British Standard: Guide to Managing Product Design*, Technical Committee QMS/4 Document 87/67900, London: British Standards Institution, January.

BSI, 1989: *Guide to Managing Product Design, BS7000*, London: British Standards Institution.

Buhl, C., 1990: Product semiotics research. Paper presented to the Design Management Forum, Copenhagen Business School, 15–17 August.

Burke, T., 1989: Year of the green revolution in Britain, *The Independent*, 27 September, 21.

Caldecote, Viscount, 1979: Investment in new product development, *Journal of the Royal Society of Arts*, October, 684–95.

Cantwell, J., 1989: *Technological Innovation and Multinational Corporations*, Oxford: Blackwell.

Carter, C. F. and Williams, B. R., 1957: *Industry and Technical Progress*, Oxford: Oxford University Press.

Caves, R., 1971: International corporations and the industrial economics of foreign investment, *Economica*, 38, 1.

Caves, R., 1974: International trade, international investment and imperfect markets. *Special Papers in International Economics* No. 10, International Finance Section, Princeton University, N.J.

Caves, R., 1982: *Multinational Enterprise and Economic Analysis*, Cambridge: Cambridge University Press.

Challis, S. and Crump, M., 1990: Design Management Study – Raleigh Industries, London: Royal College of Art, June (*mimeo*).

Chandler, A. D., 1962: *Strategy and Structure*, Boston: MIT Press.

Chesnais, F., 1986: Some notes on technological cumulativeness, the appropriation of technology and technological progressiveness in concentrated market structures. Paper presented at Conference on Innovation Diffusion, Venice, March.

Chesnais, F. (ed.), 1990: *Compétitivité Internationale et Dépenses Militaires*, Paris: Economica.

Chung, K. W., 1989: The role of industrial design in new product strategy. Unpublished Ph.D thesis, Manchester: Institute of Advanced Studies, Manchester Polytechnic, July.

Clark, K. and Fujimoto, T., 1989: Reducing the time to market: the case of the world auto industry, *Design Management Journal*, 1 (1), 49–57.

Clipson, C., Anous, C., Black, E. and Carr, D., 1986: *Design and World Markets*, Ann Arbor: Architecture and Planning Research Laboratory, University of Michigan.

Clipson, C., Bingham, T., Samuels, A., Thorp, M., Berry, J. and Williams, C., 1984: *Business/Design Issues*, Ann Arbor: Architecture and Planning Research Laboratory, University of Michigan.

CNAA, 1984: *Managing Design: an Initiative in Management Education*, London: Council for National Academic Awards.

Cole, H. S. D., 1987: Global models, *Futures*, 19, 403.

Cole, H. S. D. and Miles, I., 1984: *Worlds Apart*, Brighton: Wheatsheaf.

Cole, H. S. D., Freeman, C., Jahoda, M., and Pavitt, K., 1973: *Thinking about the Future*, London: Chatto and Windus.

Committee of Inquiry into the Engineering Profession, 1980: *Engineering Our Future* (The Finniston Report), Cmnd 7794, London: Her Majesty's Stationery Office.

Confederation of British Industry, 1984: Survey reported in *The Engineer*, 8 November.

Conran, T., 1989: quoted by C. Gardner and J. Sheppard, *Consuming Passions*, London: Unwin Hyman.

Consumers' Association, 1989: Going green, *Which?* September, 430–3.

Conway, H., 1983: An engineer's view of design, *Journal of the Royal Society of Arts*, 131 (5324), 454–69.

Cooley, M., 1983: New technology – social impacts and human-centred alternatives. *Technology Policy Group Occasional Paper No. 4*, Milton Keynes: Open University.

Cooley, M., 1987: *Architect or Bee: The human price of technology*, London: Hogarth Press.

Coombs, R., Saviotti, P. and Walsh, V., 1987: *Economics and Technological Change*, Basingstoke: Macmillan.

Cooper, R. G. and Kleinschmidt, E., 1988: Predevelopment activities determine new product success, *Industrial Marketing Management*, 17, 237–47.

Corfield Report, see NEDO, 1979.

Cox, J. and Kriegbaum, H., 1989: *Innovation and Industrial Strength in the UK, West Germany, United States and Japan*, London: Policy Studies Institute.

Cronshaw, M., Davis, E. and Kay, J., 1990: On being stuck in the middle. In J. McCalman et al. (eds), op. cit.

Cross N., 1989: *Engineering Design Methods*, Chichester: John Wiley.

Cyert, R. and March, J., 1963: *A Behavioral Theory of the Firm*, Englewood Cliffs, N.J.: Prentice Hall.

Dagger, B., Farrar, D.J. and Bridgefoot, M., 1985: *Design for Economic Manufacture*, Watford: Engineering Industry Training Board Publications.

Dalum, B. and Fagerberg, J., 1986: Diffusion of technology, economic growth and intra-industry trade: the case of the Nordic countries. Paper presented at the Second Knoellinger Seminar, Aabo, Finland, April (mimeo).

Dalyell, T., 1990: Thistle Diary, *New Scientist* (1721), 66.

Darke, J., 1979: The primary generator and the design process, *Design Studies*, 1 (1), 36–44.

Dean, J. W. and Susman, G. I., 1989: Organizing for manufacturable design, *Harvard Business Review*, January–February, 28–36.

Department of Scientific and Industrial Research (DSIR), 1963: *Engineering Design* (The Fielden Report), London: Her Majesty's Stationery Office.

Design Council (Denmark), 1985: *I D Prisen 1965–85* (Great Danish Industrial Designs), Copenhagen: Dansk Designraad.

Design Council (UK), 1977: *Industrial Design Education in the United Kingdom*, London: The Design Council.

Design Council (UK), 1988: *Designer Directory 1988*, London: The Design Council.

Design Council (UK), 1989: *The Design Solution*, London: The Design Council.

Design Council (UK), 1991: *Profits by Design: A summary of the findings of an investigation into the commercial returns of investing in design*, London: Prepared for the Department of Trade and Industry by the Design Council.

Dodgson, M. (ed.), 1989: *Technology Strategy and the Firm: management and public policy*, Harlow: Longman.

Dosi, G., 1982: Technical paradigms and technological trajectories – a suggested interpretation of the determinants and directions of technological change, *Research Policy*, 11, 147.

Dosi, G. and Soete, L., 1988: Technical change and international trade. In G. Dosi et al. (1988).

Dosi, G., Freeman, C., Nelson, R., Silverberg, G. and Soete, L. (eds), 1988: *Technical Change and Economic Theory*, London: Frances Pinter.

Dosi, G., Pavitt, K. and Soete, L., 1990: *The Economics of Technical Change and International Trade*, Hemel Hempstcad: Wheatsheaf–Harvester.

Dreyfuss, H., 1955: *Designing for People*, New York, Paragraphic Books.

Duffy, J. and Kelly, J. 1989: United Front is Faster, *Management Today*, November, 131–9.

Dyson, J., 1987: Conference transcript. Designer as Entrepreneur Conference, Bath, November.

Economist, The, 1988: From little bricks great houses grow, 27 August, 62.

Edwards, C., 1985: *The Fragmented World: theories of trade, money and crisis*, London: Methuen.

Elliott, L., 1990: £2.2bn trade gap sends stock market into shock, *The Guardian*, 26 April, financial pages.

ENDS (Environmental Data Services Ltd.), 1989: Official poll ranks environment second among government priorities, *ENDS Report*, September, 176.

Evans, W., 1985: Japanese-style management, product design and corporate strategy, *Design Studies*, 6 (1), 25–32.

Fagerberg, J., 1985: Technology, growth and international competitiveness, Report 95, Oslo: Norwegian Institute of International Affairs (NUPI).

Fagerberg, J., 1988: Why growth rates differ. In G. Dosi et al. (1988).

Fairhead, J., 1987: *Design for a Corporate Culture*, London: National Economic Development Office.

Fielden Report, see Department of Scientific and Industrial Research (1963).

Filby, I. and Willmott, H., 1988: Ideologies and contractions in a public relations department: the seduction and impotence of living a myth, *Organization Studies*, 9/33, 293–307.

Finniston Report, see Committee of Inquiry into the Engineering Profession.

Flugge, B. (Competition organizer, Danish Design Council), 1990: Personal communication.

Forty, A., 1986: *Objects of Desire: design and society 1750–1980*, London: Thames and Hudson.

Francis, A. and Winstanley, D., 1987: Organizing professional work: the case of designers in the engineering industry in Britain. In A. Pettigrew (ed.), Proceedings of the British Academy of Management Conference, Oxford: Blackwell.

Francis, A. and Winstanley, D., 1988: Designing for competitiveness. *Engineering Designer*, March/April, 18–19.

Freeman, C., 1979: Technical innovation and British trade performance. In F. Blackaby (1979).

Freeman, C., 1982: *The Economics of Industrial Innovation*, London: Frances Pinter.

Freeman, C., 1983: Design and British Economic Performance. Lecture given at the Design Centre, London, 23 March, Brighton: Science Policy Research Unit, Sussex University (*mimeo*).

Freeman, C., 1987: *Technology Policy and Economic Performance: lessons from Japan*, London: Frances Pinter.

Freeman, C., Clark, J. and Soete, L., 1982: *Unemployment and Technical Innovation*, London: Frances Pinter.

Freeman, C. and Lundvall, B.-A. (eds), 1988: *Small Countries Facing the Technological Revolution*, London: Frances Pinter.

Freeman, C. and Perez, C., 1988: Structural crises of adjustment, business cycles and investment behaviour. In G. Dosi et al. (1988).

Gardiner, J. P. and Rothwell, R., 1985: *Innovation.*, London: The Design Council.

Georgiou, L., Metcalfe, J. S., Gibbons, M., Ray, T. and Evans, J., 1986: *Post-Innovation Performance: technical development and competition*, London: Macmillan.

Gershuny, J. I., 1978: *After Industrial Society – the emerging self-service economy*, Basingstoke: Macmillan.

Gershuny, J. I., 1983: *Social Innovation and the Division of Labour*, Oxford: Oxford University Press.

Gershuny, J. I., 1988: Time, technology and the informal economy. In R. E. Pahl (ed.), *On Work*, Oxford: Blackwell.

Gershuny, J. I., and Miles, I., 1983: *The New Service Economy*, London: Frances Pinter.

Gershuny, J. I. and Miles, I., 1985: Towards a new social economics. In B. Roberts, R. Finnegan and D. Gallie (eds), *New Approaches to Economic Life*, Manchester: Manchester University Press.

Gibbons, M., Coombs, R., Saviotti, P. and Stubbs, P., 1982: Innovation and technical change: a case study of the UK tractor industry, *Research Policy*, 11, 289.

Glancey, J., 1990: *The Independent*, 15 January, 3.

Godley, W. and Cripps, S., 1983: *The Guardian*, 14 March; also in the programme *TV Eye*, 6 March 1986.

Gorb, P. and Dumas, A., 1987: Silent design, *Design Studies*, 8 (3), 150–6.

Guy, K., 1989: The UK information technology industry and the Alvey programme. In Dodgson, M. (1989), 184–201.

Hart, S. J., Service, L. M. and Baker, M. J., 1988: Design orientation and market success. In T. Robinson and C. Clarke-Hill (eds), *Marketing Past,*

Present and Future, Conference Proceedings, Marketing Education Group, Huddersfield Polytechnic, July.

Hart, S. J., Service, L. M., and Baker, M. J., 1989: Design orientation and market success, *Design Studies*, 10 (2), 103–10.

Hay, D., 1983: Management and economic performance. In M. Earl (ed.), *Perspectives on Management*, Oxford: Oxford University Press.

Heskett, J., 1980: *Industrial Design*, London: Thames and Hudson.

Holt, K., 1987: *Innovation: a challenge to the engineer*, Amsterdam: Elsevier.

Hooley, G. J., J. Lynch, R. Brooksbank and J. Shepherd, 1988: Strategic market environments, *Journal of Marketing Management*, 4 (2), 131–47.

Hubka, V., Andreasen, M. M. and Eder, W. E., 1988: *Practical Studies in Systematic Design*, London: Butterworth.

Hufbauer, G., 1970: The impact of national characteristics and technology on commodity composition of trade in manufactured goods. In R. Vernon (1970).

Hughes, P., 1991: The role of passenger transport in CO_2 reduction strategies, *Energy Policy*, March, 149–60.

Irvine, S., 1989: Consuming fashions? The limits of green consumerism, *The Ecologist*, 19 (3), 88–92.

Jones, D., 1981: Maturity and crisis in the European car industry: structural change and public policy. SERC Paper No. 8, Brighton: Sussex European Research Centre, Sussex University.

Jones, D., 1983: Technology and the UK automobile industry, *Lloyds Bank Review*, April.

Jones, J. C., 1970: *Design Methods: seeds of human futures*, London and New York: Wiley.

Kaplinsky, R., 1982: *Computer-aided Design in a Dynamic World*, London: Frances Pinter.

Kay, N., 1979: *The Innovating Firm*, London: Macmillan.

Keynes, J. M., 1936: *General Theory of Employment, Interest and Money*, London: Macmillan.

Kicherer, S., 1990: *Olivetti, A Study of the Corporate Management of Design*, London: Trefoil Publications.

Klein, B., 1977: *Dynamic Economics*, Boston: Harvard University Press.

Knights, D. and Willmott, H., 1987: Organizational culture as management strategy: a critique and illustration from the financial services industry, *International Studies of Management and Organization*, XVII (3), 40–63.

Kotler, P. and Rath, G. A., 1984: Design: a powerful but neglected strategic tool, *Journal of Business Strategy*, 5 (2), 16–21.

Kravis, I. and Lipsey, R. E., 1971: *Price Competitiveness in World Trade*, New York: Columbia University Press.

Lall, S., 1985: *Multinationals, Technology and Exports*, Basingstoke: Macmillan.

Langrish, J., Gibbons, M., Evans, W. and Jevons, F. R., 1972: *Wealth From Knowledge*, London: Macmillan.

Lawrence, P., 1987: *Winning by Design: Project Report*, Sydney: The Warren Centre, University of Sydney.

Lawson, N., 1985: Causes and implications of the deficit in the UK balance of trade in manufacturers. Evidence to House of Lords Select Committee on Overseas Trade 1984–5, HL 28 XX QQ 1618–19.

Leadbeater, C., 1989: *Financial Times*, 4 December.

Lemola, T. and Lovio, R., 1988: Possibilities for a small country in high technology production: the electronics industry in Finland. In C. Freeman and B.-A. Lundvall (1988).

Leontieff, W., 1953: Domestic production and foreign trade – the American capital position re-examined, *Proceedings of the American Philosophical Society*, 97.

Leslie, G., 1984: Designers and users in the UK lighting industry. Working paper WP-09, Milton Keynes: Design Innovation Group, Open University.

Levitt, T., 1984: *The Marketing Imagination*, New York: Free Association Books.

Levy, S., 1959: Symbols for sale, *Harvard Business Review*, 37.

Lewis, J., 1988: The distancing of design. Working Paper WP–11, Design Innovation Group, Open University and UMIST.

Lilley, S., 1949: *Archives Internationales d'Histoire des Sciences*, 28, 376–443.

Lorenz, C., 1986: *The Design Dimension*, Oxford: Blackwell.

Lorenz, C., 1987: Scrum and scrabble – the Japanese style, *Financial Times*, 19 June, 19.

Lundvall, B.-A., 1985: Product innovation and user-producer interaction, Industrial Development Research Series No. 31, Aalborg, Denmark: Aalborg University Press.

McAlhone, B., 1987: *British Design Consultancy: anatomy of a billion pound business*, London: The Design Council.

McLean, M. and Rowland, T., 1985: *The Inmos Saga: a triumph of national enterprise?*, London: Frances Pinter.

Meade, J. E., 1951: *Theory of International Economic Policy, I, The Balance of Payments*, Oxford: Oxford University Press.

Meadows, D. H., Meadows, D. L., Randers, J. and Behrens, W. W., 1972: *The Limits to Growth*, New York: Universe Books.

Miles, I., 1985: *Social Indicators for Human Development*, London: Frances Pinter.

Mintzberg, H., 1987: Crafting Strategy, *Harvard Business Review*, July–August.

Mole, V. and Potter, S., 1991: Consumers' opinions of design: a study of consumer and purchaser influence on photocopier design, *Working Paper WP. 14*, Design Innovation Group, Open University and UMIST.

Momigliano, F. and Dosi, G., 1983: Tecnologia e Organizzazione Industriale Internazionale, Bologna: Il Mulino.

Moody, S., 1980: The role of industrial design in technological innovation, *Design Studies*, 1 (6), 329–39.

Moody, S., 1984: The role of industrial design in the development of new science based products. In R. Langdon (ed.), *Design and Industry*, London: The Design Council.

Mowery, D. and Rosenberg, N., 1979: The influence of market demand on innovation: a critical review of some recent empirical studies, *Research Policy*, 8, 102.

Myerson, J., 1989: Angels fall to bottom line. The *Guardian*, 5 June.

NEDC, 1987: *Design for a Corporate Culture*, a report for the National Economic Development Council by James Fairhead, London: National Economic Development Office.

NEDC, 1989: UK trade performance, memo attached to NEDC (89) 9, London: National Economic Development Council.

NEDO, 1979: *Product Design*, a report by K. G. Corfield, London: National Economic Development Office.

NEDO, 1988: *Performance and Competitive Success in the UK Electronics Industry*, London: National Economic Development Office.

Nelson, R. and Winter, S., 1977: In search of useful theory of innovation, *Research Policy*, 6, 36–76.

Newfarmer, R. (ed.), 1985: *Profits, Progress and Poverty*, Notre Dame, Indiana: University of Notre Dame Press.

Ng, J., 1987: An investigation of the contribution users make to the design of scientific instruments. Unpublished M.Sc. Thesis, Manchester: Manchester School of Management, UMIST.

Oakley, M., 1984: *Managing Product Design*, London: Weidenfeld and Nicolson.

Oakley, M. and Pawar, K., 1984: Managing product design in small firms. In R. Langdon (ed.), *Design and Industry*, London: The Design Council.

OECD, 1981: *The Measurement of Scientific and Technical Activities* ('Frascati Manual'), Paris: Organization for Economic Cooperation and Development.

OECD, 1982: *Innovation in Small and Medium Firms*, Paris: Organization for Economic Cooperation and Development.

OECD, 1987: *Science and Technology Indicators*, Paris: Organization for Economic Cooperation and Development.

OECD, 1989: *OECD Economic Surveys 1988/89: United Kingdom*, Paris: Organization for Economic Cooperation and Development.

Olins, W., 1986: The industrial designer in Britain 1946–82. In P. Sparke (ed.), *Did Britain Make it? British design in context*, London: The Design Council.

PA Design, 1988: company brochure, London: PA Design.

Pahl, G. and Beitz, W., 1984: *Engineering Design*, London: The Design Council (Original German edition 1977).

Papanek, V., 1982: *Design For The Real World*, London: Thames and Hudson.

Parsons, S., 1988: A note on culture and meaning, Manchester: Centre for Organization, Management and Technical Change, UMIST (*mimeo*).

Patel, P. and Pavitt, K., 1987: The elements of British technological competitiveness, *National Institute Economic Review*, November, 72–83.

Pavitt, K. (ed.), 1980: *Technical Innovation and British Economic Performance*, London: Macmillan.

Pavitt, K. and Soete, L., 1980: Innovative activities and export shares: some comparisons. In K. Pavitt (1980).

Pearce, F., 1990: The consumers are not so green, *New Scientist*, 16 June, Special supplement 'The Greening of Industry', 13–14.

Piatier, A., 1984: *Barriers to Innovation*, London: Frances Pinter.

Pickering, J. F. and Jones, T. T., 1984: The firm and its social environment. In J. F. Pickering and T. A. J. Cockerill (eds), *Economic Management of the Firm*, London: Philip Allan.

Pilditch, J., 1978: How Britain can compete, *Marketing*, December, 34–8.

Pilditch, J., 1987a: NEDO action: In Proceedings of the CBI 'Design or Decline' conference, London: Confederation of British Industry, May.

Pilditch, J. (Chairman of the Design Working Party), 1987b: *Design*, London: National Economic Development Council.

Pilditch, J., 1987c: *Winning Ways*, London: Harper and Row.

Polan, B., 1989: Buying and selling a new decade, The *Guardian*, 11 November.

Posner, M., 1961: International trade and technical change, *Oxford Economic Papers*, October.

Posner, M. and Steer, A., 1979: Price competitiveness, non-price factors and export performance. In F. Blackaby (1979).

Potter, S., 1987: *On the Right Lines? the limits of technological innovation*, London: Frances Pinter; New York: St Martin's Press.

Potter, S., 1989: High-speed rail technology in the UK, France and Japan: managing innovation – the neglected factor, *Technology Analysis and Strategic Management* 1 (1), 99–121.

Potter, S., 1990: Successfully managing research, design and development. In T. M. Khalil and B. A. Bayraktar (eds) *Management of Technology II*, Georgia: Industrial Engineering and Management Press.

Potter, S. and Roy, R., 1986: Research and development: British Rail's fast trains (Units 9–10, Open University course, T 362 *Design and Innovation*), Milton Keynes: Open University.

Potter, S., Roy, R., Capon, C. H., Bruce, M., Walsh, V. and Lewis, J., 1991: The Benefits and Costs of Investment in Design: Using professional design expertise in product, engineering and graphics projects, Report DIG-03, Milton Keynes/Manchester: Design Innovation Group, Open University and UMIST.

Pugh, S., 1986a: *Curriculum for Design: specification phase*, Hatfield: SEED (Sharing Experience in Engineering Design), Hatfield Polytechnic.

Pugh, S., 1986b: Design activity models: world-wide emergence and convergence, *Design Studies*, 7 (3), 167–73.
Pye, D. 1983: *The Nature and Aesthetics of Design*, London: The Herbert Press.
Robertson, J. A. S., Briggs, J. M. and Goodchild, A., 1985: *Structure and Employment Prospects of the Service Industries*, London: UK Department of Employment.
Robinson, A., 1989: *Partners in Providing the Goods*, London: Investment in Industry (3i).
Rodgus, G., 1989: The role of the customer in new product development – a study of the enzyme industry. Unpublished M.Sc. Dissertation, Manchester: UMIST.
Rose, S. and Rose, H., 1971: The myth of the neutrality of science. In W. Fuller (ed.), *The Social Impact of Modern Biology*, London: Routledge and Kegan Paul.
Rothwell, R., 1977: The characteristics of successful innovators and technically progressive firms, *R and D Management*, 7 (3) 191–206.
Rothwell, R., 1981: Non-price factors in the export competitiveness of agricultural engineering goods, *Research Policy*, 10, 260.
Rothwell, R. and Gardiner, J. P., 1983: The role of design in product and process change, *Design Studies*, 4 (3), 161–9.
Rothwell, R. and Gardiner, J. P., 1984: The role of design in competitiveness. In R. Langdon (ed.), *Design Policy: Design and Industry*, London: The Design Council.
Rothwell, R., Schott, K. and Gardiner, J. P., 1983: *Design and the Economy: the role of design and innovation in the prosperity of industrial companies*, London: The Design Council.
Roy, R. 1984: Product design and innovation in a mature consumer industry. In R. Langdon (ed.), *Design Policy: Design and Industry*, London: The Design Council.
Roy, R., 1987: Design for business success, *Engineering*, January, 16–17.
Roy, R., 1990: Product design and company performance. In M. Oakley (ed.), *Design Management: a handbook of issues and methods*, Oxford: Blackwell, 49–62.
Roy, R., 1992: Creativity and Conceptual Design: the invention and evolution of bicycles (Block 3, Open University course, T264 *Design: Principles and Practice*), Milton Keynes: The Open University Press.
Roy, R. and Bruce, M., 1984: Product design, innovation and competition in British manufacturing – background, aims and methods. Working Paper WP-02, Milton Keynes: Design Innovation Group, Open University.
Roy, R. and Cross, N., 1983: Bicycles: invention and innovation, (Units 5–7, Open University course, T263 *Design: Processes and Products*), Milton Keynes: Open University.
Roy, R. and Potter, S., 1990: Managing design projects in small and medium-sized firms, *Technology Analysis and Strategic Management*, 2 (3), 321–36.

Roy, R. and Potter, S., with Rothwell, R. and Gardiner, J. P., 1990: *Design and the Economy*, London: The Design Council.

Roy, R. and Walker, D., 1988: Case studies: A & R Cambridge; Hewlett Packard, (Unit 2, Open University course, P791 *Managing Design*), Milton Keynes: Open University.

Roy, R., Walker, D. and Cross, N., 1987: *Design for the Market*, Watford: Engineering Industry Training Board Publications.

Roy, R., Salaman, G. and Walsh, V., 1986: Research Grant Final Report – Design-based innovation in manufacturing industry: principles and practices for successful design and production, *Report DIG-02*, Milton Keynes: Design Innovation Group, Open University.

Rutterford, C. A., 1989: The management of engineering design. Unpublished M.Phil. Thesis, London: Imperial College.

Rzevski, G., 1990: Engineering design and artificial intelligence. Inaugural lecture, Open University, May.

Sahal, D., 1981: *Productivity and Technical Change* (2nd edition), Cambridge: Cambridge University Press.

Samuels, A., 1989: Observations on the designing of projects, processes and products. In M. Diani and V. Margolin (eds), *Design at the crossroads*, CIRA Seminar Series Monograph No. 2, Centre for Interdisciplinary Research in the Arts, Northwestern University, May.

Sanderson, M., 1972: Research and the firm in British industry 1919–1939, *Science Studies*, 107–51.

Saviotti, P., Coombs R., Gibbons M. and Stubbs, P., 1980: *Technology and Competitiveness in the Tractor Industry*. A Report for the Department of Industry, Manchester: Department of Science and Technology Policy, University of Manchester.

Schott, K. and Pick, K., 1983: The Effect of Price and Non Price Factors on UK Export Performance and Import Penetration. UCL Discussion Paper 35, London: University College.

Schumpeter, J. A., 1934: *The Theory of Economic Development*, Cambridge, Mass: Harvard University Press.

Seers, D., 1982: Active Life Profiles for Different Social Groups. Discussion Paper No 178, Brighton: Institute for Development Studies, University of Sussex.

Service, L. M., Hart S. J. and Baker, M. J., 1989: *Profit by Design*, London: The Design Council.

Seymour, R., 1989: quoted by B. Polan, Buying and selling a new decade. *The Guardian*, 11 November.

Shirley, R. and Henn, D., 1988: *Support for Design: Final evaluation report*, London: Assessment Unit, Research and Technology Policy Division, Department of Trade and Industry.

Soete, L., 1985: Innovation and international trade. In B. Williams and J. Bryan-Brown (eds), *Knowns and Unknowns in Technical Change*, London: Technical Change Centre.

Stewart, R., 1987: *Design and British Industry*, London: John Murray.

Stoneman, P., 1983: *The Economic Analysis of Technological Change*, Oxford: Oxford University Press.

Stout, D. K., 1977: *International Price Competitiveness, Non-Price Factors and Export Performance*, London: National Economic Development Office.

Stubbs, P., 1979: Technology policy and the motor industry. In R. Johnston and P. Gummett (eds), *Directing Technology*, London: Croom Helm.

Sudjic, D., 1990: Shopped by the City, *Sunday Correspondent Magazine*, 6 May.

Swann, P. 1987: International differences in product design and their economic significance, *Applied Economics*, 19, 201–13.

Swann, P. and Taghavi, M., 1988: Product Competitiveness and the Ideal Consumer: Some Calculations for Consumer Durables. Discussion Papers in Economics No. 8803, London: Brunel University of West London.

Thackara, J. (ed.), 1988: *Design After Modernism: beyond the object*, London: Thames and Hudson.

Tjalve, E., 1979: *A Short Course in Industrial Design*, London: Newnes-Butterworth.

Twiss, B., 1980: *The Management of Technological Innovation*, London: Longman.

Ughanwa, D. O. and Baker, M. J., 1989: *The Role of Design in International Competitiveness*, London: Routledge.

Urban, G. L. and Hauser, J. R., 1980: *Design and Marketing of New Products*, Englewood Cliffs, N.J.: Prentice Hall.

Uttal, B., 1987: Speeding new ideas to market, *Fortune*, 2 March.

Utterback, J., 1979: The dynamics of product and process innovation. In C. Hill and J. Utterback (eds), *Technological Innovation for a Dynamic Economy*, New York: Pergamon.

Utterback, J. and Suarez, F. F., 1992: Innovation, competition and industry structure, *Research Policy* (forthcoming).

Vaitsos, C., 1974: *Inter-Country Income Distribution and Trans-National Enterprises*, Oxford: Oxford University Press.

Vernon, R., 1966: International investment and international trade in the product cycle, *Quarterly Journal of Economics*, 80, 190.

Vernon, R. (ed.), 1970: *The Technology Factor in International Trade*, New York: Columbia University Press.

von Hippel, E., 1978: Successful industrial products from customer ideas, *Journal of Marketing*, 42 (2), 39–49.

Wainwright, H. and Elliott, D., 1982: *The Lucas Plan*, London: Allison and Busby.

Walker, D., 1986: In a spin: the British car industry, *Design*, 450, June.

Walker D., 1988: Case studies: W. H. Smith; Plasplugs (Unit 3, Open University course, P791 *Managing Design*), Milton Keynes: The Open University.

Walker, D., Oakley, M. and Roy, R., 1989: Overview issues (Conclusions of Open University course, P791 *Managing Design*), Milton Keynes: Open University.

Walker, W., 1980: Britain's industrial performance 1850–1950: a failure to adjust. In K. Pavitt (ed.), op. cit.

Walsh, V., 1984: Invention and innovation in the chemical industry: Demand-pull or discovery-push? *Research Policy*, 13, 211–34.

Walsh, V., 1987: Technical change, competitiveness and the special problems of small countries. *STI Review*, 2, 81.

Walsh, V., 1988: Technology and the competitiveness of small countries – a review. In C. Freeman and B.-A. Lundvall (eds), op. cit.

Walsh, V. and Roy, R., 1983: Plastic products: good design, innovation and business success. Report DIG-01, Milton Keynes: Design Innovation Group, Open University.

Walsh, V. and Roy, R., 1985: The designer as gatekeeper in manufacturing industry, *Design Studies*, 6 (3) July, 127–33.

Walsh, V., Roy, R. and Bruce, M., 1988: Competitive by design, *Journal of Marketing Management*, 4 (2), 201–17.

Warren Centre, 1987: *Winning by Design: Technical Papers*, Sydney: The Warren Centre, University of Sydney.

Wells, L., 1972: *The Product Life Cycle and International Trade*, Boston: Harvard University Graduate School of Business Administration, Division of Research Publications.

Whitney, D. E., 1988: Manufacturing by design, *Harvard Business Review*, July–August, 83–91.

Wiener, M. J., 1982: *English Culture and the Decline of the Industrial Spirit, 1850–1980*, Cambridge: Cambridge University Press.

Willett, J., 1984: *The Weimar Years: A culture cut short*, London: Thames and Hudson.

Williams, R., Roy, R. and Walsh, V., 1982: Government and technology, (Units 3–4, Open University course, T361 *Control of Technology*). Milton Keynes: Open University.

Williamson, O. E., 1970: *Corporate Control and Business Behaviour*, Englewood Cliffs, N.J.: Prentice Hall.

Williamson, O. E., 1975: *Markets and Hierarchies: analysis and anti-trust implications*, New York: The Free Press.

Womack, J. P., Jones, D. T. and Roos, D., 1990: *The Machine that Changed the World: the story of lean production*, New York: Rawson Associates.

Woolf, E. and Tanna, S. 1988: *Understanding Accounting Standards*, London: Institute of Chartered Accountants in England and Wales/McGraw-Hill.

Woudhuysen, J., 1989: quoted in C. Gardner and J. Sheppard, *Consuming Passions*, London: Unwin Hyman.

Yorke, P., 1988: Culture as commodity: style wars, punks and pageant. In J. Thackera (ed.), op. cit.

Young, R. M., 1971: Evolutionary biology and ideology: then and now. In W. Fuller (ed.), *The Social Impact of Modern Biology*, London: Routledge and Kegan Paul.

Young, R. M., 1977: Science is social relations, *Radical Science Journal*, 5, 65–129.

Index